THE OTHER BORDER WARS

ILLUMINATIONS: CULTURAL FORMATIONS OF THE AMERICAS SERIES

JORGE CORONADO, EDITOR

THE OTHER BORDER WARS

CONFLICT AND STASIS
IN LATIN AMERICAN CULTURE

SHANNON DOWD

UNIVERSITY OF PITTSBURGH PRESS

Published by the University of Pittsburgh Press, Pittsburgh, Pa., 15260
Manufactured in the United States of America
Printed on acid-free paper
10 9 8 7 6 5 4 3 2 1

Cataloging-in-Publication data is available from the Library of Congress

ISBN 13: 978-0-8229-4808-7
ISBN 10: 0-8229-4808-7

Cover art: Horacio Zabala, *Combustión III*, 1973. Pencil on burned paper. Used with permission.

Cover design: Alex Wolfe

For my parents, Mary and Kevin, and for Richard.

CONTENTS

ACKNOWLEDGMENTS

Many people have helped make this book. Most of all, I wish to thank my many teachers, advisors, and mentors over the years, especially Gareth Williams, Kate Jenckes, and Jaime Rodríguez-Matos, for sharing their knowledge and methods with me. Likewise, Victoria Langland, Patrick Dove, Cristina Moreiras-Menor, Javier Sanjinés, Sergio Villalobos-Ruminott, and Gustavo Verdesio have contributed to the development of this book in ways large and small. I would like to thank my colleagues at Niagara University, especially Jim McCutcheon, Jamie Carr, Brian Bennett, Paula Kot, and Henrik Borgstrom, for welcoming me warmly and encouraging me to complete this project. At the University of Pittsburgh Press, I thank Josh Shanholtzer, Alex Wolfe, and Amy Sherman for expertly carrying the book through to publication and Kimberly Laurel for excellent copyediting. Likewise, I thank series editor Jorge Coronado for endorsing the book for inclusion in *Illuminations*. Two anonymous reviewers offered insightful critiques that strengthened the manuscript, and I greatly appreciate their careful reading and comments.

ACKNOWLEDGMENTS

In libraries, I owe a debt of gratitude to Barbara Alvarez at the University of Michigan and Samantha Gust at Niagara University for procuring hard-to-find materials. I also wish to thank my students, especially those who have taken versions of my Border Wars classes, for their willingness to entertain and challenge ideas in progress.

Without the indefatigable friendship of some brilliant people, this book, and my life, would be much poorer indeed. Special thanks to Corinne Prosniewski, Juanita Bernal Benavides, and Ludmila Ferrari for always being there with the right words at the right time. The encouragement of many others has been critical, especially from Pedro Aguilera-Mellado, Erika Almenara, Matías Beverinotti, Abigail Celis, Andrew Clifton, Claire Clifton, David Robinson Dwyer, Marilyn Fysh, Nanette Harmon, Gabriel Horowitz, Drew Johnson, Juan Leal Ugalde, Joel Louwsma, Ajitpaul Mangat, Mariano Olmedo, Raquel Parrine, Laura Pensa, Eric Purchase, Marcela Reales Visbal, Rachel ten Haaf, Mariana Valencia Mestre, Rachel Violanti, Travis Williams, and Félix Zamora Gómez. Special thanks also to the Soroka-Greene and Prosniewski families. At the University at Buffalo, I thank David Johnson and the Department of Comparative Literature for ongoing intellectual stimulation and engagement.

The University of Michigan's Rackham Graduate School provided fellowships for travel to Argentina, the Falkland/Malvinas Islands, and Bolivia, and the Department of Romance Languages and Literatures provided support for research in many forms, including a postdoctoral fellowship. The Niagara University Research Council provided financial support for permissions and publication. In particular, I thank Dave Schoen for his expert guidance. Andrew Ascherl assisted with manuscript preparation. Authors Wilmer Urrelo Zárate, Carlos Gamerro, and Horacio Castellanos Moya generously took time to help along the way, whether at a conference, over coffee, or in a well-timed email. For permission to use materials, I thank the Fundación Roque Dalton; directors Paz Encina, Alex Bowen, and Lola Arias; photographers Eugenia Kais and Tristram Kenton; and Gema Films. Special thanks to Horacio Zabala for permission to use *Combustión III* on the cover. I send my gratitude to all of the authors and artists whose work I examine here for their contributions. This book would not exist without them.

Earlier versions of this material appeared elsewhere, and I thank the publications for permission to reproduce it here. Chapter 1 is derived in part from "Moth-Eaten Maps and Empty Wells: Augusto Roa Bastos, Augusto Céspedes, and the Chaco War Archive," published in *Journal of Latin American Cultural Studies*, vol. 28, no. 2, 2019, pp. 179–94, copyright Taylor & Francis, available online: http://tandfonline.com/10.10 80/13569325.2019.1618800. Chapter 4 contains a portion of the article "*Los pichiciegos* on Sovereignty, Decolonization, and Democracy in the Falklands/Malvinas," originally published in *Revista de Estudios Hispánicos*, vol. 52, no. 2, 2018, pp. 551–74. Extracts and ideas from the article "*Polemos*: The Struggle between Being and History in Heidegger and Derrida," originally published in *Política común*, vol. 13, 2019, have been incorporated throughout.

Finally, this book would not have been written without a lifetime of support from my family. I cherish the memories I have of my grandmothers and the inspiration I draw from them. Family ghosts lurk in this book, I'm sure. I am endlessly grateful for my sister, Sarah, for her support and occasional ribbing, and for Zelig and the family who joined along the way. I dedicate this book to my parents and my partner. To my mother, Mary, for opening a path in life that made it worth living, and in memory of my father, Kevin, who died before he could hold this book, whom I miss every day, and whose love was boundless. And to Richard, for everything.

THE OTHER BORDER WARS

I.1. Argentine and Chilean officers and soldiers deciding on a border in the Pampas in *Mi mejor enemigo*. Alex Bowen, Alce Producciones SpA

BORDER WAR AS STASIS

In 1978, war almost broke out between Argentina and Chile. The conflict is rarely remembered, a historical blip eclipsed by the enduring legacy of South America's brutal military dictatorships. The film *Mi mejor enemigo* (My best enemy), directed by Alex Bowen, reimagined what happened in this war-that-wasn't for twenty-first-century viewers. The film follows a group of Chilean soldiers tasked with finding an old border fence in the seemingly endless grasslands. Their compass breaks, and they lose radio contact with their regiment. The lost soldiers wander through the Pampas until they come across a similarly lost group of Argentines. Both dig trenches on either side of what they imagine to be their territory, although the commanding officers are finally forced to admit, in the words of the Argentine to his Chilean counterpart: "Neither of us knows where the border is."[1]

Because they can't find the border, they decide to create one (fig. I.1). In a tense scene, the Chilean officer confronts the Argentine about selfish and unfair treatment. A tight reverse shot reduces the scale of the impending war down to a duel. Even though they had decided on the border only moments before, the Argentine declares tersely: "You are invading my territory."[2] The officer begrudgingly concedes, ordering his subordinate to take "two *small* steps toward the Atlantic," clarifying to the obviously confused soldier, "That way, man."[3] The soldiers decide to burn a line of fire in the grass to seal the pact. But the wind suddenly picks up, carrying the fire across the dry grass. Panicked soldiers hurry to stamp it out and avoid territorial losses. Effectively, they recreate the process of border arbitration in miniature. Their border is a fiction, but a fiction they believe in—a fiction for which they risk their lives.

The Other Border Wars argues that the border is this fiction, sustained on both sides by steady belief even in the face of death. It examines twentieth-century border wars in Latin America and their circulation and negotiation in culture. Latin American borders—some established and upheld since the colonial period, some since the nineteenth century, some only since the 1930s—organize political and cultural space, shaping both internal and external conflicts. Once they are established, they tend to be reinforced by these same internal and external forces. This book departs from the hypothetical question: What happens if we examine border conflict while suspending belief in the border? After all, like the lost soldiers, the closer one gets to the border, the more difficult it is to find. Today's borders are especially diffuse, sometimes overwhelmed by frequent crossings of goods and people, sometimes frustrated by unclear or disputed demarcations. Globalization has made contemporary borders more ambiguous but also more contentious.

None of this is new to the Mexico-US border, which has long been viewed as an area of contention and a rich object of study. Since Gloria Anzaldúa's seminal *Borderlands/La frontera*, the northern Mexican and southern US border has been understood as a space of rich cultural exchange. For Anzaldúa, the border is a metaphor, traversing categories of race, ethnicity, language, and sexuality. Yet scholars of Latin American studies have been slow to apply Anzaldúa's approach to other borders in the region. Latin American borders are generally considered peaceful, and problems are often minimized either by focusing on domestic unrest or by invoking *hermandad*, fraternity, among Latin American nations, especially in opposition to Global Northern powers. Political scientists in particular celebrate the region as peaceful compared to Europe. For instance, David Mares contrasts the relative infrequency of international disputes to the ongoing low-intensity insurgency and civil warfare that he calls Latin America's "violent peace" (ix-xiv).[4] This "violent peace" has been an implicit focus in much of Latin American cultural studies as well, with literature and film seen primarily as useful depictions of internal conflicts like civil wars, revolutions, and armed insurrections. As a consequence, twentieth-century border wars have been considered minor or incidental. *The Other Border Wars* pushes back against this current, instead casting border conflict as critical to understanding Latin American culture.

After all, internal conflicts are inextricably entwined with external ones. Domestic pressures in the United States, for instance, shape the relationship to the Mexican border as much as, or perhaps even more than, international relations. Returning to the Beagle Conflict depicted in *Mi mejor enemigo*, the dispute between Argentina and Chile encapsulates in miniature the political and legal legacies at work in Latin American border conflicts and serves as an introduction to the common language and themes undergirding border disputes in this book. A variety of factors—internal, external, colonial, and contemporary—influenced the development and outcome of the conflict. Its origins in colonial territorial divisions, independence-era statecraft, and response to European and US pressures make it a model of the simmering tensions at borders throughout the region during the twentieth century.

For most of the century, both Argentina and Chile had sporadically claimed the islands of Picton, Nueva, and Lennox at the eastern edge of the Beagle Channel and the southern tip of South America. In 1971, both countries submitted their arguments to a binding arbitration court overseen by a neutral mediator, who was, as determined in previous treaties, the British sovereign, Queen Elizabeth II. Why, after decades of apparent apathy, did the sovereignty of the islands seem suddenly important? An Antarctic land grab was looming with the threat of encroachment from powerful countries seeking to argue that some territories did not belong to anyone—were res nullius—and were therefore claimable. Both Argentina and Chile sought a definitive resolution in their favor to avoid neo-imperialism in the region. At stake was the definition of property and the question of how international law determines an area as either unowned or sovereign territory.[5]

In 1977, the British court handed down its binding decision, with all three islands awarded to Chile.[6] Argentina withdrew its support from the mediation and planned to invade the islands and other strategic locations in Chilean Patagonia. They called the attack, set to begin December 22, 1978, Operación Soberanía, "Operation Sovereignty." The name reveals that Argentina viewed the border as the limit of sovereignty and its claim to the islands as justified under an international system in which sovereignty is inviolable. A threat to sovereign waters necessitated a response on sovereign soil. In a final effort to avoid bloodshed, Pope John Paul II offered to arbitrate the dispute under the auspices of the Vatican. The two clearest incarnations of sovereignty—queen and pope—had been called on to settle this dispute that came from the continent's imperial past. They embodied the staying power of political theology, imported from Europe to the Americas with the first European settlers and still decisive centuries later. The pope's arbitration was ultimately successful in avoiding armed conflict between the military governments led by two of Latin America's most notorious dictators, Jorge Rafael Videla and Augusto Pinochet. When, in 1984, Pope John Paul II's arbitration court came to largely the same conclusion as the queen's, awarding the three islands to Chile but giving Argentina maritime rights, Argentina accepted. The country had been soundly defeated in the Falklands/Malvinas War of 1982 and had little appetite for conflict. Argentina and Chile subsequently signed and ratified the Treaty of Peace and Friendship.

Contrary to the film *Mi mejor enemigo*, there was no bloodshed. Electoral democracy returned to Argentina in 1983 and to Chile in 1990. This minor border conflict—and the major border wars this book examines—depended on a definition of sovereignty, and hence bordering, that emerged from much older legal systems. Sovereignty was transferred from the Spanish empire to independent nations via the principle of *uti possidetis juris*, providing for the transfer of territorial limits from colony to nation-state at independence. When the dispute flared again in the twentieth century, the imperial powers of pope and queen—icons of political theology—in negotiation with newer autocratic sovereigns—US-backed anti-communist dictators—were again called upon to resolve the border question, eventually giving way, at least nominally, to the people. The Beagle Conflict epitomizes the tension between sovereignty and democracy characteristic of all of the armed border conflicts that *The Other Border Wars* examines. Each of the conflicts raises major political and cultural questions, including the nature and importance of sovereignty in light of European political theology and imperialism; the balance or imbalance of internal and external forces, past and present, legal and cultural; and the meanings of democracy in relation to violence.

I explore these questions by approaching border conflict from the perspective of stasis, meaning civil strife, rather than from the perspective of *polemos*, or international conflict.[7] This terminological shift implies a method, adapted from Mexico-US border studies and globalization studies, that privileges the border as a site of conflict, exchange, negotiation, and differential enclosure and flow. Yet it does not take the border as a given. Although it may seem counterintuitive, approaching border wars from the perspective of internal conflict imparts a rich field of meaning through which to understand past and present conflicts. *The Other Border Wars* uses the following three related definitions of stasis to argue for a suspension of the border as the organizing principle of cultural and political life.

The first definition of stasis explored here: stagnation, stoppage, lack of change, status quo. Long before the twentieth century, national and international legal systems coalesced around European definitions of sovereignty exported to the Americas during the colonial period. The Beagle Conflict, for instance, emerged from treaties and systems that settled into place over the course of centuries. As German jurist Carl Schmitt writes, Latin America's legal sphere was seen as essentially European: "The Latin American states that arose [during the nineteenth century] assumed that they, too, belonged to the 'family of European nations' and to its community of international law" (Nomos 286–87). During the early nineteenth-century wars of independence and the later nineteenth-century international wars—notably the War of the Triple Alliance in 1864–1870 and the War of the Pacific in 1879–1883—Latin America established largely static limits between territories. By the turn of the twentieth century, Latin American borders were substantially the same as they are now, with the critical exception of the Bolivia-Paraguay border, finally decided after the Chaco War. Subsequent territorial disputes were mostly confined to the diplomatic sphere, and Latin American states assumed a fixed shape.

Over time, political scientists argue that territorial stagnation brings unity and coherence to bordered land masses, leading to regional and national senses of identity (Hassner). If the territory is in dispute, however, this cohesion increases the likelihood of conflict. Intractable disputes, such as the conflict over the Falklands/Malvinas Islands, become more contentious as a result. As Ron Hassner writes of intractable territorial disputes, "As these conflicts mature, the perceived cohesion of the disputed territory rises; its boundaries are perceived as becoming more clearly defined; and the availability of substitutes for the territory appear to decline" (110). The border's physical stasis makes negotiation and compromise less likely. The gradual process of entrenchment sharpens the disputed territory's boundaries and increases its perceived value, leading to war as an outlet for unfinished business, as described most famously in Carl von Clausewitz's 1832 treatise *On War* as "the continuation of policy by other means" (87).

By the twentieth century, Latin American political geography had become static and many border disputes had been settled. Geographical limits were codified into law. As Walter Benjamin's "Critique of Violence" argues, "If . . . conclusions can be drawn from military violence, as being primordial and paradigmatic of all violence used for natural ends, there is inherent in all such violence a lawmaking character" (283). Military violence, whether the violence of imperialism or of warfare, creates the law, and the law then maintains the status quo. Michel Foucault's 1975–1976 lectures advance Benjamin's observation by inverting Clausewitz's proposition in the present: "Politics is the continuation of war by other means. Politics . . . sanctions and reproduces the disequilibrium of forces manifested in war" (16). The legal order becomes the unquestioned violence that undergirds society. War is no longer just at or beyond the border; it has saturated political organization. Force is inscribed in everyday life.

This situation leads to Latin America's "violent peace," only visible in rare moments of overt confrontation. These moments of violent confrontation then illuminate a collage of forces coming to bear on the border. As we will see in chapters 1 and 2, the emergence of a stagnant geographical border implies the tenuous hold of the map on national space and the written word as an enclosure of cultural difference that is necessarily partial and incomplete. Geographically stagnant borders serve as key sites for examining the violence of enclosure. As Fredric Jameson writes, "War is . . . the potentiation and becoming-actual of . . . occulted virtualities: the presence of those absent enemies which peacetime and daily life confined to newspaper or television news when their existence intersected at all with my own" (*Valences* 595). With the outbreak of hostilities, latent conflicts spring into view, calling into question the codified violence of the legal and political order. Border wars provide a unique opportunity to carry out "the interpretation of society and its visible order [in] the confusion of violence, passions, hatreds, rages, resentments, and bitterness" (Foucault 54). Fiction, film, poetry, plays, and visual art depict these moments of simultaneous violence and stagnation, emphasizing ongoing tension at borders and within the legal order.

This leads to the second definition of stasis: an internal conflict, uproar, or internecine dispute. This second definition is perhaps the most difficult to grasp when considering border conflict because, since ancient times, European thinkers working from classical models have insisted on the categorical difference between internal and external conflict, *stasis* and polemos. Famously, Thucydides laid the foundation for a differentiation between civil and external wars in his account of the Peloponnesian War.[8] In Book V of *Republic*, Plato likewise distinguishes between war among the Greeks and war with barbarians. The former is considered *stasis*, a civil war that manifests an illness in the polity, whereas the latter he terms polemos, a war with a true enemy. Aristotle considers and modifies this distinction when he elaborates on its opposite, friendship, in *Politics*.[9] Since ancient Greece, the border has long served the key function of dividing an ordered polity from its barbaric exterior. More recently, classicist Nicole Loraux's *Divided City* presents *stasis* as an important precursor to democracy, describing how amnesty in the wake of civil conflict formed the basis of Athenian politics. Schmitt has also expanded the significance of *stasis* in political theology to mean an uproar or rebellion of the One against itself (*Political Theology II*), so that for Loraux, *stasis* precedes democracy and for Schmitt, it marks the unfolding of political theology.[10] For both, *stasis* profoundly affects the shape of the political order.

Since the classical period, two world wars and later globalization caused political theorists and philosophers to reconsider categories of violence. In the wake of the Second World War, philosopher Emmanuel Levinas began to use the term *polemos* to describe violence not only engulfing the European continent but also permeating the Western philosophical tradition. In *Totality and Infinity*, Levinas interprets two Heraclitus fragments as the basis for the philosophical view that posits polemos, or war, as the foundation of existence.[11] For Levinas, polemos unites key thinkers in continental philosophy, leading most damningly to Martin Heidegger, who explicitly refers to Heraclitus's fragments on polemos when writing in Nazi Germany. Heidegger's association with the Nazis beginning in 1933 resonates with his rendering of polemos into German as *Kampf*, later abandoned for its Nazi resonances not least with Adolf Hitler's autobiography *Mein Kampf* (Fried 30–32). As a result of this contaminated Western philosophical tradition, Levinas argues that ethics must supersede ontology. For Levinas, polemos and the conflictual nature of existence must be set aside in order to make way for the ethical relationship with the other.

Levinas's observation has also been taken up in Latin American studies, where it has become foundational in decolonial theory. In *Against War*, Nelson Maldonado-Torres critiques European modernity as originating in and expanding through a "paradigm of war," where "by paradigm of war I mean a way of conceiving humanity, knowledge, and social relations that privileges conflict or *polemos*. . . . The paradigm of war can be characterized in terms of the privilege of conflict or the celebration of the reduction of the singularity of individual entities and subjects to the generality of the concept, to Being, to an ethnos, or to a totality in philosophical reflections" (3). Polemos manifests the violence intrinsic in the Western philosophical tradition, especially translated into the Global South. With Levinas, Maldonado-Torres sustains that ontology is violence, but he goes a step further to claim that philosophy, especially European philosophy, causes physical violence. For him, philosophy sits at the base of empire, which is itself a machine for eliminating difference. Imperial remnants in the Global South must be philosophically decolonized.

The problem with Maldonado-Torres's approach, explored further in chapter 3, is that the oppositional—polemical—structure of war is inscribed in the book's title: *Against War*. Maldonado-Torres, and decolonial theorists more generally, sustain a polemic against polemic—a war against war. In order to overcome this circularity, Maldonado-Torres proposes an "ethics of love" that approaches others as singularities. The world is not knowable through a universal concept of humanity or a central division of friend and foe but rather through a universality of difference. As in the case of the border, however, claiming resistant differences risks reinforcing these differences. The very distinction between self and other, identity and difference, is often the cause of violence.

The Other Border Wars argues that theoretical work that opposes war cannot argue against war. It cannot make war the enemy. Instead, conceptual work must consider the philosophical, legal, and historical circumstances that come to bear on specific conflicts while questioning their categorization and function in the present. By examining war from within rather than viewing it as a condition imposed from outside, Latin American border conflicts speak to the philosophical and political currents shaping the region and its idea of borders into the present.

This leads to the third definition of stasis: displacement, redirection, and multiplication. Resonant with recent changes under globalization, this third definition comes from the rhetorical tradition, in which stasis is an argumentative procedure used to define and work through a dispute. Border mediation typically follows a similar process in order to define physical boundaries and sovereign rights. Contemporary bordering in particular often also involves movement and negotiations about trade and labor. In *Border as Method*, Sandro Mezzadra and Brett Neilson suggest that contemporary borders are shifting and multiplying. Borders increasingly differentiate flows of people and goods so that border enforcement stretches into remote corners; for instance, when government agents raid a workplace hundreds of miles from the nearest border. The border comes to the people. In US Latinx communities, the phrase "We didn't cross the border; the border crossed us" has become a rallying cry (qtd. in Mezzadra and Neilson xi, 270). Mezzadra and Neilson describe this contemporary situation as "a proliferation but also a heterogeniza-tion of borders" (3). The border serves to control labor and consumption so that, as Mezzadra and Neilson explain, borders are points of both stoppage and flow (3). Borders articulate contemporary global capital-ism, organizing space, labor, politics, and culture.

While borders are changing rapidly now, a gradual shift has been going on for quite some time. Two world wars eroded the legal princi-ples of territorial integrity established in the 1648 Treaty of Westphalia, and a new system emerged that slowly transformed understandings of sovereignty. Rhetorical stasis became part of geopolitical positioning. Writing in 1953, Schmitt decries the decisive shift away from a concrete order based on territory: "Every legal system, every unity of order and orientation requires some concept of property guarantees, of *status quo* and *uti possidetis*. The Geneva institution also appeared to guarantee the territorial integrity of each member. . . . Yet other, not formally rec-ognized, but nevertheless effective principles, such as the right of free self-determination of peoples, stood in the way of the legitimacy of this territorial *status quo*, and essentially jeopardized its unproblematic and unequivocal nature. . . . The essential difficulty . . . lay still deeper, and concerned the question of what the *status quo* should be" (Nomos 245). The territorial status quo comes into question with the emergence of principles such as self-determination that interrupt the essentially impe-rial order. Schmitt assumes that the European legal framework carries over to the Americas but runs into difficulty when the territorial status quo is threatened. A staunch opponent of both communism and liberal democracy, Schmitt hears the threat of the people in this change and foresees a dark future, heightened under globalization as the balance of power shifted toward the United States. As he feared, the understanding of the nation-state as a "bordered power-container" (Anthony Giddens, qtd. in Elden, *Birth* 3) would decay so that the state no longer had a mo-nopoly on violence.[12] Under this new regime, the democratic power of the people would become a threat to the international legal order.

In 1963, the near-simultaneous introduction of the concept of "global civil war" in Hannah Arendt's *On Revolution* and Schmitt's *The-ory of the Partisan* revealed that the nature of organized violence was changing in political theory as well as international jurisprudence. Ac-cording to some commentators, the classical difference between polemos and *stasis* had become obsolete. The emergence of political bodies such as the League of Nations, Organization of American States, and United Nations revealed what Schmitt feared; namely, that sovereignty—along with inherited concepts of borders and war—was becoming diffuse, spread into supranational organizations. As international cooperation grew along with softer forms of neo-imperialism, borders weakened and warfare became subject to greater influence from other countries. Some, like Schmitt, sought to hold on to the assurances of bordered sovereignty. In *Walled States, Waning Sovereignty*, however, Wendy Brown shows that the proliferation of border-based violence, heated rhetoric, and lengthening walls are a direct and paradoxical outgrowth of the diminishing power of the border under globalization. People seek to reinforce the border because of its weakness. Like Schmitt, they fear a threat to sovereignty and territorial integrity.

Today, the border has been undermined, displaced, multiplied, and moved. *The Other Border Wars* examines the antecedents of this contemporary situation in chapters 4 and 5 as a border beholden to imperial political geography transforms from dictatorship to democracy, through the neoliberal consensus and into the present. The displacements characteristic of rhetorical stasis appear in cultural production through figures of ecstasy—etymologically ecstasis, or displacement outside of the self—and metastasis—the border's spread to new sites. Hence, while borders may seem unchanged, *The Other Border Wars* examines the often drastic changes in their political and cultural importance.

The three definitions of stasis used here aim to explain how bordering works in present-day Latin American culture and politics, examining the past to understand the current configuration of borders in dialogue with Latin American cultural studies, border studies, philosophy, and political theory. The argument is that stasis is the underlying force in border conflict, and that stasis is the foundation of the political sphere manifested in culture. The method is to examine border conflict in context while suspending the force of the border. This approach requires the double movement of acknowledging the border as a source of conflict while taking care not to assume that the border is in a specific geographical place, has a specific importance, or organizes politics and culture in a particular way. After all, border wars imply conflict about where the border really is and how it functions.

The coming chapters consider contested borders in Central and South America in order to examine the political and philosophical concepts that underpin notions of sovereignty and globalization. Instead of viewing the border as a space of articulation through identity and difference, *The Other Border Wars* departs from the idea that crossing, recrossing, and interrupting metaphorical borders between categories of identity often reinforces the divisions these borders create.[13] This insight emerges from Mexico-US border studies—the site of the most contentious and visible border conflict in the United States—and resonates with questions about the nature of sovereignty, labor, language, migration, representation, and consumption. *The Other Border Wars* takes aim at the conceptual foundations of bordering through stasis. Dimitris Vardoulakis writes that stasis is the basis of the political: "Stasis underlies all political praxis" (*Stasis* 121). Drawing on Loraux and Jacques Derrida, Vardoulakis argues that it is important to consider stasis before the state because "*stasis comes before any conception of the state that relies on the ruse of sovereignty*" (*Stasis* 11). By foregrounding stasis, this book highlights conflicts that have been obscured by preestablished borders, political theology, and sovereignty claims.

Three case studies track the development of the border through stasis: the 1932–1935 Chaco War between Bolivia and Paraguay; the 1969 Soccer War, or Hundred Hours War, between El Salvador and Honduras; and the 1982 Falklands/Malvinas War between Argentina and the United Kingdom. Chapters 1 and 2 focus on the Chaco War, which is particularly important because the end of the war marks the last major change in Latin American territorial borders. The war also involved European and US intervention on behalf of diplomatic and oil interests while shaking soldiers' religious, philosophical, and political beliefs, much as the First World War did in Europe. In chapter 1, I use hypostasis, the assumption of form in philosophy and theology, to describe the formation of the border as boundary of the national body politic. In Christianity, hypostasis refers to the word made flesh, God's incarnation in human form. I argue that Augusto Céspedes challenges complete bodily enclosure in the stories "El pozo" (The well) and "La paraguaya" (The Paraguayan woman) from the collection *Sangre de mestizos* (Mestizo blood) while Adolfo Costa du Rels's *Lagune H.3*, released in Spanish as *La laguna H.3* (Lagoon H.3), reveals the Chaco as an expansive void, both physical and spiritual. Most tellingly, Augusto Roa Bastos's *Hijo de hombre* (Son of man) filters the war through the Christian salvation story to show that Paraguayan national incarnation, assumed to be finished after the war, remained incomplete. The Chaco border represents the partial enclosure of the nation in flesh, depicted by Roa Bastos as Paraguay's living death. Hypostasis grounds later conceptions of stasis, rooted in the political theology of God and king.

Chapter 2 examines the more recent legacy of the Chaco War. After the war, neither Bolivia nor Paraguay had coastal outlets, and geographical isolation cut both countries off from commerce. Landlocked, the soldiers' thirst in the arid Chaco turned into a thirst for oil, development, and trade in more recent decades. Wilmer Urrelo Zárate's novel *Hablar con los perros* (Talking to dogs) depicts the violence of consumption through the trope of cannibalism borrowed from indigenous Tupi and Brazilian avant-garde traditions. For Urrelo Zárate, the mouth is a site of consumption, consumerism, and narrative. Urrelo Zárate leaves no space for the vanguard. Instead, the desire to consume oil and flesh leads to violent extraction. Static social class and an unequal division of wealth represent the war's legacy. In contrast, Paz Encina's experimental film *Hamaca paraguaya* (Paraguayan hammock) portrays mouths as apertures and sites of narrative discontinuity. The Chaco War appears in the relationship between two people sitting, together yet separate, in a hammock that represents the temporal suspension between the Chaco War and the present moment.

Chapter 3 moves to the 1969 Soccer War, also called the Hundred Hours War, between El Salvador and Honduras. While short and sensationalized, the war offers a glimpse into how Cold War economic integration and peacekeeping efforts backfired, contributing to an ongoing low level of violence in Central America. Roque Dalton's poetry from the time of the war to his untimely death in 1975 presents the hostilities as the result of a demographic and wealth imbalance. Dalton sets out to correct this imbalance and account for the people's perspective. In a strongly etymological sense, he conducts demographic writing, in which he accounts for the movement of the people, the Greek *demos*, through what he sees as a Central American stasis. Yet Dalton also hints that something escapes his text, mimicking the squatters and undocumented migrants who lacked textual proof of belonging to land and nation. Horacio Castellanos Moya picks up on Dalton's approach in the novel *Desmoronamiento* (Breakdown; Collapse). The novel charts the arc between Honduran political discord before the war, the Soccer War itself, the Salvadoran Civil War, and ultimately, the liquidation of fixed assets and flight from Central America by middle- and upper-class people who could afford to migrate north to Mexico and the United States. For Castellanos Moya, the 1969 war feeds into El Salvador's prolonged internal conflict and Central America's ongoing economic and political hardship.

Chapter 4 turns to the 1982 Falklands/Malvinas War between Argentina and the United Kingdom.[14] The war can be traced back to Argentina's peculiar relationship to Spanish and British imperialism, which

I explore through Susana Thénon's "Poema con traducción simultánea español-español" (Poem with simultaneous Spanish-Spanish translation). Likewise, Rodolfo Enrique Fogwill's *Los pichiciegos* (The armadillos; published in English as *Malvinas Requiem*) establishes the major tropes of the war as an anti-imperial and anti-authoritarian conflict, as Malvinas structures the Argentine state and nationalism. Carlos Gamerro's *Las Islas* (The islands) transposes the Malvinas War to sites on real and virtual planes in Buenos Aires during the 1992 commemoration of the tenth anniversary of the war and the five hundredth anniversary of Columbus's arrival, incorporating videogames, hackers, and transnational finance. For Gamerro, the only escape from the war is an extreme out-of-body experience, a type of ecstasy—ecstasis—brought on by MDMA, the recreational drug also known as Ecstasy. The spread of Malvinas into every corner of the country by the late 1990s shows that borders, even old imperial ones, have undergone a significant symbolic shift by the end of the twentieth century. What was once an old imperial conflict has now become a source of ongoing discord as the political body of the Argentine state is displaced outside of its own borders.

Chapter 5 examines the legacy of the Falklands/Malvinas War after 2001. From 9/11 in the United States to the political and financial crisis in Argentina, 2001 marked a rearrangement of political and economic structures. In Argentina, Malvinas returned to mainstream political discourse with the support of popular films like *Iluminados por el fuego* (Enlightened by fire; released in English as *Blessed by Fire*). Yet global political shifts also made Malvinas more difficult to pin down than earlier testimonial accounts were. Now, the war's legacy appears at unexpected and incongruous sites, as in medical metastasis when cancer manifests in distant organs. Lola Arias's trilingual play *Minefield/Campo minado* and subsequent film *Theatre of War/Teatro de Guerra* disarticulate testimony and translation as mechanisms of solidarity. Patricio Pron's *Nosotros caminamos en sueños* (We sleepwalk; We walk in dreams) uproots the Malvinas conflict completely, laying bare its connections to the military-industrial complex. Together, Arias and Pron suggest examining the past from the perspective of an outsider. They advocate taking a third-person perspective to challenge the role of the border under globalization as borders shift and multiply.

Throughout the book, I trace the emergence of the border as a locus of stasis: a geographical status quo accompanied by cultural and political nuance and dynamism. The borders wars I examine are rooted in Spanish colonialism, a legal and discursive background that continues to operate in spite of changes during the twentieth and twenty-first centuries. Against this backdrop, I have selected conflicts that are especially resonant with issues in contemporary border studies. For instance, the question of consumption, especially oil consumption and smuggling, appears in the Chaco War; labor, migration, and documentation appear in the Soccer War; and the confrontation between Spanish and English, Global South and Global North, appears in the Falklands/Malvinas War. These "other" border wars are not meant to be comprehensive and do not encompass all of Latin America's twentieth-century border disputes. Notably, the conflicts between Peru and Ecuador in 1941 and 1995 do not appear nor do border disputes involving Nicaragua, Brazil, or Colombia. The book does not aim to be a compendium of cultural studies of all Latin American border conflicts. Rather, the aim is to examine border conflicts to see how to study the border without affirming the border—that is, how to understand the border through stasis rather than polemos. Throughout the book, I gesture to a constant tension between a variety of forms—legal, textual, philosophical, political, and embodied—and what escapes them as nothingness, lack, omission, or undocumented vacancy.[15] By analyzing these tensions, I argue that replacing polemos—tied to border binaries—with stasis—a more ambiguous and plural conflict—allows a richer portrait of the border today.

CHAPTER 1

THE CHACO WAR AND ARCHIVAL HYPOSTASIS

Viejo vicio, este de la escritura. Círculo vicioso que se vuelve virtuoso cuando se cierra hacia afuera. Una manera de huir del no-lugar hacia el espacio estable de los signos.

—**Augusto Roa Bastos,** *Hijo de hombre*

Augusto Roa Bastos creates a narrative collage of Paraguayan history in the novel *Hijo de hombre* (Son of man), examining the 1932–1935 Chaco War with Bolivia in the final sections. In one of these chapters, Roa Bastos prints the diary of Miguel Vera, a military prisoner stuck in a jail that seems outside of the flow of time, where nothing happens and even the river seems to stand still: "The days pass by monotonously, all the same. . . . We're anchored in the middle of the slow, tiger-striped current, more than a kilometer wide. . . . When you look at it fixedly, at certain times of the day, it too seems halted, immobile, dead" (221).[1] In the midst of this dead time, news begins to filter in of students massacred in a pro-war rally in Asunción amid rising tensions with Bolivia.

Vera and the other prisoners begin to speculate on the reasons for the increasing likelihood of war, each presenting a theory about the true nature of the conflict. El Zurdo (Lefty) Medina, so-called for his Marxist views, claims that Paraguayans have been forced to fight for the vast expanses of land held by the likes of Argentine rancher Carlos

Casado: "Halfway through the Chaco, we're still on his land. Now we have to ask him for permission to go and die for it" (245).[2] According to Martínez, however, Casado has nothing to do with it: "We're going to fight and die for patriotism!" (245).[3] In response to Martínez's patriotism, el Zurdo offers another theory; while Paraguay defends Casado's lands, Bolivia pushes into the Chaco under pressure from oil companies. As el Zurdo replies to Martínez, "But our patriotism is going to end up smelling a lot like oil. . . . Big companies have good noses. They smell the mineral sea buried in the Chaco from far away" (245).[4] Another theory notes that the Bolivian attacks aim east toward the river: "Clearly, the Bolivian incursion aims at cutting off the Paraguay River, our vulnerable, watery spine. If they get control of it, they can fold the country in half and put it in their pocket" (246).[5] Landlocked since the 1879–1884 War of the Pacific, Bolivia aimed for the Paraguay River as an outlet to the Atlantic Ocean.

In his novel, Roa Bastos gives a snapshot of the most common explanations for the war that dragged on for three years and caused the death of tens of thousands in South America's poorest countries. Bolivia suffered more losses in its eventual defeat, while Paraguay, initially hesitant to fight, greatly expanded its official territorial reach into the northern Chaco. This was the first war in which modern military armaments like tanks were used in the Americas, yet historians believe more soldiers died of thirst and poor infrastructure than in direct combat. As a consequence, the war has been called *la guerra del petróleo* (war of oil) and *la guerra de la sed* (war of thirst). Roa Bastos emphasizes the soldiers' frustrations as they stand under the sun, noting that they're more likely to find oil when they dig a well than water.

Another prisoner, Noguera, proposes a theory that seems more historical, impressionistic, even poetic. Half-jokingly, Noguera says that hundreds of years before, the Spanish mapped the border between Alto Perú, which would eventually become Bolivia, and the Governorate of Paraguay, which would eventually become Paraguay. But an insect infestation in the archives at the Audiencia de Charcas rendered the documents illegible: "Those bugs bored holes through the Royal Documents. They ate up the primitive border signs, the landmarks, *uti possidetis*, they drank down the rivers. Everything. Now no one can figure it out. Not our scholars of borders. And not theirs . . ." (245).[6] The royal record succumbed to the tiny bookworms. Imperial enclosures were rendered illegible by bugs who ate through the representational suture of the map to its territory, making the decay of the legal limit literal and its enforcement impossible. In this poetic rendering of the legal history of the

Chaco, soldiers use force to fill in the holes and assert sovereignty. War restores imperial legal principles and spatial order, filling the vacancy at the heart of the South American continent and claiming the space left by the haphazard decay of empire.

In fact, an exact continuity with imperial limits was always impossible. Since the Spanish map was drafted, Bolivia and Paraguay had both gained independence but also suffered severe losses in late nineteenth-century wars with neighboring countries. The 1864–1870 War of the Triple Alliance against Argentina, Brazil, and Uruguay decimated Paraguay's population. Bolivia had already lost its seacoast to Chile and Peru as a result of the 1879–1884 War of the Pacific. Paraguay was hesitant to fight for the Chaco after enduring such major losses, while Bolivia was landlocked and eager to find a port. The attempt to recover the borders from the Audiencia de Charcas, and therefore ensure uti possidetis as the principle behind territorial division, was impossible from the start, even as it remained a guiding aim. The proper shape of American nations, mapping clearly and without holes onto the Spanish idea, sought continuity with the past while conveniently holding the promise of future resource exploitation in border zones.

Historically, the Chaco War has been seen as part of a broader continuity between imperialism and neo-imperialism as well as the stunted promises of modernizing infrastructure and progress. Roberto Querejazu Calvo's *Masamaclay* emphasizes that Bolivia in particular suffered from a disastrous combination of weak, fumbling politicians and cunning businessmen. This combination allowed transnational oil investors to start a race into the Chaco. In different versions of this story, Standard Oil of New Jersey is portrayed as Bolivia's backer, while Royal Dutch Shell is seen as Paraguay's. After peace negotiations, however, it became clear that the Paraguayan portion of the Chaco lacked significant oil deposits.[7] In his fictional account, Roa Bastos prefers to point the finger at large landholders, especially foreigners like Casado, who were more certain to lose from a Bolivian occupation than oil speculators. Despite many competing versions of war motives, the people living in the Chaco are almost never mentioned.

Paraguay greatly extended its reach into the Chaco territory after three years of combat. The principles of uti possidetis and status quo, which Carl Schmitt claims confer property guarantees and concrete spatial order to the system of international law as we saw in the introduction, were powerless to halt the outbreak of warfare. Nor could the newer League of Nations, with its more liberal ideals of self-determination, avoid bloodshed.[8] Bolivia, retreating toward the Andes once again, ne-

gotiated to keep the oil fields it had before the war but endured international humiliation. Finally, the border between the two countries was
agreed upon in peace negotiations, settling the largest territorial dispute
in twentieth-century Latin America.

In literature, the Chaco War is portrayed as unrelenting violence
that made promise and idealism impossible. Paraguayan history appears
in fragments braided with myth and reality, progress and destruction,
Spanish and Guaraní in the novel *Hijo de hombre*. Roa Bastos places a hole
at the heart of the South American continent, marking the Chaco as an
unknown or unrepresented point. Politicians and historians imagined
the Chaco as an untamed wilderness or state of nature that was formless
and eternal. Like the colonizers before them, they sent representatives
of the state to enclose it, to tame the unruly space at the heart of the
South American continent. The independence-era problem of civilization against barbarism returned with neo-imperial fervor, updated in the
rush to extract oil in the 1930s.

As an unenclosed territory at the heart of South America, the Chaco
illustrates the emergence of geographical, political, and embodied form
through enclosure.[9] In particular, the introduction of modern military
armaments in what was considered a primitive place makes the Chaco
War a stark exercise in contrast between the conquest-era imaginary
of untamed nature and modern political violence. The literature of the
Chaco War ironizes the violent transition from undifferentiated ground
to bordered territory as bloodshed shapes the land on maps. Ultimately,
the Chaco becomes the last part of the nation to be subdued and incorporated in a metaphysical incarnation likened to national birth. At the
same time, the border is decided as the philosophical foundations of the
modern political and geographical order begin to crumble, rattled by the
violence of the First World War and accelerating modernization. The
Chaco War sits at the crux of the final consolidation of sovereign borders in South America, even as the intellectual basis of this consolidation
weakened in the face of violence. Literature about the war reflects the
legacy of the Spanish colonial past, foundational uncertainties rocking
continental philosophy, and economic and political domination by powerful nations in the Global North.

This chapter begins the examination of stasis by looking into what
lies beneath: hypostasis. Whether what lies beneath the Chaco is oil,
water, or just more dirt, the Chaco War causes writers to revisit this
question through origin stories refracted in modern politics and philosophy. In philosophy, *hypostasis* means underlying substance, often related
to the emergence of form, while in Christianity, it refers to the word

becoming flesh, as in Roa Bastos's Biblical title. Narrative published during and just after the war—including Adolfo Costa du Rels's novel *La laguna H.3* (Lagoon H.3); Augusto Céspedes's short stories "El pozo" (The well) and "La paraguaya" (The Paraguayan woman) from *Sangre de mestizos* (Mestizo blood); and *Hijo de hombre*—is often realist in style. These works describe the violence of war with skepticism, causing a break with foundational fictions in religion, philosophy, and politics. In this chapter, I argue that the Chaco War presents the simultaneous appearance of sovereignty and its unworking in the undecidable and incomplete enclosure of territory. As the war aims to solidify and clarify national form, authors investigate the Chaco as a site of unintelligible enclosure, allegorized as holes in the map. They question hypostasis and the nature of representation in literature, philosophy, and politics.

THE CHACO WAR ARCHIVE

Roa Bastos's archival bookworms demonstrate how the dispute over the Chaco originates in texts like the disintegrating royal decrees. Spanish imperial maps inherit three of the foundational myths present in the Chaco archive: God, sovereign, and capital. With the frontier closing, myths of origin and destiny emerge as major tropes, especially through religious conceptions of heaven and hell. Throughout *Hijo de hombre*, Roa Bastos balances the two, mentioning a seventeenth-century treatise, *El paraíso en el nuevo mundo* (Paradise in the new world) by Antonio de León Pinelo, that affirms that the lost Eden lies in the heart of South America. For the soldiers in the Chaco, "these must be the ashes of Eden, burnt by Sin, over which the sons of Cain make pilgrimage now dressed in khaki and olive green. . . . From that mud emerged this dust" (265).[10] The war represents a return to paradise after expulsion, a return to the site of creation after the punishment of sin. A people emerges from the ruins of Eden, site of creation and incarnation, but, as we will see, their return makes faith falter. And Eden is just one of many origin stories that figure in one way or another in the perforated Chaco War archive.

Political myths also posit an origin, whether narrative or axiomatic, depicting anarchic and unsubdued territory prior to the emergence of order. Famously, for Thomas Hobbes, the origin of the political is in the state of nature, which is a chaotic and unbearable war of all against all. In exchange for protection, people submit to hierarchical organization, and the Leviathan is born. The return of war is an unfortunate resurgence of primordial violence that temporarily suspends sovereign protection, causing doubt in the validity of the state's protective promise. For Schmitt, the fiction of political origin can be supplanted by an axiom:

friend or foe. Describing the opposition displaced into the Chaco, Roa Bastos states: "On the other side is Kundt, the Teutonic mercenary. Two European schools of war will come face to face in the savage American desert, with primitive means, for less than primitive ends. It is also a way of enacting civilization on an uncultured periphery, stalled in the backwardness of the first day of Genesis" (*Hijo de hombre* 253–54).[11] The Chaco War is an update to the old stories of civilization and barbarism, melding myth with modernity. Both Hobbes and Schmitt draw on key elements of the broadly defined political realist tradition emphasizing the conflicted or oppositional aspects of politics, especially in international relations, rather than an idealist or liberal view emphasizing cooperation.[12]

The war likewise presents a conflict between those who see the origin of civilization as cooperative harmony and those who see it as unchecked conflict. Like their European counterparts after the First World War, Chaco War authors reflect on the nature of existence, metaphysical ground, and the nation. During the interwar period, Europe sought to rebuild and foster international cooperation through the League of Nations, operating at the time of the Chaco War and active in trying to mediate the dispute. Yet, as Schmitt mentions in a footnote, the League accomplished little but the twin prohibitions of conquest and war in the Chaco.[13] The League wanted to create a coalition against the recurrence of war but had no mechanism to enforce it. This would become its perennial problem: the incompatibility between a cooperative model and the inevitable resurgence of conflict, between an idealist and realist understanding of politics and international relations.

As conflict returned, narratives that emerged from the Chaco emphasized war's fruitless destruction with such insistence that some critics considered the authors condemned to be realists as well.[14] The land appeared untamable, burying, disappearing, and otherwise consuming the soldiers who sought to define an unambiguous border . This enclosure of land, in turn, holds another origin story. In Marxism, enclosure forms a key part of the origin of capitalism: primitive accumulation. Criticizing Adam Smith, Marx writes that, without a historical basis, the phase of wealth and resource accumulation "plays in Political Economy about the same part as original sin in theology" (*Capital* 873).[15] For Smith, according to Marx, the phase represents the mythical fall from grace, introducing economic inequality, which, for Marx, must be historicized and placed in context.

Out in the Chaco, stark contradictions emerged from the attempt to enclose, once and for all, the land at the heart of the continent. On the Paraguayan side, for instance, soldiers were forced to fight without shoes for privately held estates, including the strategic base of Puerto Casado. On the Bolivian side, soldiers fought with little water and, in the case of dramatic sieges such as the long battle at Boquerón, almost no supplies whatsoever. In Bolivia, the works of the so-called Chaco generation sparked political change during and soon after the war. Critical of combat conditions, racial inequality, and government neglect, the authors who recounted battle scenes began to foment a social consciousness that would set up the long track to Bolivia's 1952 revolution.[16]

Many Chaco generation authors wrote to raise political consciousness. Some of the Chaco generation Bolivians showed the vast inequalities in political and economic systems based on accumulation by dispossession, to use David Harvey's updated term for Marxist primitive accumulation. Others chose to focus on the material difficulties the soldiers faced on the battlefield, writing of a constant conflict, whether among the troops, against nature, or against the enemy. Postwar skepticism forced writers to question the nature of ground under the guises of metaphysics, incarnation, and ontology, with profound effects on conceptions of territory and sovereignty. Against the enclosure that the Chaco War sought to effect and the literary realist responses the war elicited, I focus in the coming pages on incomplete enclosures and representations, examining the places where the foundational fictions of God, sovereign, and capital hold and where they falter. Changes in presentation affect representation as, ultimately, Chaco War narrative exposes the hollow foundations of the state at its moment of greatest crisis and greatest strength: at war. The authors seem to depart from origin stories to share "the suspicion that war is ultimately unrepresentable" (Jameson, *Antinomies* 233).

THE ARCHIVE AND THE GROUND

In spite of the dubious representability of war, numerous Bolivian and Paraguayan authors wrote works based on combat. These form the basis of the Chaco War's literary archive, emblematically collected in Jorge Siles Salinas's book *La literatura boliviana de la Guerra del Chaco* (Bolivian literature of the Chaco War). Siles Salinas presents a contextualized study of the war's effects on Bolivian letters, remarking that there is a broad tendency in the stories, novels, and testimonies of the time to claim that the true Bolivian enemy is not the Paraguayan but the Chaco itself. In fact, in much Bolivian Chaco literature, the enemy rarely appears. Occasionally the authors give a glimpse of the battlefield, but on the whole, the novels bear more resemblance to survival than war stories. In this way, the literary representation of the Chaco War collapses the categories of friend and enemy, nature and culture, and international and civil war. The war is a question of ground that calls the ground into question.

Siles Salinas—along with much popular historiography, political speeches, and media reports, even now—refers to the war as an absurd, tragic event that should be remembered as an unfortunately lethal family row rather than a truly international war, noting the absence of any sort of hatred toward the Paraguayan enemy (*La literatura* 29).[17] He calls the Chaco War a civil war, even a fratricide, carried out by people too ignorant or easily manipulated to realize that Latin American nations are, in fact, brothers. He accuses other critics who find enmity between the two sides of being unable to recognize "in the case of Spanish-speaking countries on our continent, a blood brotherhood based on historical and cultural experience" (*La literatura* 78). He continues, "Consequently, the war between the two peoples is a civil war, a fratricide, like a conflict between two provinces of the same nation" (*La literatura* 78). The blood, culture, and history of the continent form the basis of a borderless American bloc. At first glance, Siles Salinas's interpretation may seem to support the guiding thesis that border wars can be considered as stasis rather than polemos, yet it fails in key regards.

In reading the cultural production that emerged from the war, Siles Salinas tends to find cooperation foiled by misunderstandings. He believes in the text's capacity to reveal the best of intentions, constructing a literary archive that attempts to recover a lost Spanish spatial order under threat of warring anarchy. Between the prepolitical origins of Spanish domination, in which the true enemy is a threatening landscape, and the seemingly inevitable but unnecessary war, Siles Salinas tends toward a shared language rather than a different nationality. At the same time, as in Roa Bastos, the historical archive thwarts the search for authentic, original, recoverable borders. Continuity with imperial enclosure is impossible, a creole heritage that ignores difference and reaffixes itself to a Hispanic space that has gradually become unrecognizable. Characterizing the conflict as a household row accepts the myth of an originary imperial family, failing to account for the question of ground that soldiers encounter in the Chaco.

A similar strategy of displacing conflict from the city onto the family dates back to ancient Athens. Giorgio Agamben, drawing heavily on Nicole Loraux, finds confusion between the intimate and foreign, especially in the threat of civil war, during which "the killing of what is most intimate is indistinguishable from what is most foreign" (14). In the case of the Chaco War, the retrospective inscription of kinship attempts to confound Bolivian and Paraguayan nationalisms, to place them in the same house.[18] As in ancient Athens, the civil war, or *stasis*, creates leaps *"through which the house is exceeded in the city and the city is depoliticised in the family"* (Agamben 16).[19] This process "functions in a manner similar to the state of exception" (Agamben 22) as inclusion through exclusion. If war makes the house indistinguishable from the city, represented in national and textual forms, then Siles Salinas's reading merely depoliticizes the border, appealing to a genealogical sense of cooperation.[20] In addition to finding no enmity toward Paraguayans, he finds no culpability on the part of diplomatic and business interests that many politicians blamed for the war. Siles Salinas considers this perspective part of an "excessive politicization" of war authors, and he decries the influence of Marxism (*La literatura* 42). He also describes a lack of faith that leads these authors to espouse a "pacifism [that] responds to something like an abstract and universal idea that considers *all* peoples of the earth brothers" (*La literatura* 31). Secular myopia leads them to translate class struggle universally without regard to cultural and linguistic heritage. For him, Hispanic fraternity outweighs other group identities, such as class. The erasure of enmity between Bolivia and Paraguay affirms a cooperative model of Hispanic brotherhood while erasing class struggle, indigenous heritage, and sexual difference.

Against this widely disseminated view, the rest of this chapter presents Chaco texts as questioning everything from the ground up. Soldiers question their captivity in a model of sovereignty rooted in political theology, layered with class conflict, and weighed down by imperial inheritance. In concert with European responses to widespread violence, Chaco authors use the coincidence of conflict in political and literary realism to reinterpret the mythical foundations upon which war depends, starting with enclosure. They reconsider the relationship between ground and territory, void and form, open and closed. The texts that emerge present the ground as undifferentiated space, proving that conflict cannot be so easily dismissed as an unfortunate row between Hispanic brothers, as for Siles Salinas. Ontological questions cannot be pushed aside when the foundation of the political order in hypostasis is at stake.

ANXIETY IN THE CAMERA OBSCURA

Some of the most famous accounts of the war come from Bolivian author Céspedes, who fought in the Chaco and whose writing and later political career were profoundly shaped by the war. His reports from the battlefield are collected in *Crónicas heroicas de una guerra estúpida* (Heroic tales of a stupid war). His story "El pozo," from the 1936 collection *Sangre de mestizos*, takes the form of a diary of soldiers who spend months excavating the earth in search of water, "with more thirst than hatred" (22).[21] The deeper they dig into the dry earth, the more desperate they become. After months of work, the supervising officer reaches the conclusion that, in spite of excavating meters and meters of soil, they will never find water. The frustrated officer repeatedly asks the men if they've found anything, and they inevitably return a negative: "Always nothing, same as the war . . . This nothingness will never end!" (42).[22] Céspedes's well is a bottomless pit, the fruitless labor of men slowly dying of thirst, and a symbol of the infernal Chaco: endless, dry, empty, hot, and hopeless.

Céspedes's story also seems to lend itself to Siles Salinas's interpretation of war, using the well's emptiness as a straightforward metaphor for the meaninglessness of war. For the soldiers on the ground, the push into the empty and unyielding land is frustrating, and abstractions such as title and right to property quickly fade. Historian Roberto Prudencio writes that the experience of the Chaco more broadly injected soldiers with a tragic anxiety: "Martin Heidegger says that anxiety is the encounter with nothingness. I'd say that the tragedy of the Chaco has been the tragedy of anxiety, that the men have encountered nothingness [*se han encontrado con la nada*]" (qtd. in Siles Salinas, *La literatura* 19). This nothingness in the Chaco might demonstrate that war bases itself on a nihilistic forging ahead under senseless orders without hope of victory or salvation. Nihilism proves that wars use inadequate means to achieve their often impossible ends, showing that the Chaco is merely an exemplary case of the lack of substance at the heart of violent confrontation.

More than merely declaring war empty, however, both Céspedes and Martin Heidegger circle the same questions: What happens in this encounter with nothing? What does it mean? For Heidegger, the anxiety produced in nothingness is shaped not by liberal cooperative ideals or fraternity but by the conflict between nothing and something as beings come to be. Heidegger's sustained reflection on the philosophical principle of sufficient reason—*nihil est sine ratione*, "nothing is without reason"—reflects the anxious encounter with constitutive nothingness that Prudencio describes in the Chaco. Diego Mattos Vazualdo has called this phenomenon "the poetics of absence" in Chaco War literature, a poetics that conflicts with the border as limit. Taking up the question a few years earlier from the other side of the Atlantic, Heidegger's interwar essay "On the Essence of Ground" follows the history of metaphysics, from Aristotle through Leibniz's principle of reason to Kant, as ground is inextricably linked to being and truth—a timely reflection given the reconfiguration of conceptual and geographical ground in Europe. As

Heidegger explains, the principle sets forth a rationalist paradigm: "The principle makes an assertion *about beings*, and does so with regard to something like 'ground.' Yet what constitutes the essence of ground is not determined *in* this principle" (100). Heidegger asks about the essence of ground by turning to ontology and epistemology, questioning the principle of sufficient reason through the ontological difference, the difference between beings and Being.[23] In the Chaco, Céspedes approaches a similar problem but changes the focus, asking: Why is there nothing instead of something?

For Céspedes, the Chaco's deepest well points to a precarious convergence of abyss and ground, reason and unreason. The point of contact between the soldiers and the ground undercuts the territorial distinctions of the state, as the deeper the soldiers dig, the more elemental and less differentiated the earth becomes. As they come in contact with the ground and the nature of their existence, they find themselves stuck between a war under the modern interstate framework, with its multiple and conflicting national anchoring points, and the ground of the Chaco as an anarchic underbelly of the more ordered progress taking place in urban centers.[24] Céspedes then uses the metaphorical, literary ground to approach the philosophical ground that Heidegger traces, digging into the idea that nothing is without reason or that, terrifyingly, thanks to war, everything is without reason. As Heidegger sketches the limits of reason in philosophy, Céspedes sketches them in literature, and the Chaco War, an outgrowth of modern national and economic reason, poses an anxiety-inducing encounter with irrationality and nothingness.[25]

In one of the most enigmatic episodes of "El pozo," the rational hold of war comes to a breaking point. At a depth of forty-one meters, the soldiers begin hallucinating light, water, and serpents. The narrator describes the well becoming the dark room of a camera obscura, the distant top its aperture that allows the soldiers to see, or at least imagine, another world. Using the light from this tiny opening, the soldiers develop their visions like photographs:

> Strange things happen. That camera obscura imprisoned in the depths of the well reveals images of water, catalyzed by dreams. The obsession with water is creating a peculiar, fantastic world, starting 41 meters below the surface, manifesting itself in a strange occurrence that took place at that depth.
>
> El Cosñi Herbozo . . . had fallen asleep at the bottom of the cistern when he saw a silvery serpent flash up. He grabbed it, and it disintegrated

> in his hands, but others appeared and started to gush up until they formed
> a spring of sonorous white bubbles, growing, filling the dismal cylinder
> like an enchanted serpent that had lost its rigidity and become as flexible
> as a column of water, upon which Cosñi felt himself lifted up until he
> was poured out onto the resplendent face of the earth. (*Sangre de mestizos*
> 37–38)[26]

El Cosñi Herbozo's mirage fills the well, lifting rather than drowning
him as he rises back to the level of the ground. He had ended up so
far down in the earth, plunged into his desire for water that he found
himself in a state of "groundless floating" (Heidegger *Being and Time*
170). When he reaches the surface, he tells the other soldiers about the
vision, sparking what the officer declares an "epidemic" of water delusions. Cosñi's vision reveals how Céspedes's story treads a fine line
between lack and plenitude, where, alongside Heidegger, the soldiers
discover the region in which "excess and withdrawal become transcen-
dentally attuned to one another" ("On the Essence of Ground" 129).
The soldiers hallucinate openness in water and light in the midst of their
underground imprisonment. The hallucination stages an encounter with
plenitude at the same time that it injects the soldiers with the anxiety
that begins to take hold of them as the ground entraps them and the
world recedes.

Rather than turning to idealism, the narrator mentions nothing but
frustration; the war that aimed at complete territorial enclosure gets displaced, from the horizontal push into the Chaco onto a vertical push
into the ground, from the superficial to the transcendental. And yet as
the men continue to dig down into the bind between sovereignty and
territory, they discover an unbreachable void, a lack of closure precisely
at the point where closure should be violently completed. They become
more literal versions of Roa Bastos's bookworms. This abyssal gap conditions their hallucination—a gap in both presentation, where beings
come into contact with Being, and representation, where reality and
hallucination converge.[27] The hallucination might be read as symbolic of
the emptiness of war or the metaphysical grounding of nationalism—the
absent center of an imagined community. The well might also provide
a metaphor for the lack of water—condition of life—that structures the
Chaco as a war of thirst and the Bolivian state in its frustrated search for
a port. Yet again, the vision might be cast as an aberrant discovery that
emerges from the dredging of ground, somehow creating an impossible
conversion of dirt and a sliver of light into serpents and water.

In these interpretations, the well becomes a version of the Platonic cave, the realm of ideal forms. The author of the diary likewise repeatedly returns to the image of a camera obscura in which light projects moving but distorted and inverted images of what happens above.[28] As the supervising officer explains when he finally decides to descend into the well himself, "I've tried to work, striking furiously with the pick, in hopes of accelerating with quick work the passage of time. But time is fixed and invariable in this place. Failing to reveal the change of hour with light, time stagnates underground in the black uniformity of a camera obscura. This is the death of light" (Céspedes, *Sangre de mestizos* 37).[29] The Chaco itself becomes the still point of modern progress. The reign of the image appears in the stagnation of time, or what Roland Barthes calls the stasis of the photographic image. The paradoxical still point at the heart of modernity becomes visible in photography where modernity records movement through immobilization, interiorizing its contradiction. The photo stops time, and death appears in what Barthes calls the "image's finitude" (90).[30]

The inelegant dance within nascent modernity's stillness over an emptying ground keeps "El pozo" from repeating the maxims of metaphysics, the image or idea of the cave, turning instead to the point of slippage between fantasy and reality. Once the water appears for the first time, the officer, concerned with the contagious hallucinations, asks rhetorically, "Such pain, such searching, such desire, so many thirsting souls concentrated in the deep hole give rise to these burgeoning springs?" (Céspedes, *Sangre de mestizos* 39).[31] The soldiers' hallucinations reveal that the well weakens their grasp on reality and perverts their desire. The well increasingly overwhelms them, especially since they have invested so much libidinal energy in it, as the earth—*Pachamama*, "Mother Earth"—threatens to devour them.[32]

Their fear is realized in the final lines of the story. The narrator describes the fate of the well from a hospital in the rearguard where he's recovering from a severe malaria relapse. Remembering the last time he saw the well, the officer recalls a sudden attack on the Bolivian lines. Thirsty Paraguayans, referred to as *pilas* from *pata pila* because their distinguishing feature was their barefootedness, hear rumors of the legendary well and make a push toward the water: "The pilas' gunfire grew and between explosions we made out their savage cry, the rage of the attack intensifying around the well. But we didn't retreat even a meter, defending it, *as if it really had water!*" (Céspedes, *Sangre de mestizos* 43).[33] The hallucination penetrates reality. Thirteen men die in the battle for the empty well, and their bodies are tossed into it, "swallowed up by shadows" and covered over with dirt (Céspedes, *Sangre de mestizos* 44).[34]

These thirteen soldiers fuse with the ground. In a curious twist, they die not for their country or even to save themselves but to protect the empty well that holds the unfulfilled promise of water in the midst of drought and the discovery of madness in the midst of the battlefield. They only discover this promise thanks to the extreme thirst in their own bodies, which forces them to act and symbolically unbind ground from territory, hollowing out an empty space in which the accidental encounter with nothingness and anxiety in hallucinatory desire and the devouring mother becomes possible. The accident, then, causes their raison d'être to pass from the state to their own survival and then to the preservation of the empty promise that lies deep in the well—the unfulfilled, unfulfillable promise of the sovereign state.

THE LAUGHING TOTEM

In another classic Chaco War story, *La laguna H.3*, a group of Bolivian soldiers, under attack by legions of Paraguayans, manages to escape siege in the nick of time. Their task is to supply water to the fort they had just abandoned, using only a compass and hazy memories of the maps they left behind in their rush to retreat. Originally written in French by Bolivian diplomat Costa du Rels in the immediate aftermath of the war, the novel was later amended and published in Spanish in 1967.[35] The soldiers have only a vague notion of the location of their water source, a lake or pond called H.3, presumably based on its coordinates on the lost map. Much like in "El pozo," the soldiers always expect to find water soon, but they never actually arrive at the lagoon. Rather than being trapped in the ground, the men wander through the desert, following commanding officer Borlagui, who eventually reveals to his subordinate, Contreras, that the instrument he has been using to guide them is actually a pedometer instead of a compass. Borlagui had been periodically consulting it as if it were a compass, yet carefully shielding it from the rest of his men's view. Similarly, the men defending the well in "El pozo" did so as if it had water; those reading the decaying maps in the Spanish archives did so as if they were complete. In each case, there is a measure of belief and a measure of deception. Borlagui had lost all sense of direction but had tried to keep up appearances to maintain order in the ranks.

Like in "El pozo," *La laguna H.3* stages a crisis of faith, particularly overwhelming at the beginning of the novel. Borlagui, whose Christian faith and military career make him seem almost monastic, argues with Contreras, whose religious and, to a lesser degree, political skepticism make him the cynical counterweight, exemplar for Costa du Rels of the modern, rational subject. As Contreras and Borlagui try to convert each other, tests of faith in the unseen, transcendent powers of God and the unifying powers of the state punctuate the novel, pushing the officers to consider proofs of politics and ontotheology. They probe the borders that contain them and the hierarchical structures that create order in their lives.

At the forts along the border, Borlagui begins to doubt: "Borlagui felt the first prick of doubt. Accustomed from the beginning of his career to the precarious existence of forts in dreadful, uninhabited territories, standing guard between inexistent borders, cause of future conflicts, Borlagui had coated himself in cool impassivity" (Costa du Rels, *La laguna* 59).[36] Yet, apart from this short lapse, Borlagui generally maintains faith in the cohesion that the weightless, inexistent borders offer. He explains that belief-trickery pairs, such as the compass and the border, are the only things capable of maintaining order. They turn his men into well-handled puppets thanks to an air of authority and the men's desire to believe in an organizing structure. According to Borlagui: "My authority here doesn't come from talent or rank, but from my knowledge and the confidence it inspires. Granted, my power consists of an imaginary compass. At the expense of a . . . swindle, it has maintained discipline, cohesion, and shaped the hope of all of my men. In the face of danger, everyone looks for the object or image that solidifies and retains fate" (67).[37] The men cling to the objects that might save them. Unable to recover the map, they imagine that Borlagui's memory of the coordinates along with his compass represent survival, salvation, order, and orientation.[38] Between them, with a measure of imagination and luck, the lagoon takes on shape and weight; it can be discovered and exploited. Without the compass, the *laguna* is empty, purely figurative, and lacking, as its other definition suggests: a lack, or lacuna.

As the need for water grows dire, the Chaco becomes more unbearable. Its vast openness in the day contrasts with the bright, menacing eyes shining in the scrub at night. Man and beast turn on each other and among themselves, staging the prehistoric war of all against all with the conquistador's eye toward nature as anarchic space awaiting enclosure and exploitation. In the wilderness, Costa du Rels imagines a reverse discovery scene in which Contreras acts as one of Columbus's men, on the lookout for water instead of land. From high in a tree rather than the crow's nest of a ship, "[Contreras] hurried down, but stopped on one of the last branches. There, he gathered strength and cupping his hands in the shape of a megaphone, shouted, like Columbus's sailors, instead of land: Water! Water!" (*La laguna* 155).[39] Costa du Rels rewrites the discovery into his Chaco war novel. Yet centuries later, the conquest's ever-inward drive has exhausted itself. Latin American states, now independent, have yet to escape the farcical repetition of their colonial history or rid themselves of the view that further discovery will lead to salvation.

Costa du Rels draws this continuity through the instruments of spatial representation, pairing the fake compass with the memory of the lost map. A high-ranking diplomat, active in the League of Nations at the time of its dissolution, Costa du Rels himself was tasked with preserving the spatial order set in previous centuries with compasses and maps. In order to prevent warfare, in practice the League was forced to preserve the status quo in the name of diminishing loss of life through rational dialogue in a common space. The organization tried to tame anarchy using deception, making the low-level violence inherent in the preservation of order invisible.[40] Reading Costa du Rels's novel alongside his biography, the fraudulent compass might correspond to the League of Nations, over whose final session he presided. With Contreras as neo-Columbus in the Chaco, the novel makes clear that there is no peace, at least since the arrival of Europeans in the Americas.[41] The League, a purely figurative compass tasked with organizing spatial order and fostering dialogue, cannot do anything other than make limp declarations, citing past precedent and encouraging peace. Powerless to stop the subsequent three years of bloodshed in the Chaco, it would be similarly powerless to stop rekindled war in Europe, which Costa du Rels would observe firsthand from Paris.[42]

Echoing the futility of diplomacy and the frustration of Céspedes's well, the discovery of water in *La laguna H.3* again proves to be a mirage. As the men keep looking, the Chaco becomes a version of hell. Having barely escaped the impending Paraguayan counteroffensive at Boquerón, the land entraps them. The Chaco makes them feel that they are moving forward, even though they are only ever walking in circles. The men finally realize the futility of their erring through the desert when they come upon the body of a comrade, swarmed by buzzards and insects and stuck high in a tree like a prize of war. They imagined themselves walking away from him but realize they have been encircling him all along. They are unable to escape the eternal return of the damned in this circle of hell. In spite of the limitlessness of the desert, it imprisons them.

Contreras, the representative of rationality, eventually has a modern crisis of faith, a crisis in his ability to reason. After he has definitively lost his mind, the other men consider killing him to save his ration of water, but Borlagui keeps them at bay. Stuck out in the sun, Contreras sits near a bulging toborochi tree with a cut in the center of its trunk: "He had had his gaze fixed, with partly closed pupils, on the old hieratic tree for over an hour, wondering about the source of its strange wound. He discovered an air of majestic sadness in it. A deposed king, perhaps humiliated by age and the ingratitude of the younger generation. Contreras spoke to it pityingly, wanting to tease out the source of its misfortune" (Costa du Rels, *La laguna* 121).[43] The injured majesty of the tree at first inspires compassion with its natural sovereignty, its power and age. But then it inspires violence. Contreras "turns twice around the *toborochi*, as though waiting for the exact moment to ask it a question or deliver a blow. Is he really in his right mind, constant arbiter of his thoughts and actions? Brusquely, he strikes the tree, and with his hands tensed, in an effort of which he no longer seemed capable, he insists on transforming the cavity into an immense, half-open mouth, nearly leaving his nails behind in the bark" (124).[44] He sculpts a mouth into the tree, scratching the bark with his fingernails to liberate its form. Reason stands in question. In his madness, rather than dig a dark chamber in the ground or bore a hole through a map, Contreras wants to know about its misfortune, so he carves out an opening for speech, turning his madness into the possibility of conversation with the deposed toborochi king.

Contreras's fascination with the humanoid form he liberates from the tree trunk places him in a quasi-religious ecstasy: "Everything vibrates. Everything gleams in the dawn phantasmagoria. Contreras feels thrown out of himself, upon seeing that the mouth, the horrible gob, work of his hands, dripping with light, laughs!" (126).[45] The laughter is meaningless, conveying mocking, madness, confusion, and thirst but without substance. Later in the novel, in a part heavily amended from the original French, Contreras identifies this as the moment in which part of his personality stays behind in the tree and another continues on through the Chaco.[46] Contreras's ecstasy has placed him at the limit between rationality and irrationality, connecting him to forces beyond the supposed ground of reason, beyond the reality and realism of the Chaco.

Contreras's encounter with madness can be understood as an encounter with the beyond, a religious ecstasy brought on by extreme heat and thirst. Under this lens, the novel has been considered "a Catholic novel built around that tragedy" (Siles Salinas, *La literatura* 131). Biblical allusions, as in Roa Bastos, are undeniable, especially as the men wander in the desert. The toborochi is also likened to the Tree of Jesse. And there are references to Columbus's *Diaries*, Dante's *Inferno*, and other works from the European Christian tradition. Presumably, the Catholic nature of the novel comes from its author's personal convictions along-side the salvation scene, in which a sudden providential storm drops pebble-sized hail that the few remaining soldiers, including Contreras, gather and eat. Yet, the novel also seeks to modernize the religious prob-lem, presenting the war's brutality as an inflection point at which skep-ticism and deception become part of the modern state.[47]

In the Christian interpretation of *La laguna H.3*, Contreras's skep-ticism might be seen as a modernized test of faith, reaffirmed when, in the second edition of the novel, he returns to war having recovered his sanity. Nevertheless, there is an undeniable breakdown between the supernatural and reason at the moment that the sculpted mouth laughs. The illusion of realism and transparent representation disappears when Costa du Rels abandons his realist style as Contreras loses his grip on reality. The missing lagoon—lacuna—coincides with the formless node of madness inside the tree's swollen trunk. Contreras recognizes the mo-ment as pivotal because it disrupts his self-identification. Realism fails because of the weakness of the body or the mind, and there is a hypo-static encounter. There is already heterogeneity and unintelligibility in the sculpted, totemic form of the mouth emerging from the tree trunk. Yet the story of sovereignty quickly swallows it up. As a consequence, skepticism and a degree of self-criticism and heterogeneity become in-tegral to the enclosure.

The war gradually moves to smaller scales. Like nesting dolls, Bo-livian narrative shows how the conflict's toll pushes further down, from the level of international conflict to the Bolivian troops among them-selves to the individual soldier who no longer identifies with himself. The ever smaller scale and split self-identification appear at the narrative level as an interruption of representation, making way for a kernel of un-intelligibility that exceeds the goals of communication and pacification that Costa du Rels espoused as a diplomat. Something escapes the field of representation, rendering liberal diplomacy ultimately ineffective. Cen-turies after the conquest, the Chaco still holds elements unintelligible to compasses and maps, a hypostatic node that is not fully captured in representation or speech.[48] In spite of the ideal of cooperation, it is im-possible to recognize the tree as a subject or its laughter as communica-tion. The tree's laughter exposes wrinkles in the smooth, selfsame space that the compass presupposes, revealing the rationalization of space and communication as a fraud.

From this perspective, the novel functions as much more than a mere rewriting of Biblical stories in the context of Latin American warfare. It is a critique of the state and interstate systems from the very moment of enclosure, from the time a thirsty Columbus stumbles through the ashes of Eden in the Chaco. Diplomacy and literature stretch and falter at the imperfect seam between narrative realism, seen in the description of the Chaco, and political idealism, seen in the affirmation of fraternity and cooperation. Both modes fail: the literary deviating into fantasy and ecstasy and the political degenerating into unremitting conflict. The mouth in the tree, instead of consuming the representation of territory like the archival bookworms, becomes the mouth of the man-eating, madness-inspiring Chaco, in which ants and beetles swarm abandoned corpses and buzzards pick at the war's festering human carrion. The Chaco becomes more menacing than the enemy, capturing its victims as in José Eustasio Rivera's classic *La vorágine* (The vortex). Costa du Rels could have easily included Rivera's famous last line: "los devoró la selva" (203), or "the jungle devoured them," modifying it slightly to "los devoró el Chaco," or "the Chaco devoured them," as Francisco Xavier Solé Zapatero writes, drawing from Carlos Fuentes's analysis of the *novela de la tierra* (qtd. in Solé Zapatero). Borlagui eventually succumbs to the Chaco, and Contreras is left guarding the fake compass and leading a diminishing number of increasingly fractious men in search of water. In the end, the liberation of the sovereign shape, unintelligible and hidden in the tree trunk, becomes the voracious mouth of the Chaco, consuming the soldiers while ensuring Bolivia and Paraguay's landlocked enclosure in the South American continent.

CAPTIVITY AND SPECTRAL TRANSPARENCY

Céspedes and Costa du Rels's narrative realism could not contain the outburst of the fantastic, just as the soldiers cannot stop their creeping captivity in and captivation with the Chaco. As the empty well fills with silver serpents and Contreras finds himself absorbed in ecstasy, stories reveal that enclosure necessitates escape. It is this same enclosure, ciphered in sovereignty, that vexes contemporary political theory: "A picture holds the study of politics captive. It is a picture of politics organized into sovereign states" (Havercroft 1).[49] Political theory can identify, but not fully escape, the matrix established in wars such as the Chaco. It can hear but not make sense of the unintelligible cries that escape this matrix. The two disputed motives for Bolivian aggression adhere exactly to the conflicting desires of enclosure and release: on the one hand, the desire to safeguard resources in order to facilitate accumulation and modernization and, on the other hand, the desire for an exit to a viable port to ship primary materials and other resources overseas. This contradictory and static picture, whether in the form of a map or an institution like the League of Nations, represents the failed mediation between open-ness and closure. The problem, in other words, is not just that there is a modern European mode of warfare playing out in a mythically primitive desert as German General Kundt directs Vickers tanks sinking into the mud of Eden. Nor is it that the fantastic interrupts the real. Rather, the problem is that the encounter between void and form that Chaco narra-tors portray—the problem of the assumption of form or hypostasis—is the terrain over which the "picture of politics" captures and combines affirmation with skepticism, theism with atheism. This split drives Con-treras mad and makes self-identity impossible. It is a contradictory, even perverse, combination of the origin stories of conflict (Hobbes), enclo-sure (Marx), paradise (Eden), and the metaphysical beyond.

In wartime, the "picture of politics" distills this muddle of fictional origin stories into the order of sovereign states. From Céspedes's primi-tive camera obscura in the deepest well in the Chaco, the technology of the state creates an unmoving image of borders, citizens, and soldiers, mimicking photography in its capture. One could replace the word "photograph" with "sovereign state" in Barthes's remarks on the frozen time of the photo: "That the Photograph is 'modern,' mingled with our noisiest everyday life, does not keep it from having an enigmatic point of inactuality, a strange stasis, the stasis of an *arrest*" (91). Photographic capture depicts the modern picture of politics, arrested by sovereignty.

"La paraguaya," also from Céspedes's *Sangre de mestizos*, follows the portrait of a mysterious woman recovered from a Paraguayan soldier's body.[50] From the opening line, the story suggests the question of prop-erty and the proper: "That photograph of a woman belonged to a dead Paraguayan" (233).[51] The picture is the property of this dead Paraguayan. The rest, whether the woman depicted is Paraguayan or even the dead soldier's lover or wife, is up to conjecture. The Bolivians inventory the dead Paraguayan officer's possessions, taking what they see fit, including the picture of the mysterious woman and a lock of hair wrapped in silk. These last two objects become a sort of talisman for the Bolivian officer, Lieutenant Paucara, who takes them. He refuses to give the picture to a comrade, who snatches it out of his hands, insisting that it brings him luck. At the end of the story, Paucara is gunned down in battle, and the picture again crosses enemy lines and passes into the hands of two Para-guayans, who remark to one another, "She's pretty, the Bolivian's wife" (251).[52] They note that she's a widow now, and Céspedes closes the story: "And they marched on through the woods, carrying off the portrait of the 'widow'" (251).[53] The reader is left wondering how many times her photo has crossed from cadaver to cadaver as a talisman—possibly as long as the war has gone on—and whether she was originally Bolivian or Paraguayan.

The story might easily be integrated into the larger narrative of tragic warfare among people who, at heart, belong to the same fraternity of Latin American nations, unwittingly caught in a modern disaster. The woman could easily be Bolivian or Paraguayan, her portrait and strands of hair moved to the bodies of officers from either side. She is a widow many times over on both sides of enemy lines, a representative of unnecessary heartache inflicted on the home front. Her image always lands on the wrong side of the friend-enemy line, which the photo easily crosses. Deprived of the comforts of the opposite sex, the men on the battlefront fetishize her as an exotic other, yet she always escapes their grasp. She stands outside of their fraternity.[54] She cannot be pinned down and becomes a wandering signifier of national fluidity as her image gets plucked from the bodies of dead soldier after dead soldier.

In this sense, the woman undercuts the promise of photography. The photo promises to represent the person pictured transparently, as in the portrait of her captivating face: "Dense, black, flowing hair . . . softly rounded face . . . immense eyes" (235).[55] In the story, however, the index fails; the woman cannot be identified except contextually in association with a corpse. The portrait is supposed to form part of a stable system of signification anchored in reality and experience, yet there is a disconnect between Paucara's title, *teniente*—literally, one who possesses (lieutenant; placeholder)—and the spectrality of his possession: "His life in flames accepted, without feeling it, the fact of his romantic relationship with this unknown, mute woman, with the distant Paraguayan lodged in the intimacy of his wallet as the only woman in the void the others hadn't been able to occupy" (239–40).[56] The woman is a phantasm in the void. The system of signification has come unmoored on the battlefield, and the woman's image occupies the emptiness that opens up at the intersection of sexual difference and war. At the same time, the physical proximity of the photograph to death is evocative. More than representing the deep similarity between warring nations, the photograph reveals that when violence intervenes in the system of signification, even the most transparently indexical and modern forms of representation escape into the unknown and mute.

If in Céspedes's "El pozo" there was a radical presentation, a failure of reason, and the near impossibility of representation, then "La paraguaya" approaches the war from another angle. The image's ambiguous belonging is ill-suited to the typical explanations for war. In the photograph, the war appears as neither meaningless nor meaningful. It is not a tragic fratricide, given the officers' cold approach to the spoils of war, unfeeling toward the dead enemy and possessive of the woman pictured. Nor are the men truly enemies; rather, they are traversed by a shared traitorous desire. They are neither brothers nor friends nor enemies. All they possess is the promise of an illusory and impossible relationship with an excluded, desirable other. The photographic capture proves inadequate to anchor signification, holding a representative captivity, which, while seemingly indexical, can be easily unchained from its signified.

This point is the threshold of politicization in Agamben's approach to *stasis*. Following Loraux, civil war, or *stasis*, mediates between *polis* and *oikos*, city and family, public and private, politics and economics (Agamben 23–24). This space between polis and oikos is the same one portrayed in "La paraguaya." The woman's portrait creates a juncture that can bring together or pull apart the home and the nation, catalyzing or depoliticizing conflict. Agamben picks up on this point, arguing that, given the existence of the nation, etymologically linked to birth, the only way that life can be politicized at the moment of *stasis* is in its exposure to death, in his signature concept of "bare life" (24).[57] Similarly, the image, standing in for the threshold of politicization in the cross between polis and oikos, is only released from its captivity, its possession by the lieutenant (teniente), in death.[58]

Yet this woman never appears in relation to a body, so she is never exposed to death. Rather, her image exists at the point where spheres of enclosure meet but fail to signify. The photographic capture, most real of realisms, has divorced representation from the hallucinatory void in "El pozo" and the sculpted liberation of form in *La laguna H.3*. The woman's "immense eyes" stare out of the portrait unflinchingly at each officer and at each exchange across enemy lines, through all of the slippages between polis (in this case, the nation-state rather than the city-state) and oikos (part of ongoing primitive accumulation rather than the household economy). But the woman does not experience birth pangs at the border between these two nations and spheres of enclosure. No one witnesses the emergence of the nation as a political body; it is merely assumed. While the enclosures create the "picture of politics" that captivates the soldiers like the picture of the woman, in the borderlands of the Chaco the picture merely floats back and forth across the border. Both images stutter at the edge of realism. Again, representation fails. Stuck in a cycle that signifies only in relation to corpses, the moment of capture fades into the past. Agamben assumes that the division into city and family is sealed prior to the *stasis*, even as it remains at the service of a more fluid politicization. Disarticulated by the closure of the Chaco frontier, the image of politics based on fraternity is dissociated from any referent.

On this account, the soldiers' fixation on the Paraguayan woman's portrait resonates with the emphasis on the face for Emmanuel Levinas. In his early lectures collected in *Time and the Other*, Levinas describes hypostasis as the experience of the ontological difference, defining it as the moment when an existent comes into contact with its existence in the evanescent present of the encounter with the other (51–54). In setting out from the self and returning to the self, the subject performs the "work of identity" from which temporality arises (52). Based on this progression, Levinas arrives at an ethically inflected critique of Heideggerian ontology.[59] In "La paraguaya," however, the work of identity is impossible because the woman exists merely as a representation of light and shadow on paper. As in each of the stories in this chapter, contact with enclosure is disrupted by a gap, a space vacated by the existent. Again and again, the Chaco seems to present the inscrutable anxiety of this vacancy. It can be covered over with the veil of fraternity, but the suture comes undone in the face of sexual difference.[60]

Consequently, the realism of war literature cuts more deeply than just representation of experience. Chaco literature passes through territory and enclosure to the very question of ground and the moment of hypostasis, grappling with the articulation between birth and death, hypostasis and the stasis of war—no longer the Greek civil war but rather stasis emptied of identitarian terms and in all of the meaning it acquires in this book: stagnation, internecine conflict, and rhetorical displacement. Returning to Jameson's "suspicion that war is ultimately unrepresentable" (*Antinomies* 233), we find that there is always already a disjuncture in sovereignty, an atheism in political theology, an imperfection in hypostasis. Unrepresentability at this threshold creates a static time that arrests the border at the moment it emerges. Hypostasis is in a seemingly sealed, atemporal state, like the picture of politics, but stasis is not the same as stillness. Stasis must have a temporal vector or risk reproducing the purported timelessness of sovereignty. This timelessness is what the literature of the Chaco War exposes as a fraud, such as fraternity, the compass in *La laguna H.3*, the rational space of dialogue, and the uncontested transit between house and city in Agamben's version of *stasis*. Instead, constructions and disarticulations of time, birth, and death have to be made to appear, as they do at last in Roa Bastos's fragmentary portrayal of Paraguayan history in *Hijo de hombre*.

THE FRAGMENTED PASSAGE OF TIME

In many ways, *Hijo de hombre* echoes the earlier Bolivian stories of the 1930s, including the struggle against nature, lack of water, and overall hopelessness of the troops. In the lead up to the war, Miguel Vera is a military prisoner charged with subversive activity. Ostracized and stigmatized for having leaked a plan of rebellion during a night of excessive drinking, Vera is forgiven when, soon after the conversation the prisoners have about the destroyed maps from the Audiencia de Charcas, he is released back into the ranks to fight in the Chaco. Eventually, he and his men get lost somewhere near the ongoing siege at Boquerón. They come upon a clearing that seems to be the meeting point of several well-traveled paths, and so they haphazardly decide it has "a certain operational importance" (Roa Bastos, *Hijo de hombre* 263).[61] As if in a miniature Chaco, the men fumble upon something perceived to be valuable but that is, in the end, worthless.

Trapped behind enemy lines with scarce provisions and a demagnetized compass, Vera and his men await the slow white death of thirst. They send out scouts who never return, but by connecting two sections of the novel, the reader sees that these scouts must have made it back to camp and given the officers information about the lost detachment's location. The officers decide to send Cristóbal Jara at the head of a water convoy, considering the mission at best a suicide mission. Back in the scrub, Vera holds out until the very end, while the men around him gradually die. He sees the water truck approach, having driven through hell, tires aflame, Jara's hands tied to the steering wheel. But Vera, weak and tired, thinks the truck is a hallucination and shoots at it "without managing to destroy that monster of my own delirium" (Roa Bastos, *Hijo de hombre* 272).[62] Unlike the Bolivian narrative written in the immediate aftermath of the war, in which hallucinations destabilize reality, Roa Bastos's version sees Vera confuse reality with hallucination. Reading his journal entry along with the story of Jara in the novel's next chapter, the reader sees that Vera has killed his savior, sealing his fate as a traitor. For his part, Jara seems unfazed by the suicide mission. He considers the biblical dust in the weight of the earth, covering the bodies of two fallen men with dirt, "thinking perhaps that all the dead earth of the Chaco wouldn't be able to cover them, to fill in those holes the size of a man" (304).[63] Expanding like a map folded out to match the ground, the holes have grown from the small ones eaten into the archival paper to the size of men, so expansive that they cannot be filled with all the dirt in the Chaco.[64]

40

Of all of the pieces missing from the fragmentary story, however, perhaps the most obviously absent in a novel that treats the transition from mythical to modern times is the story of salvation: the moment of tragedy and triumph in which Jara saves Vera.[65] By the time the water convoy is on its way, Vera is desperate and on the verge of suicide, writing in his journal: "It's better to end it once and for all . . . But how difficult it is to die!" (Roa Bastos, *Hijo de hombre* 272).[66] When he remarks on the experience years later, it is as if his escape from the edge of the abyss remains inexplicable: "I found myself sitting at a table in a bar, next to other human spoils of war, without being like them. Like in that remote ravine in the Chaco, scorched by thirst, bewitched by death. That ravine had no exit. But nevertheless I'm here. My nails and hair keep growing, but a dead person cannot withdraw, give up, relinquish a little bit more and more . . . So I keep living, in my own way, more interested in what I've seen than what I have left to see" (361).[67] Vera sees himself as part of the human spoils of war, surrounded by others yet without any shared likeness. He reflects on his entrapment in the gully before a sudden temporal ellipse covered up with "But nevertheless . . ." during which he escapes and survives, but he never gives an account of his salvation. Instead, he notes that his hair and nails have continued growing, as they would immediately after death. He survives in a liminal space between life and death in which his organism continues functioning, unable to retract or withdraw, but the nature of his existence has been irrevocably called into question by the encounter with the *salida*, "exit": the escape from the ravine, from the Chaco, from the earth. He has been rendered an animated residue of the past, lodged between life and death, existence and nonexistence.

Vera ultimately had survived the ordeal and made it back to the town, where he became a politician. He continues writing, haunted by the past, insistently returning to the shame of his betrayal and trying to justify his survival. He gradually falls into increasing desperation. By the final pages of his manuscript, continuing his search for an escape, he writes, "There must be some escape from this monstrous nonsense of man crucified by man. Because otherwise one would be forced to think that the human race is eternally damned and that this is hell and we can no longer expect salvation. There must be some way out, because otherwise . . ." (Roa Bastos, *Hijo de hombre* 369).[68] The sentence is left unfinished, and a note included with the text reads, " . . . This concludes Miguel Vera's manuscript" (369).[69] Vera dies of a gunshot wound to the spine, and his words are copied down in a legal document testifying to his death. In drawing up the report, there are two versions of what happened: the first, that the gun fired while Vera was cleaning it; and the second, that a boy playing with the mayor's gun accidentally shot him.

In a fragment excised from the edited and reissued version of the novel, Roa Bastos writes in the final note from that Vera "was an incurably tortured man, his spirit disgusted by the world's ferocity, but he rejected the idea of suicide. 'A Paraguayan never commits suicide . . . ' he wrote to me in one of his final letters. 'At most he lets himself die, which isn't the same thing . . . '" (*Hijo de hombre* 402 [2008]).[70] And yet, Vera was on the verge of suicide when Jara arrived and again as he scribbled his final words on the freshly inked pages found near his mortally wounded body. History has embittered Vera, whose diary had promised to serve as the "stable space of signs" (Roa Bastos, *Hijo de hombre* [2012], 237). But after the war, the "old vice" of linguistic capture remains incomplete, inadequate for explaining death.

The terrestrial translation of the Christian salvation story onto the accursed repetition of "man crucified by man" causes Vera to feel trapped. He is caught between a desire to resolve into time, to write and rewrite the past making it palpable and representable, and a desire to resolve away from time, obscuring betrayal and salvation to make his pain disappear. He is caught in the Christian tradition of the word made flesh—his own existence as failed hypostasis—and the incarnation of speech referenced in the novel's epigraph from the Guaraní hymn of the dead: "And I will make language [*el habla*, speech] reincarnate . . . / After this time is lost and a new time dawns" (Roa Bastos, *Hijo de hombre* 31).[71] Once incarnation has taken place, there seems to be no exit. Even suicide, "the final mastery one can have over being" (Levinas, *Time* 50), appears to offer an, at best, ambiguous solution, and the reference to suicide, even to refute it, is put under erasure in the revised edition of the novel.

Here, Roa Bastos's novel intervenes in the philosophical problem of how to approach existential foundations when modern technological violence has ripped them apart. Levinas examines the problem by emphasizing the limitless, which does not admit suicide. Against Heidegger's anxiety and nothingness, Levinas focuses on the impossibility of an exit from being: "The notion of irremissible being, without exit, constitutes the fundamental absurdity of being. Being is evil not because it is finite but because it is without limits. Anxiety, according to Heidegger, is the experience of nothingness. Is it not, on the contrary—if by death one means nothingness—the fact that it is impossible to die?" (Levinas, *Time* 50–51).[72] Between "how difficult it is to die!" and "a Paraguayan never commits suicide," Vera's diaries hesitate between the finite and infinite.

Roa Bastos makes Vera's testimony a gesture toward this threshold at which philosophical foundations and mythical certainties, shaken and dislodged by bloody wars, rework the relationship to ground, even as the ground sinks away into bottomless pits.[73] This process is only visible at the edges of the text, in the connections between fragments, versions, and revisions, but eventually, it comes into view. Just as after the war there is a treaty, a line, a final enclosure, so the novel arrives at an uncertain stability portraying the war and its consequences. In the heat of battle, Vera writes in his diary: "Our lines have stabilized somewhat precariously. It's more of an unstable equilibrium" (Roa Bastos, *Hijo de hombre* 258).[74] Perhaps the lines are not just the trenches but also the lines of writing in Vera's diary, the lines that pass into the novel and, eventually, with the publication of the revised edition, achieve an equilibrium that both includes and suppresses ellipses and omissions.

Stasis acquires a temporal vector, having passed through the questions of origin and enclosure in hypostasis. Enclosure seeks a complete shape or form, and finitude, poised on the edge of anxiety and nothingness, undoes it. Time appears in death, crisis, conflict, and decay, as fragment and multiplicity as well as impalpable lack. In the final pages of his manuscript, reflecting on the toll of war on its survivors, Vera points out that "in Guaraní, the word *arandú* means *wisdom* and indicates *feeling the passage of time*" (Roa Bastos, *Hijo de hombre* 368).[75] This "feeling the passage of time" keeps stasis from becoming frozen, lodged in the past like the human spoils of war or the modern picture of sovereignty. The passage of time exposes borders to their own decay, to their necessary and inherent self-deconstruction.

Reading the literary archive of the Chaco War means peering into the depths of the well with a nod to the inevitable forces of unreason, the insufficiency of realism, and the uncontained void at the heart of representation. The task of reading the incomplete and fragmented Chaco archive is to identify the convergence between literary and political enclosures, to recognize the representative functions that lay claim to the region. It is to exploit the breach in these enclosures in the face of sexual and linguistic difference, unrepresented in the liberal diplomatic field. It is to become the bookworms wrecking the maps in order to feel the ground, all without falling into a facile pacifism that assimilates the violence of enclosure through Hispanic fraternity. It is to this familial violence that chapter 2 turns, examining a very different temporality that works to pacify unintelligibility, gradually incorporating, sublating, and consuming it in the twenty-first-century legacy of the Chaco War.

THE CHACO WAR AND THE CONSUMPTION OF STATUS

Boquerón es un hueso difícil de digerir. El movimiento peristáltico de nuestras líneas trabaja inútilmente para deglutirlo. Hay algo de magia en ese puñado de invisibles defensores, que resisten con endemoniada obcecación en el reducto boscoso. Es pelear contra fantasmas saturados de una fuerza agónica, mórbidamente siniestra, que ha sobrepasado todos los límites de la consunción, del aniquilamiento, de la desesperación.
—**Augusto Roa Bastos,** *Hijo de hombre*

Early in the war, Bolivian troops captured the Paraguayan fort at Boquerón in order to advance their position into what is today Paraguayan territory. The Paraguayan army planned a counterattack and laid siege to the fort for weeks in September 1932. The heroic resistance of the vastly outnumbered Bolivians became the stuff of lore. As the siege wore on, Bolivian soldiers ran short of every possible supply, even killing and eating the mules that carried heavy machinery to the remote fort. In the end, the remaining soldiers were taken prisoner, and Bolivia was defeated. Paraguay achieved a decisive, albeit extraordinarily bloody, victory, igniting hopes for a swift end to the conflict. The battle was also future Paraguayan dictator Alfredo Stroessner's first major battle at the age of nineteen. In Bolivia, stories of Boquerón echo into the present, perhaps because the besieged, waterless fort resembles Bolivia's territorial siege by its neighbors.

During the war, the shifting border between Bolivia and Paraguay was infested with man-eating creatures. Buzzards, mosquitoes, ants, and jaguars threatened to consume, infect, and swallow the soldiers as they attempted to set firm national borders. Picking up on themes of enclosure and national incarnation in the last chapter, the contemporary legacy of the Chaco War appears as an intensification of thirst and consumption while claustrophobically enclosed within national limits. The long siege at the Battle of Boquerón serves as a paradigmatic example of this contemporary condition. *Boquerón*, after all, indicates a large mouth but also the bite-sized anchovy, and the verb *boquear* means to gape or gasp, as in the harrowing stories of the white death of thirst in the Chaco.

Bolivia's relationship with territory has long been one of enclosure, extraction, and consumption. Since colonial times, the region encompassing present-day Bolivia has been economically dependent on the extraction of underground resources, especially from the mountains and, most famously, the silver mines at Potosí. The Chaco became part of a broader reclamation of subsoil resources before, during, and after the war. The Standard Oil Company of New Jersey was accused of incitement, and in 1937, the Bolivian government appropriated the company's assets, accusing the firm of tax evasion and undermining the war effort.[1] The landmark 1937 decision to nationalize the industry set a precedent for Mexico's oil nationalization the following year. In the decades to come, Bolivia alternated between privatizing and nationalizing oil until, in 2006, Evo Morales's government declared another nationalization of oil and gas. The decree echoed popular demands from the Bolivian resource wars, notably the 2000 Water War and the 2003 Gas War, to get rid of exploitative transnational corporations, and so echoed the anti-corporate sentiment that the 1937 nationalization shared with Morales's Movimiento al Socialismo (MAS). Accordingly, Morales named the decree for the "Héroes del Chaco," who are described as representatives of the collective defense of hydrocarbon resources. The declaration begins: "In consideration: That in previous periods of combat the people have earned, through bloodshed, the right for our hydrocarbon wealth to return to the hands of the nation and be used to benefit the country." The declaration, while ambitious, resulted in a modest public-private hybrid rather than full nationalization (Webber 89).[2] Nevertheless, it reinforced the commonly told story that the Chaco War was a critical turning point in the way Bolivia considers its natural resources (B. Gustafson 29).

The contemporary legacy of the Chaco War, and especially the Battle of Boquerón, connect entrapment—territorial and military siege—with consumption—the mouth and hydrocarbon usage—on material and symbolic levels. In contemporary culture, this convergence appears in Wilmer Urrelo Zárate's 2011 novel *Hablar con los perros* (Talking to dogs). The novel details a fictional origin story for contemporary ritual cannibalism in Bolivia, starting with the Battle of Boquerón. Trapped in the fort for weeks without supplies, one of Urrelo Zárate's characters bludgeons another soldier to death and eats his flesh. In the following decades, the perpetrator continues to practice ritual cannibalism and recruits a cannibal "family," becoming one of La Paz's many crime gangs in the novel. True to form, *Hablar con los perros* figuratively cannibalizes everything from underground pop culture to canonical literature, incorporating them into the narrative in unexpected ways. The novel implicitly builds on Brazilian author Oswald de Andrade's famous avant-garde "Manifesto antropófago" (Cannibal manifesto) of 1928. Andrade transferred the impetus of the European avant-garde to the Americas using indigenous symbols and customs, especially the much-mythologized Tupi cannibal, to incorporate, digest, and sublate European history and literature. This consumption occurs thanks to the cannibal's entrapment of his victims and extraction of their strength, and it binds consumption to a declaration on how past and future, Europe and the Americas influence each other historically and aesthetically.

The avant-garde and vanguard bridge military and artistic vocabularies. To take the most obvious example, an early skirmish between Bolivia and Paraguay before the outbreak of war took place in 1928 at a fort aptly named Vanguardia, in the same year Andrade published his manifesto.[3] It was one of the early, presciently named incidents that would lead to war, along with others that marked the methodical Bolivian occupation of the Chaco amid tentative but growing Paraguayan resistance (Querejazu Calvo 25–29). In Paraguay, conventional wisdom goes, the War of the Triple Alliance dealt the country a decisive blow so that it closed in upon itself. In the military, this manifested as a hesitancy to resist Bolivian occupation of the Chaco; in art, it manifested as a lack of participation in region-wide aesthetic vanguards. Hugo Rodríguez-Alcalá describes the phenomenon, echoing the words of Josefina Plá, as part of a bellicose history that "explains not only that 'history devours literature' but also that the country turned its back to the future, living a decapitated time without that essential aspect of human existence that is the future" (243).[4] Trapped in the past and cut off from the future, national culture came to an impasse. The desire to break free of entrapment—the definitive closure of the frontier—causes the consumption of literature by history.

This chapter shows how two contemporary representations of the war discredit the traditional story of a heroic fight for progress. Taking up themes from the Battle of Boquerón—the historical import of the siege and Paraguayan victory, the symbolic import of soldiers' gasping and gaping mouths—the chapter reflects on the mouth as a site of consumption and speech, enclosure and narrativity. Mouths are important tropes in Urrelo Zárate's *Hablar con los perros* as well as director Paz Encina's film *Hamaca paraguaya* (Paraguayan hammock), and they force a confrontation with the war's violent legacies in the twenty-first century. As chapter 1 showed, realist accounts of the war revealed that the attempt to enclose the land remained incomplete over holes and gaps interrupting models of cooperation and fraternity, leading to a thorough examination of hypostasis. However, spatial enclosure seems so complete by the twenty-first century, national form so static, as to be besieged and self-consuming. Continuing to reflect on incarnation as *carne*—"flesh" or "meat"—Urrelo Zárate's reworking of the anthropophagous Brazilian avant-garde model of Euro-American cultural relations accelerates and transforms under contemporary finance capitalism. Subsequently, Encina's use of the mouth exposes the incomplete hypostasis of the war in her use of asynchronous sounds and images of spoken Guaraní. Both texts examine status—social status but also the status of language and consumption in the modern order of largely fixed borders and extractivist-financial stasis. The conflicts between siege and entrapment, consumption and incorporation appear in the strained connection of artistic, military, and political vanguards as they are salvaged and reshaped in the modern legacy of the war.

THE CONSUMPTION OF DIFFERENCE

When Urrelo Zárate rewrites the history of the Chaco War through cannibalism, he implicitly invokes the conflict between civilization and barbarism that the earliest Chaco generation authors present, while simultaneously casting back to the theological, philosophical, and aesthetic traditions associated with cannibalism in previous centuries. Arguments about cannibalism formed part of Christian theology before the advent of natural law. Theologians considered the relationship between body and soul in the Christian tradition with questions such as: During the promised resurrection of the flesh, whose body will God resurrect if one man eats another? And what will happen if this second man dies and his body is in turn consumed by worms and beetles (Avramescu 41–69)? In Christian theology, once God creates a human with a soul, its identity must remain constant, body and soul together. The gradual physical dispersion of flesh in other flesh makes this impossible. The consumption of human flesh, whether by a person or animal, threatens the integrity of the border set at the skin. As a result, cannibalism threatens the shaping of the body, the assumption of flesh as form, becoming a strong prohibition during the conquest of the Americas.

As a tool of European political philosophy, cannibalism helped justify the colonial edifice as an imposition of civilization (Castro-Klarén; Avramescu). The European taboo on cannibalism helped explorers and conquistadors establish indigenous Americans as others, and cannibalism served as a key part of the Spanish crown's justification for indigenous enslavement, famously presented in Juan Ginés de Sepúlveda's arguments against Bartolomé de las Casas at Valladolid in 1550–1551. The prohibition of cannibalism—an offense against natural law—justified conquest and subjection because, according to Sepúlveda, the Spanish were contributing to the cultural and spiritual development of indigenous peoples (Ginés de Sepúlveda 155). The cannibal trope reinforced perceptions of the barbarism of the Americas, whether real or imagined, and became the perfect testing ground for natural law, either to prove a point about the innocence of "natural man" or to make an argument about indigenous monstrosity.[5] Although at odds with each other, both served to justify political and religious domination through the concept of *just war*. At the edges of European theological and political thought on cannibalism, it becomes clear that the fear of cannibals stems from their destabilization of the distinction between self and other. The cannibal's perversion is not his otherness; rather, he is marked as "other" because he threatens to destabilize identity.[6]

Centuries after the natural law debates, the 1928 "Manifesto antropófago" radically reworked this tradition into an aesthetic movement that valorized rather than scorned cannibalism. In the manifesto, Andrade, a central figure of Brazilian modernism, makes a typically vanguardist gesture, suggesting that cannibalism might be "the world's single law. Disguised expression of all individualism, of all collectivisms. Of all religions. Of all peace treaties" ("Cannibalist Manifesto" 38).[7] Peace appears when the cannibal takes the nutrients from another body to nourish his own, violently bridging individualism and collectivism. This process is all-consuming as seen in the repetition of "all," and it functions through a dialectic in which the cannibal (thesis) consumes his enemy (antithesis), strengthening himself (synthesis).

If the dialectic is important to Andrade's cannibalism, so too is the question of the future, as in all *vanguardias*. The future-oriented avant-gardes are best exemplified in the 1909 Italian Futurist Manifesto that threatened to "destroy museums, libraries [and] academies of every kind" and "glorify war—the world's only hygiene—militarism, patriotism" (Marinetti 22). It exalted speed without history and violence without object. Andrade's manifesto also calls for a violent approach to history in the name of the future, though perhaps taking a milder tone than the Futurists. Andrade assimilates the historical object, and in this sense his anthropophagy is past- rather than future-oriented. The "Manifesto antropófago" remedies the problems of the periphery by announcing that from now on, art will cure American exclusion through incorporation. Modern art will be subsumed to its American instances. The future of *antropofagia* as an aesthetic idea is more antropofagia, a violent marriage of past with future in the Americas.

In the manifesto, artistic creation straddles past and future. Andrade sees this temporal union as another conflict: "The struggle between what we might call the Uncreated and the Creation—illustrated by the permanent contradiction between Man and his Taboo. Everyday love and the capitalist way of life. Cannibalism. Absorption of the sacred enemy. To transform him into totem" ("Cannibalist Manifesto" 43).[8] There is a contradiction between the shapeless uncreated and creation, negated in the taboo or exalted in the totem. The possibility that a creature might come into existence emerges from the circumstances of the present, specifically, the capitalist modus vivendi. As with peace treaties, the laws of cannibalism express tension in the language of statecraft, where modus vivendi refers to an informal treaty or armistice, a way to continue living with the enemy, of assimilating enmity without outright hostility.

This modus vivendi in the cannibal dialectic is also geographically inflected. Taking the canonical travelogues of Europeans that claimed to witness Tupi cannibalism, Andrade makes indigenous American elements consume classical European culture, especially in the manifesto's most famous line, in which the Tupi "cannibalize" Shakespeare's *Hamlet* in English: "Tupi, or not tupi, that is the question" ("Cannibalist Manifesto" 38).[9] The historical and textual cannibalism in this line destabilize European identity formations and the European literary canon, staging the complexity of the developing relationship between Europe and America from the colonial period to the early twentieth century. Depending on how the consumption of difference takes place, the line can be read in three ways. In the first, American cannibalism reverses the Eurocentric view of culture and history. The American supersedes the European, and civilization and barbarism become inextricably melded. Anthropophagy issues a counterhegemonic corrective to history. This perspective prioritizes the antithesis. In the second, the manifesto might be an argument for an inclusionary, syncretic nationalism. Under this reading, the "cannibal" would be the Brazilian state, assimilating ethnic difference into a heterogeneous, hybrid melting pot. From this nation-alist perspective, the state is capable of a violent, witty assimilation that operates according to a logic of completion and wholeness. This view prioritizes synthesis. Finally, in the third, Andrade's manifesto might be read as a failed attempt at transvaluation in which the Tupi, representa-tive of subjugated subaltern knowledge, disrupt the avant-garde propos-al; ironically, they cannot be assimilated into the project that emerges from their ritual cannibalism (Castro-Klarén). This view represents a radical incompletion—a fetish or trace excluded from the dialectic.

The following sections examine each of these formations—antithe-sis, synthesis, and trace—as they appear in Urrelo Zárate's contemporary depiction of cannibalism after the Chaco War. Of course, the capitalist modus vivendi has shifted toward financialization since Andrade first wrote his manifesto. With the end of the Cold War, Francis Fukuyama, drawing on Alexandre Kojève's seminars on Hegel, famously declared history over.[10] The capitalist modus vivendi allegedly settled into a histo-ry without enemy or future, even as increasingly decentralized, techno-logically advanced resource conflicts such as the Chaco War proliferated. The closure of territory and the closure of history seemed illusorily com-plete. And once territorial enclosure appeared irremediable, Bolivia and Paraguay's fates as landlocked nations were sealed: Bolivia cut off from a *salida al mar*, "outlet to the sea," and Paraguay isolated as what Augusto Roa Bastos calls an "island of land / surrounded by land" (*El naranjal* 44).[11] Contemporary work on the Chaco War examines the question: Is it possible to recover a sense of the future under conditions of siege, with limited alternatives to consumption, status, and consumerism?

CANNIBALISM AND ANTITHESIS

The stories passed from generation to generation in *Hablar con los perros*, including the dark secret of ritual cannibalism, emerge from the siege at Boquerón and ripple out to affect each of the five narrative threads, ranging from 1932 to 2007. They converge around protagonist Alicia Soriano's investigation of the past after her grandmother's funeral. To-gether with her bandmate, Perro Loco, Alicia moves around the city of La Paz following what turns out to be an elaborate scheme designed to bring them closer and closer to Papá, patriarch of the cannibals. The closer they get, the more information they discover about the hidden stories of the past. As it follows the broad arc of a detective novel, *Hablar con los perros* combines stories of war, kidnapping, sex trafficking, rape, murder, and corruption alongside more banal stories of family quarrels, unrequited love, teenage malaise, and metal bands forming and splitting up. The novel slips between first-, second-, and third-person voices, talking to living, dead, famous, and fictional figures, as the reader begins to see the convergence of its characters. In Urrelo Zárate's contemporary version of the Chaco War novel, the anxiety of nothingness becomes a more banal adolescent angst, full of fretting about friends, lovers, and suffocating families, and filled with strange details like Alicia's job as a taxidermist. Satanism is the only religion represented in the novel, and the body is the site of immense violence but also a physical, even metaphysical, freedom. A street war fueled by violent criminals and corrupt police officers fills Urrelo Zárate's ironically named version of La Paz.

At the heart of the novel, the relationship between war and peace comes into view. Even seventy-five years after the siege, Urrelo Zárate explains, there is no peace. Papá describes the supposed peace as silence, one of the war's worst and longest lasting consequences:

> It was the war. the war never ends when the treaty is signed. and it doesn't end with our food either. it keeps going here. like the illnesses that eat away at the old. in the hearts of the veterans. they return home and the war they carry inside them spreads. plaf! it infects everyone that lives there. it attacks the wives. sacrifices them. kills the sons. the daughters. the paraguayan bullet doesn't kill anymore. not fever. not malaria. not the heat of the chaco. not hunger. not thirst. what kills now is the veteran himself, and he does it in his own home. his strength is hatred. they kill wives. crime. it was hatred. it was fear. it was the war still living in them. and even though they deny it, it's still alive to this day. the youth of 1935 now old like me. or nearly dead. or dead. now the war kills their grandchildren. those who don't know or don't care to know about their grandmothers' suffering. that story is closed. dead. now the war is hypocrisy, miss, and that's even more deadly. (*Hablar con los perros* 332–33)[12]

The war's violence has returned to the city, its legacy engrained in Bolivian society where it disproportionately affects veterans' families. The enemy has become internal, hypocritical, silencing and stifling the more sinister aspects of the war to replace them with stories of heroism, but as Papá says: "Why do they call those of us that went to war heroes if all we did was kill people?" (Urrelo Zárate, *Hablar con los perros* 332).[13] There is no inherent honor in murder.

Instead of making Boquerón represent bravery and honor, *Hablar con los perros* makes it stand in for Bolivia's landlocked status, with no maritime or fluvial exit, no hope, and no narrative beyond a hollow and, in Urrelo Zárate's view, false story of heroism. Papá's view stands in direct opposition to Chaco generation authors who exposed the horrors of war in chronicles and fiction during the 1930s and whose work was later incorporated into the political movements that led to oil nationalization and, eventually, the Revolution of 1952. Historically, Chaco narrative placed indigenous exploitation in the foreground of fictional and nonfictional representation, so that excluded elements of society became suddenly visible, such as in the classic Chaco novel *Aluvión de fuego* (Downpour of fire) by Óscar Cerruto, in which a young bourgeois army deserter develops a political and social consciousness in the tin mines. In the wake of an accident, the novel evokes a "shriek that seemed to rise from the very depths of the mountain" (230).[14] This unidentified voice represents the excluded miners, many indigenous, whose voices began to be heard in the wake of the war, a war-to-revolution link that Cerruto's novel makes explicit. The cry is inarticulate and muffled but indicates the presence of the uncounted actors upon whose lives the violence of extraction is founded. Subsequent political changes forced the widening circle of the state to consider these silenced voices, and so traditionally, the Chaco War became aligned with not only defeat but also a narrative of progress through social transformation and revolution.

Urrelo Zárate's novel takes a different approach. The external war has not morphed into an uprising or revolution following the logical progression anticipated by Cerruto's strain of Marxist narrative. Rather, the war has become an undeclared civil war, as if a besieged Bolivia had turned inward, not to take in a widening swath of citizens but instead to endure the silenced consequences of the internal conflicts that the Chaco War both emerged from and generated. Whereas in Nicole Loraux's study of ancient Athens, civil war, or *stasis*, must be followed by amnesia, serving as a foundation for democracy, in Urrelo Zárate's novel, amnesia is presented as silence, an inability to narrate appearing in Alicia's muteness after the car crash that killed both of her parents.[15] By the time of the third generation after the war, Urrelo Zárate shows that war has been embedded in the city. Alicia and Perro Loco comment on how little they learned about Bolivian history in school because they were more interested in the histories of their favorite bands (*Hablar con los perros* 63). Gradually realizing that the historical episode is critical to the mystery, Perro Loco finally looks up the Chaco War and the Battle of Boquerón to help Alicia solve the mystery (151–52). Meanwhile, the characters travel La Paz's streets, some named for major battles, in their search to understand what's going on; the war has become an unremarked part of the urban space of La Paz, folded into its geography.

As Alicia and Perro Loco begin to find out more, and especially when Papá recounts his life before and after the Battle of Boquerón, the novel turns toward monstrosity. Urrelo Zárate forgoes the positive progression—traditional stories of inclusion as seen in Cerruto—for a negative one: decadence. In the words of Alicia's grandfather: "What happens is that everything gets worse with time in this country" (*Hablar con los perros* 79).[16] Even in music, everything revolves around this decay. Alicia's ex-boyfriend's band was called Sífilis, or "syphilis." Alicia and Perro Loco's metal band, Aguas Putrefactas, or "putrefied waters," is no longer a reclamation of an exit to the sea but rather an homage to the stench of stagnation. In Urrelo Zárate's version of the war's legacy, there is a celebration of physical and moral decay—a spectacular embrace of the imagery and figuration of death, decay, and disease.

As Papá says, it is no longer bullets and malaria that kill. Instead, it is hypocrisy, embedded in the abuse and exploitation that goes unremarked. In a decadent La Paz, this hypocrisy and celebration of death are shuffled into metal subculture and decontextualized. Perro Loco obsessively cites Mexican grindcore band Brujería, literally meaning "witchcraft," whose lead singer Juan Brujo (whose last name translates to "sorcerer"), and emblematic decapitated head Coco Loco, or "crazy coconut," Perro Loco addresses in the second person, as if they were demigods listening to his story. He often cites Brujería's 1993 album *Matando güeros* (Killing whiteys), whose tracks are about killing US Americans, crossing the Mexico-US border, narcos, and Satanism, revealing the sinister persistence of a transnational enemy: the *güero* for Brujería and the Yankee capitalist in post-Chaco Bolivia.

This spectacular enemy becomes more difficult to pinpoint over time, moving from place to place through Mexico, the United States, and Bolivia. Yet the figure of the enemy as antithesis is embedded in cultural expression. Kostas Kalimtzis describes *stasis* as an illness in the polity (xiii–xvii), and this illness persists in the metal subculture Urrelo Zárate describes. Here, a decapitated head, for instance, or the words *gore* and *slime* or names of various venereal diseases that form the metal lexicon are nonspecific and interchangeable metaphors for decay. The narco-Satanist-*metaleros* might substitute one term for another because what matters most is the striking display of decadence and violence. At the same time, these are merely figures without a cause or narrative. The violence is flat and infinitely reappropriable, especially in Perro Loco's version of events, in which almost everything relates back to Brujería. Perro Loco's first-person narrative, laced with a metal soundtrack, lacks purpose and directionality, reiterating the violence of an absolute and unintelligible present, here and now. The enemy is everywhere.

If the enemy has been made into a metaphor or spectacle, both everywhere and fully assimilated, then is this still truly an enemy? In Carl Schmitt's *Concept of the Political*—originally published in 1927 just a year before the "Manifesto antropófago," with significant revisions in a 1932 edition with the ascendence of Nazism—having an enemy is the condition of the political. There is no need to account for temporality in Schmitt's axiomatic since temporality begins from this decision. Schmitt specifies that the possibility of killing an enemy must exist in war, defined as "the existential negation of the enemy" (*Concept* 33). Any reconciliation or alliance would require another enemy. In Urrelo Zárate's novel, Papá's enemies are the rich—La Paz's few, abhorrent millionaires. Ultimately, Papá decides that the group's cannibalism will transform from the opportunistic murder and consumption of indigents into a calculated, class-based cannibalism, killing and eating a wealthy banker. By the twenty-first century, the capitalist enemy has become internal to Bolivian society and thus consumable: Bolivians working within the market logic that spawned the war's need for resources and transportation are consumed by the cannibals that the war created. Ultimately, Perro Loco undergoes the same transformation. Alicia's former best friend, secretly in love with her, is killed and eaten, an internalization of both enmity and the friend-turned-enemy. The temporality of enmity begins with the comrade becoming an enemy during the Battle of Boquerón, initiating a sequence in which the political internalizes the enemy again and again.

In this sense, the illness that has returned to La Paz with the veterans echoes some aspects of the Marxist novels of the late 1930s as Papá's litany of laments about his life include his mother abandoning him in the market as a child, his abuse by wealthy bosses, and the death of his dog Rayo, his only companion in misery. Papá's former bosses account for much of his rancor toward the rich, as in traditional Chaco War stories. The class differences that became visible in the wake of war form the basis of targeted violence toward a structural, social enemy. This enemy is a minion of the capitalist modus vivendi that the "Manifesto antropófago" describes. At the same time, this cannibalism exceeds mere class antagonism and defies the earlier novels' optimism for social progress. Nearing death, Papá makes plans to bring Alicia closer to the group, where she will become their next leader as they begin making social status the foundation of their choice of victims. Papá's cannibalism emerges from the nagging antagonism of history.

After incorporation, the question of the enemy lingers. Papá's story goes back time and again to the pains he has endured, and in this regard, *Hablar con los perros* "cannibalizes" Miguel de Cervantes's *El coloquio de los perros* (The dialogue of the dogs), mimicking the lament of canine main character Berganza as he complains to Cipión. At the same time, Urrelo Zárate adds cannibalism as a key dimension of social relationships. Anthropologist Eduardo Viveiros de Castro, who theorizes ritual cannibalism in the Brazilian Amazon, describes incorporating the enemy: "If it is always necessary to imagine an enemy—to construct the other as such—the objective is to *really* eat it . . . in order to construct the Self as other" (149).[17] In Papá's case, this "other" pays reparations for the damage done to him. Papá's cannibalism thus fits with ritual cannibalism as "social *poiesis* . . . the ritual production of collective temporality (the interminable cycle of vengeance)" (Viveiros de Castro 149).[18] In the fusion of the capitalist modus vivendi with ritual, the enemy becomes difficult to see as a historically constructed alterity, and so it is difficult to move beyond the "collective temporality . . . of vengeance" toward a future that exceeds repetition of the past. The antithesis cannot be taken up as part of a progression, as in Hegelian dialectics, nor a regression, as in Urrelo Zárate's focus on rot and decay. It is a stagnant temporality based on antithesis, founded on a ritualized, violent relationship between self and other.

CANNIBALISM AND METAPHYSICAL SYNTHESIS

Instead of privileging antithesis, a second interpretation of aesthetic anthropophagy through *Hablar con los perros* might emphasize metaphysical synthesis. Instead of eating for sustenance, in this view, ritual cannibalism creates spiritual or divine union. In Urrelo Zárate's novel, Papá combines human and divine, friend and enemy with the modern story of cannibalism, while, little by little, incorporation builds toward the climax. Papá's section of the novel records his side of a lengthy conversation with Alicia. They tell each other about important events in their lives, and Papá explains how he watched from a distance as Alicia grew up, waiting for her to experience enough heartache and sadness to become mature enough to lead the group. Papá describes his first cannibal meal, explaining that, toward the end of the siege at Boquerón, he was extremely hungry, like all of the other soldiers. Another soldier came up to him begging for food, which Papá found infuriating, and enraged, Papá bludgeoned the other man, nearly to death, with a rock in the graveyard. Then he cut out pieces of his still-living body as the man kicked and screamed. Papá's first meal came not out of hunger but out of anger, out of the transformation of his former comrade into a victim during the siege.

Initially, it was less about food and more about power, but Papá quickly discovered that the consumption of human flesh brought him unadulterated happiness. He had been miserable and had enlisted in the army to face what he saw as almost-certain death, a halfhearted attempt at suicide. But from his first bite, he had recovered the will to live. He found pure happiness in that first meal, as he explains to Alicia, who he refers to as "señorita": "There, in that moment, the doors that were always closed to us opening up forever. peace overwhelming the heart. so much loving for what. so much suffering for love for what. and suddenly the door opens. and behind it is happiness. . . . new life. september 28, 1932, miss. the birth of everything" (249).[19] The consumption of his comrade—the enemy within—strengthens him and causes him to fully recover his will to survive. It represents freedom and endless possibility. He experiences a rebirth, baptizing himself Papá and declaring Ananías Paredes, his former self, dead at Boquerón.

In Papá's account of that first meal, fatherhood and rebirth meld with cannibalism's metaphysical pretensions. While cannibalism might be interpreted as nationalist, unifying a diverse, even seemingly incompatible group under a single banner, in *Hablar con los perros*, cannibalism creates a different kind of family. The cannibals in Papá's family have returned from the front lines to a society that, while at peace, feels as besieged as Boquerón: "The ones that came were always lonely. solitary people. ruined for life. people with an emptiness they didn't know how to fill and the meat [*carne*] helped them, rescued them, pulled them out of that well" (379).[20] The war has shattered the relationships that these people had, and Papá draws them in. Anthropophagy begins to fill the space left by the emptiness, anxiety, and desperation after the war. In place of Cespedes's empty well, Urrelo Zárate describes a cannibal family.

By the time Alicia arrives, Papá has been practicing cannibalism for seventy-five years. Over time, he fully uncovers the mechanism through which cannibalism creates an addictive, metaphysical ecstasy, bringing strength, words, and freedom:

> What does flesh have to offer, miss? what does it give us that opens up new paths? what's in it that revives us all? why, if before we were timid and ignorant, afterwards we're the opposite of that?
>
> After swallowing the words appear. the same ones I said to you before what happened with your friend perro loco. exactly the same. without a single change. like never before words awaken in me like after a dream. whichever idiot. whichever moron. there the wise words explode. all my loneliness. all my suffering . . . evaporating. leaving my body. that was it. thinking all these years I'd been waiting for flesh [*carne*].
> (Urrelo Zárate, *Hablar con los perros* 249)[21]

In the enlightenment and rebirth that comes from eating flesh, cannibalism connects with the word, a spoken, repeated scripture, the same after the death of the petulant soldier at Boquerón as after the death of Perro Loco. In the phrase "after swallowing the words appear," Papá signals a type of muse or divinity, mediating the inverse processes of consumption of flesh and narrative production through the mouth.[22]

As Papá initiates Alicia into these secrets with their first victim, she describes the overwhelming love she feels in a similar moment of ecstasy: "Papá opens his mouth again and there's the warmth, his infinite, unselfish love, chew, miss: there, the only and the authentic love that was worth anything in this world and I was feeling it in the flesh, Papá" (Urrelo Zárate, *Hablar con los perros* 627).[23] As Alicia eats Perro Loco, who has spent most of the novel pining after her, she finds this pure love, a love Andrade described decades before as an authentic "antropofagia carnal"—a high, carnal cannibalism that eludes Freud's distinction between totem and taboo ("Manifesto antropófago" 7). She becomes one of the cannibal elites, as Andrade describes them: "Yet only the pure elites managed to realize carnal anthropophagy, which brings the highest sense of life, and avoids all the evils identified by Freud, catechist evils. What happens is not a sublimation of the sexual instinct. It is the thermometric scale of the anthropophagic instinct. From carnal, it becomes elective and creates friendship. Affectionate, love. Speculative, science. It deviates and transfers itself. We reach vilification. Low anthropophagy agglomerated in the sins of the catechism—envy, usury, calumny, murder. Plague of the so-called cultured and Christianized peoples, it is against it that we are acting. Anthropophagy" ("Cannibalist Manifesto" 7).[24] The difference between high and low cannibal instincts is the difference between Alicia and Perro Loco. The latter's desire for Alicia remains frustrated as she betrays him. She instead chooses this family, united around the "love" of high, carnal anthropophagy and values that come from another particularly Bolivian strand of underground culture rather than the high culture and Christianity that Andrade describes plaguing the European tradition.

This high anthropophagy seems to be an autochthonous American practice in both the vanguardia and Urrelo Zárate; it also engages the Christian and metaphysical traditions. For instance, in the Catholic doctrine of transubstantiation, Christ becomes the bread and wine that the faithful consume, and even though the idea of cannibalism in the Mass was declared heretical, the act represents the symbolic communion of divine and human, word and flesh. In the history of philosophy, in turn, there is a synthesis of previous ideas, a sublation that emerges from Christianity. As Jacques Derrida describes the history of philosophy: "The figures of incorporation in hermeneutics and speculative philosophy are what I call the 'tropes of cannibalism.' Nowhere is this clearer than in Hegel, but these tropes are at work everywhere in Western thought. Eating is, after all, the great mystery of Christianity, the transubstantiation occurs in the act of incorporation itself: bread and wine become the flesh and blood of Christ. But it is not simply God's body that is incorporated via a mystical eating—it is also his words" (Birnbaum and Olsson). This mystical eating takes a slightly different turn in Urrelo Zárate. In Christianity, the word was made flesh, while here, the flesh provokes words. Incorporation elicits sacred speech, and this speech is the product of a metaphysical union of self and other that founds a new spiritual tradition unique to post-Chaco generations.

While in the Judeo-Christian tradition, the word of God is codified in the Bible, Alicia's search begins with her grandfather Valentín's scripture-like account of his first meal with Papá at Boquerón. Reading the account piques her interest, propelling her toward Papá. Alicia finds a photograph with the journal, and in another thread of the novel—a flashback to Alicia's parents' wedding day—we find that the photo represents Valentín's paradoxical condition as a prisoner of war but also a soldier who has just been freed from his earthly cares by his first taste of human flesh. Valentín explains to his son, Alicia's father Julián, that he wanted to keep the photo as a memento: "Afterward they lined us up and led us out of the fort, and just when I thought they were going to execute us they pardoned us. . . . They gave us food and took pictures of all of the officers. When I was a prisoner in Asunción, a Paraguayan officer showed me mine, . . . and I thought, why wouldn't I want [to have that picture]? Wouldn't it be a nice souvenir? Wouldn't it be nice to have something to remind me of the moment I found out what it meant to be happy for real, son? . . . From that moment on, we were all prisoners" (Urrelo Zárate, *Hablar con los perros* 584–585).[25] The photograph captures Valentín as he transforms into a metaphysically free prisoner of war. It marks his entrance into a "true" language in the wake of consumption and accompanies the diary that serves as his cannibal scripture. Unlike the photograph in Augusto Céspedes's "La paraguaya," which remains ambiguous and even traitorous in its duplicity, this photograph becomes part of the divine, infinitely digestible cannibal corpus.

By the time the legacy of this modern-day metaphysics arrives at Valentín's granddaughter, it has become unspeakable. Alicia, entrusted by the end of the novel with the direction of the cannibal group, is mute. Her muteness is the result of the car crash that killed her parents, but according to the doctor, it has no physical cause; as he explains to her grandmother when she was a child, "Well there's nothing wrong, Zoila ma'am [Alicia's grandmother], physically, I mean . . . seems to me she doesn't want to talk, that's the problem" (Urrelo Zárate, *Hablar con los perros* 571).[26] Her muteness, however, is far from a lack of communication. After the accident, she goes to a sign language school called Renacer, meaning "rebirth," foreshadowing her new lease on life after she becomes a cannibal. She communicates with Perro Loco in sign language or writes in a small notebook she carries with her. As Urrelo Zárate builds the plot toward the metaphysical experience of eating human flesh, the reader begins to suspect that perhaps after eating some of Perro Loco's flesh, Alicia will speak again. Papá had already said, "After swallowing the words appear" (249). Thankfully, such a turn, verging on the mawkish, fails to appear. She continues to communicate through sign language and writing. Her aphasia does not indicate a lack of communication but rather marks the final enclosure of Boquerón. The mouth no longer speaks but only incorporates, consuming enemies and, later, exclusively capitalist enemies. This aphasia is not a mark of amnesia, as it would have been in ancient Greece where *stasis* could only be overcome by amnesia. Rather, it is an alternative written and photographic history of how the enclosure at Boquerón reaches its metaphysical aspiration through violence.

CANNIBALISM AND FETISH

After metaphysical synthesis, the third and final way that the "Manifesto antropófago" might be read through *Hablar con los perros* is as a fetish, neither a firm opposition as in the antithesis nor sublated into synthesis. Urrelo Zárate explores this aspect of cannibalism through the history of literature, as a symbolic economy of traces not appropriated into a larger system. In one passage, for instance, main characters Alicia and Perro Loco meet two-bit criminal Vallejo in a basement bar called Petróleo. Vallejo is lying low between jobs and agrees to help Alicia and Perro Loco. Alicia shows Vallejo her grandfather's notebook, but because Petróleo is a hub of underground music, she can't help remembering her ex-boyfriend Axl with whom she first discovered the musical world beyond vapid pop. Alicia recalls their relationship and remembers rebuking Axl for reading poetry, which she claimed made him sullen. He was obsessed with Argentine poet Alejandra Pizarnik and French surrealist André Breton. Axl disappeared one day without a trace, and Alicia blames the poets, thinking to herself, "Pizarnik and Breton, couple of bastards" (101).[27] Once Axl is gone she refuses to grant poetry any power: "Not believing in that old witch Pizarnik or that idiot Breton anymore" (110).[28] She recalls all of this in the presence of Vallejo, whose name more than hints at Peruvian poet César Vallejo (269–71). In this way, Urrelo Zárate mocks poetic renown as he cannibalizes Cervantes's *El coloquio de los perros*, all in a bar, Petróleo, named for hydrocarbons connected to the legacy of the Chaco War. Poetry is a scorned trace, while petroleum is Bolivia's liquid gold.

The tension between a trace that cannot be converted into something else—here, poetry—and an easily exchangeable resource—oil— animates Urrelo Zárate's exploration of the fetish and body under a violent regime of value extraction. The nation's borders, definitively set after the end of the war, organize exchanges with a crime organization called Los Infernales, "the infernal ones," in the novel. Vallejo and his associates form a kidnapping and human trafficking ring, abducting beautiful, wealthy women to extort money from their families with the help of the police chief ominously named Lucio Lobo, which literally translates as "Lucius Wolf." Vallejo, who is Bolivian but fakes a Mexican accent, is responsible for arranging these border crossings. The group transfers the bodies of abducted women to Peru, using the border to avoid police pursuit and launder money. Depending on their success at extracting the ransom, the gang either rapes the women and returns them or forces them into sexual slavery in Peru. In the Infernales' mindset, the Bolivian border serves as a convenient mechanism through which men circulate women's bodies in a brutally misogynistic economy of sexual exploitation. No longer the contested border with Paraguay as in the Chaco War, the national limit is now a selective frontier that facilitates the extraction of value and concealment of resources in the most brutal fashion.

Vallejo's job depends on the exchange of female bodies for cash. These exchanges are generally fluid and equivalence uninhibited. The more lucrative the business becomes, however, the more careless and violent the Infernales are toward their victims. Interspersed with stories of the many aspects of their business and personal dramas, Urrelo Zárate presents a particularly gruesome scene in which two of the group's underlings gang-rape a television presenter they were tasked with taking over the border, killing her and leaving her lifeless body on the side of the road (*Hablar con los perros* 293–316). This transnational, savage extraction traffics in an underground market of bodies, an illicit corporal corporation based on a straightforward exchange of cash for those it preys upon, especially the families of women they see as naive and unaware. The Infernales sees the resource they appropriate and sell back— the female body—as virtually unlimited and infinitely exchangeable.

Yet the violence seems to take on a life of its own, and the men become increasingly destructive, injuring and killing the women they depend on for extortion. The kidnapping ring falls apart, not because of a shortage of victims but because of infighting. Vallejo's wife Nancy steals his money and runs away with his partner, Villagrán. The pair end up in Buenos Aires, where they spend all of their money trying to fit into *porteño* superficiality. Vallejo pays a visit to Buenos Aires to kill his ex-partner and maim his ex-wife. With no way of making money, Vallejo starts working for Alicia in search of the mysterious people who start harassing her after her grandmother's funeral. Together with Perro Loco, the three find out that Papá and his group of cannibals were responsible for ransacking Alicia's apartment in search of the notebook containing the cannibal scriptures. After becoming an unwitting bystander to the murder and consumption of Perro Loco, Vallejo, stone-cold criminal though he is, blames Papá and his "family" for a sudden digestive indisposition: "I almost became vegetarian thanks to you" (*Hablar con los perros* 321).[29] In spite of his objections to the practice, however, Vallejo agrees to help the cannibals, who are looking for a thug to get them their meat. This transition, from criminal extortionist to meat procurer, marks a transition from the market of general equivalence to a procurement of materials for a particular purpose. While still doing the same job—kidnapping—Vallejo refashions himself with different libidinal and economic functions. Instead of profiting from the cash equivalence of the female body, he now profits from the fetish, removing flesh from circulation.

The fetish is, after all, distanced from the larger economy of desire. As a particular object or situation that excites desire, the fetish has an irreplaceable specificity. In Urrelo Zárate's novel, Perro Loco pines for Alicia. Then there is the cannibalistic fetish, in which flesh becomes object and food. Instead of participating in the traditional story of unrequited love, Alicia cannibalizes her friend. After all, following Derrida: "To love without wanting to devour must surely be anorexic" (Birnbaum and Olsson). The cannibal fetish—like the abuse and trafficking of women—involves preying on the weak. In Papá's words to Alicia: "The flesh of the weak like that boy is necessary for us, miss" (*Hablar con los perros* 74).[30] Weakness does not transform into strength but rather draws in the low and abject. It also requires an ascetic attitude according to Papá. Over the course of the novel, Alicia begins to piece together Papá's influence on her life, and she realizes that he has been the master puppeteer pulling at threads to make her life ever more miserable. Papá, she finds out, believes that healthy doses of suffering, especially poverty and unrequited love, make the ecstasy of cannibalism possible. He had asked her grandparents to mistreat her when she went to live with them after her parents died. She also discovers that Papá had a hand in Axl's disappearance so that she suffered heartbreak at a young age. After these experiences, he tells her, she can fully participate in their ritual. The fetish requires a specific set of conditions, devouring weak victims in an otherwise frugal and dissatisfying life.

The fetish in *Hablar con los perros* echoes Marx's commodity fetish: a material concept secularized from the "misty realm of religion," dissociating products of labor from their human relationships (*Capital* 165).[31] The commodity fetish makes materials seem to float around in the marketplace, unrelated to labor. In addition to taking bodies out of circulation, Urrelo Zárate sees cannibalism as a reminder of wartime trauma. In this sense, Urrelo Zárate's cannibalism favors a strand of interpretation in which the Tupi cannibal becomes a fetish in Andrade's manifesto. Sara Castro-Klarén, for instance, analyzes the dissonance in the relationship between Europe and the Americas, arguing that if Tupi praxis were truly acknowledged, it would "destabilize" and "subvert" the "Manifesto antropófago" (313).[32] It appears in the manifesto, but it cannot be understood. Thus, unwittingly, Tupi cannibalism undoes fluid, if violent, Euro-American cultural exchange. Tupi cannibalism creates an unbridgeable gap as a practice that cannot be assimilated between the two continents. Ritual cannibalism destabilizes the dialectic and signals the abyssal loss of this particular indigenous praxis from the time of conquest.[33] Tupi praxis is not the only thing destabilized either. The premise of European speculative philosophy was that it could account for everything with no remainder, or as Derrida puts it: "Nothing is inedible in Hegel's infinite metabolism."[34] Yet cannibalism becomes a systemic excrescence, akin to an appendix, a vestigial organ that indexes places where the metabolic system is excessive or inoperative.

In *Plasticity at the Dusk of Writing*, Catherine Malabou discusses this point at which an infinite metabolism comes into conflict with inconvertibility. She analyzes conflicting interpretations of inconvertibility in Derrida and Emmanuel Levinas: "I comment on Levinas's expression 'the trace is inconvertible into forms,' stating that if the trace is inconvertible, then it acquires the status of a substance or a fetish. The assertion of inconvertibility lies, for Marx, at the heart of fetishism. On the face of it, the fetish always occurs outside the operation of exchange, outside the market. From then on, when otherness is fetishized by its resistance to plasticity, when hospitality continues to be thought as the 'counter' to plasticity or, in other words, against form, it is no longer possible to distinguish cosmopolitanism rigorously from hypercapitalism" (*Plasticity* 76–77). Malabou identifies the point of convergence that Urrelo Zárate sees in the contemporary legacy of the Chaco War as lived in La Paz in the early twenty-first century. The cannibal group probes the idea of the fetish in the contemporary moment through the consumption of the rich. The otherness of the cannibal, like Tupi otherness, folds into hypercapitalism as a paradoxical excrescence.[35]

In the character of Vallejo, Chaco ritual cannibalism—picking up conquest stories and vanguard aesthetic ideas—converges with the brutality of general equivalence exposed in human trafficking and fetishization. In their final, triumphant meal, the cannibals consume one of La Paz's wealthiest bankers. Vallejo had broken into his home, threatened his family, kidnapped the man, and brought him back to the cannibal house. Vallejo thus helped the cannibals consume the agent of surplus value and financialization. They fetishize and remove the excess capital skimmed off the top by reducing the banker to the constituent parts of his body, which are no longer convertible into anything other than the material basis for their desire. This fetishism or inconvertibility mimics the hypercapitalism of the Infernales, who traffic in women's bodies until their market functions are no longer relevant; they become nothing more than sites of corporeal violence.[36] It likewise mimics the cannibal group's turn to capitalists as victims, serving as retribution for systemic historical injustice. The fetish stands apart from the model of war (antithesis) and progress (synthesis). The idea of innovation, progress, and even the viability of the manifesto can no longer be incorporated into the broader social system.

THE EXHAUSTION OF THE MANIFESTO

The 2006 proclamation named for the Heroes of the Chaco, mentioned at the beginning of this chapter, aimed at nationalizing hydrocarbons. However, the declaration fell short of nationalization, instead instituting a public-private partnership that involved exporting gas for profit while subsidizing national consumption. The Morales government named the Chaco War as a turning point in the fight for hydrocarbons and equitable wealth distribution from natural resources. A few years later, in December 2010 as Urrelo Zárate was finishing *Hablar con los perros*, Bolivia's vice president Álvaro García Linera signed the controversial "Decreto Supremo 0748," dubbed the *gasolinazo*, ending government subsidies of most hydrocarbons in order to block subsidized gas from seeping out of Bolivia's porous borders. The decree amounted to an immediate and massive price increase, because, the government said, it was not interest-ed in supporting smugglers who profit from gas and oil consumption in neighboring countries. Several days of intense protests in Bolivian cities forced the government to rescind the declaration a few days later and re-instate the subsidies in "Decreto Supremo 0759," but the experience laid bare the precariousness of the government's market- and border-con-trolling abilities. It revealed the practical limits of the state's powers of incorporation.[37]

This more recent episode in the legacy of the Chaco War reiterates the practical problem of the limits of the state, especially as these limits escape control and affect consumption. In the immediate aftermath of the war, the lines established through mediation arrived at a modus vi-vendi, but when those lines were once again challenged, another type of spatial fix, as David Harvey would call it, was enacted. The goal was to remedy the insufficient sovereign power containers' hold on re-sources necessary for social and economic function in the twenty-first century. In the MAS government, this type of truce became an ongoing contradiction for the state to resolve, beginning with Morales's historic election to the presidency. In a 2011 essay from *Las tensiones creativas de la revolución: La quinta fase del Proceso del Cambio* (Creative tensions of the revolution: the fifth phase in the process of change) in the wake of the gasolinazo, Vice President García Linera writes that there are impasses in socialist theory that were not considered by Marx, Lenin, or Mao. These contradictions come from the contemporary situation, provoking conflicts between the Bolivian state and social movements, hegemonic flexibility and social firmness, general social and specific or private in-terests, and the so-called communitarian socialism of *vivir bien*, or "liv-ing well." García Linera casts these tensions as creative, even necessary to keep the revolutionary process in check. Yet each amounts to a ten-sion between the state apparatus and a way of living that escapes it. The state needs this creativity to be able to better capture the effervescence of social movements. At heart, this tension is one of incorporation; the state seeks to incorporate that which is outside of it and continually escapes it.[38] The gasolinazo revealed the limit to the state's incorpora-tion, still configured by its borders even as these become weaker under globalization.

Structurally, this weakness inheres in the manifesto model as well. Whether an avant-garde manifesto, a declaration of war, or a decree of hydrocarbon nationalization, manifestos intend to alter the past by im-plementing a future program. The initial nationalization suffered from a disconnect between desire and reality, as revealed in the gasolinazo.

García Linera implies that late capitalism bears a specificity that seems to frustrate understandings of the past. Even Marx seems inadequate to the task of analyzing the present Bolivian economic situation. The new legacy of the Chaco War, in other words, presents a theory-praxis divide spread across history. It accounts for contingency and change yet attempts to remedy the problem at the heart of the contradiction by establishing a truce between state and capital. In the case of national oil subsidies, the state prevents multinational corporations from enacting their own spatial fixes, from de- and reterritorializing capital for maximum profit; capital "deviates and transfers itself," as Andrade says of cannibalism in his manifesto ("Manifesto antropófago" 7).[39] The manifesto attempts to soften the blows of an otherwise savage and all-consuming capitalism, the kind that ravaged Bolivia with the help of elites for centuries. The Morales government aimed to correct the massive wealth inequalities by enacting their own spatial fix, a process that was interrupted in the gasolinazo and again in the 2019 political crisis.

Yet the question of a physical or formal limit remains—specifically, the border that is overly porous to gas smugglers and, more generally, the limits to the state's powers of incorporation. In the national history of consumption, inflected through Boquerón, there is always a container struggling with excess. In different ways from the Battle of Boquerón to the gasolinazo, general equivalence and fetishism exhaust the vanguard paradigm of issuing a corrective to the past to announce the future. The manifesto or declaration cannot fix the past. Bolivia's fraught relationship with the sea, for instance, has not been remedied. The manifesto model quickly comes up against formal limits, whether of state, artistic form, or body. This paradigm, in turn, is exposed in Urrelo Zárate's novel as a tool that helps the community consume—its culture, its resources, itself. Whether these traces might be transformed into something else—such as a different type of friend-enemy relationship, access to the sea, or a more just and equitable distribution of hydrocarbon wealth—remains handicapped by a linear view of progress and an unwitting debt to consumption.

In retaking the history of the Chaco War through these constraints and limits, Urrelo Zárate experiments with and manipulates time into split but converging narratives that pile onto each other. He rewrites the story of metaphysical union or capture, collapsing speech and body into sacred trace and aphasia. The fetish fuses with a hypercapitalist drive to place objects into the market or remove them and to use and evade the territorial and subterranean borders that are the legacy of war. Urrelo Zárate thus disarticulates the stories of heroism and progress typically associated with the Chaco War. In this cannibal and cannibalized fiction, we glimpse the future of the literary trace without the exaltation of the masters (in the novel, Pizarnik, Breton, and Vallejo) and without the manifesto's progressive *telos*. Under the capitalist conditions of siege that appear so entrenched to everyone from the fictional Infernales to García Linera, one wonders if there might be a way of revisiting the legacy of the war while imagining an a-teleological, unbesieged futurity.

Urrelo Zárate provides hints. As the title *Hablar con los perros* suggests, there is a small stray dog who comes into the novel toward the end. He lives with Vallejo until Vallejo gets his comeuppance from his ex-wife Nancy, who castrates, mutilates, and stabs her ex-husband as revenge for the murder of her boyfriend Villagrán. The dog ends up living with Vallejo's ex-wife and her new girlfriend, Anita, who name him Kaiser. The dog embodies the sovereign's becoming-animal. He is a happy, nomadic observer, whose thoughts the audience reads but who can only translate his feelings of anxiety or contentment as different types of barking. In Urrelo Zárate's world, speaking to dogs is akin to speaking to a domesticated sovereign. By deposing the leader to the role of dependent companion and encouraging interspecies communication, the novel ends on a lighthearted note. The semipermeable barrier of communication between human and animal overtakes the challenges of communication registered in written and oral speech, sacred text and aphasia. Alicia's aphasia becomes a dead end, with a focus centered on the mouth as the limit between the consumption of flesh and production of speech.

For Urrelo Zárate, the question of the incorporation of the future, one not dependent on consumption, remains open. By introducing Kaiser the dog, Urrelo Zárate clarifies that the options of antithesis, with its cyclical vengeance; synthesis, with its metaphysical fusion; and fetish, with its capitalist and hypercapitalist tendencies, are not the only ones available. The novel hints at a post-humanist, postwar legacy that does not become a trace, does not repeat the "end of history," and does not presuppose teleological progress. These are traces that do not disappear into aphasia and are not metabolized into a merely mimetic relationship between culture and war. The cycle of vengeance is wholly unintelligible to Kaiser. The abyssal trace of the loss of the sea, the struggles over oil, and the territorial system inaugurated with nineteenth- and twentieth-century interstate wars have constrained Bolivia while letting its resources leak out. They have created a formal tension, an ongoing state of siege, that cannot be remedied with a declaration.

FROM APHASIA TO PHASE DIFFERENCE

Encina's experimental film *Hamaca paraguaya* (Paraguayan hammock) revisits the war from a vastly different perspective and in a different medium. Instead of focusing on the Battle of Boquerón as Urrelo Zárate does, the film approaches the end of the war and a single day: June 14, 1935, two days after the ceasefire.[40] Filmed in the Paraguayan countryside and in Guaraní, the movie takes a much slower pace than the fast urban intrigue in Urrelo Zárate's novel. Its protagonists are a couple, Cándida and Ramón, who are the parents of a soldier, Máximo. They are so far removed from the front that they do not even receive news about the war. They are left waiting to find out what has happened, hoping for the safe return of their son, a change of season, and a better life.

The film's thematic center relies on the twinning of *esperar*, "to wait" but also "to hope," with *desesperar*, "to despair" but also, transitively, "to exasperate or infuriate." As Cándida and Ramón wait for their son, there is very little action. Ramón works the land; Cándida washes clothes. They talk to each other about the weather, commenting on the heat and lack of rain, about the war and its depressing effects, about their son and when he will return, and about a dog's irritating barking. Otherwise, there is nothing much more than waiting. As such, the film resonates with Samuel Beckett's *Waiting for Godot*, and Encina claims to draw inspiration from Beckett, Roa Bastos, and Juan Rulfo (Courthès). Like the work of these authors, her story is elliptical. It relies on dialogue and yet uses a different medium to call into question the synchronicity of this dialogue. Throughout the film, Encina dissociates voice and image, at times inserting close-ups of the main characters in profile that reveal motionless lips against voiceovers in Guaraní. At other times, the camera shoots from behind, obscuring the face entirely. The mouth, which was so important in *Hablar con los perros* and in the realist narrative of *La laguna H.3* from chapter 1, no longer holds even the representative function of speech. The conversation between Cándida and Ramón likewise seems disconnected, often as if they were talking past each other or as if their conversation had somehow become jumbled, out of sync, or out of order. They constantly ask each other what they can hope for, what they can do, whether there has been any news. Cándida is much more cantankerous than her husband, trying to act undisturbed by the prolonged wait for news of her son, though she often lashes out, saying things that sound frustrated but also idiosyncratic like "hope loses you, Ramón" (*Hamaca paraguaya* 00:35:12).[41] In contrast, Ramón seems

2.1. Long shot of Cándida and Ramón in their hammock in *Hamaca paraguaya*. Cristian Nuñez / Paz Encina

2.2. Ramón in front of the veterinarian's door in *Hamaca paraguaya*. Cristian Nuñez / Paz Encina

mostly hopeful, explaining that he is a farmer and therefore knows that rain, and consequently relief, has to come sooner or later.

The noncoincidence of word and image makes *Hamaca paraguaya* a meditation on the relation of self to other and story to image (Courthès). It reflects the disarticulations between the stories we tell and the way they are received, between the history of the war lived on the battlefield and recorded in books and the one communicated to contemporary audiences. In order to do this, the film works with images of openings. In its carefully constructed scenery, the eponymous hammock with which the film opens and closes hangs between two trees in a clearing (fig. 2.1). The shots tend to be long and show the trees arching over the hammock to form an oval, an aperture. During one of the few sequences of events in the film, the persistently irritating dog stops barking. Cándida begins to worry that the dog is sick and asks Ramón to take her to the vet. It turns out that the dog is dehydrated, but since the rain hasn't come yet, there's no water for people, never mind the dog. During his visit, Ramón finds out from the veterinarian that the war ended two days ago but that not everyone had been informed. In a moment of hope, Ramón says that he must cure the dog because she belongs to his son, and Ramón imagines his son will be back soon for her. As he waits outside the veterinarian's house, daylight shines through a dark passage. The door frame and another open door behind reveals a dark chamber (fig. 2.2). It is an opening toward hope, through which the end of the war might bring life.

In a visual echo, Cándida sits next to a domed brick oven. The oven also has openings on either side, sometimes letting light through and sometimes obscuring it, depending on the angle (fig. 2.3). Like Ramón, she sits in profile facing right. They are both alone, suggesting that their waiting takes place simultaneously even though the episodes are successive from the viewer's perspective. Cándida hears the voice of a messenger looking for the Caballero family. The messenger himself never appears, and she speaks curtly as if wishing he would leave. He says he is looking for the family to inform them that Máximo Caballero died at the front. But Cándida says that her son's name is Máximo *Ramón* Caballero, and then she tells him that everyone in the area has the same name anyway so he probably means someone else. In her denial, she refuses the indexicality of her son's name. She says that her son can't have been killed by being shot in the heart off to the left, because her son's heart was in the center of his chest. As the messenger insists on delivering his news, repeating himself in spite of Cándida's evasiveness, Cándida withdraws into herself and the camera pulls in with her, shot by shot closer to her face, the profile making her unmoving lips create an even more

2.3. Cándida in front of a brick oven in *Hamaca paraguaya*. Cristian Nuñez / Paz Encina

striking contrast to her sourceless words. As the viewer is drawn closer to her, the news from the disembodied messenger's voice seems to sink in.

When Cándida and Ramón finally meet again in the hammock, they do not want to take away each other's hope, so she doesn't tell him about the messenger—or perhaps she imagined the messenger or wishes she had imagined the messenger (Johnson 224). Similarly, when she asks Ramón for news about the war, he tells her that it stopped: "'The war ended, Papá?' 'No, Cándida, my chest pain!'" (*Hamaca paraguaya* 00:54:20–00:54:27).[42] They tell these half-truths to make the waiting more bearable. Rather than a war story, *Hamaca paraguaya* ends as a love story based on partial lies and omissions, memories, and habit. It recovers a rural past in place of a vanguard future yet in a cinematically experimental form. There is no pretension to certainty through mimetic representation; even Cándida and Ramón agree that they can't really know anything, like when Máximo or the rain will come. Interspersed shots of a dark sky, heavy with clouds and rumbles of thunder make it seem as though the characters are looking up toward the possibility of salvation. But there is no salvation. We are confronted with two char-

acters stuck waiting—waiting and hoping as in esperar—whose enemy is none other than history, whose messiah is the promised rain that
never arrives, whose sacred trace is Máximo's shirt that the messenger
brings as a remembrance and Cándida burns, and who lack a horizon
since Ramón refuses to watch the sun set. One by one, the film discards the structure of the war declaration and manifesto. A brief resolution comes only in the sound of a thunderstorm that plays behind the
rolling credits.

As the film thwarts causality, it substitutes a different temporality:
one of contingency and phase difference.[43] It translates the photographic capture, as in Céspedes's "La paraguaya" in chapter 1, into a narrative mesh, so that the images of apertures mimic the hammock netting,
holding the film together in a porous form. At the beginning, the hammock is unfurled and tied. Then the couple separates, each to their daily
chores, during which they begin to suspect the death of their son. At the
end, they come back together and get ready to bring the lamp and hammock in for the night. Without having recounted the news of their son's
likely death to each other, they affirm that they have each other, in spite
of everything. The titular hammock forms the netting that supports
the simultaneously close and distanced relationship between Cándida
and Ramón. Its holes stand in for the many gestures of openness in the
cinematography and the gaps in what remains unsaid. They also reveal
Máximo's uncovered and uncoverable absence. Fragile like the old hammock, the story itself might rip apart along its asynchronous seams at
any moment during the wait for better days. During this wait, the image
of the hammock stands in for a modus vivendi, coming-together-apart,
suspended over a different kind of ground—the ductile mesh of finitude
and futurity without manifesto, trace, or messiah.

The exit from the historical condition of siege, then, is not the
capitalist modus vivendi, tempered by ritual or proclamation. Instead,
it is something more subtle. In both Urrelo Zárate and Encina, Bolivia's
and Paraguay's landlocked enclosures lead to a suffocating siege. Urrelo
Zárate's novel suggests that a purely causal relationship between culture
and war would continue this enclosure, confining future generations
to aphasia and, eventually, an amnesia that would filter into ongoing
stasis under globalization and hyperextractive capitalism. The focus on
the mouth, the desire to consume, the circulation of blood and capital, the enclosure in form, the inability to speak, and the asynchronous word and image converge in the recent legacy of the Chaco War
to portray the stuttering and irregular transition to a brutally violent
transnational capitalism. In Encina, the relationship of this past to the

present is framed as the coming-together-apart of two temporalities in the malleable form of a hammock. The moment of capture that the war attempted to seal is, in fact, unworked in this final phase difference between netted singularities, then and now. Against stories of progress and heroism, through the body, nation, and work of art, this mesh leaves open the question of *la espera*—"the wait"—for the future and an acceptance of *desesperanza*—"despair" and "exasperation." The hammock's malleability beckons Cándida, Ramón, and the audience that watches them to decide on the future of this war beyond state incorporation. Instead of a cannibalism that devours the past, Encina asks her audience to recover, tentatively and with care, the possibility of waiting, hoping, and despairing without knowing what will happen. Rather than history devouring literature in the contemporary condition of global stasis, she evokes what Rodríguez-Alcalá calls that essential dimension of time: the future.[44]

CHAPTER 3

THE SOCCER WAR AND DEMOGRAPHIC STASIS

Los muertos están cada día más indóciles.

—Roque Dalton, "El descanso del guerrero"

From July 14 to July 18, 1969, El Salvador and Honduras engaged in a short border war, sensationally called the "Soccer War" or "Football War." According to the story broadcast in the international press, fans of the Honduran and Salvadoran national teams kept their opponents awake all night before two World Cup qualifying matches in hostile territory. Losses were attributed to the interference of overzealous fans and a firmly held sense of national pride that fueled antagonism on and off the field. The war itself baffled commentators and political scientists who found it difficult to classify because it was fought over "issues that could not be easily labelled as racial, religious, ideological, linguistic or anticolonial and which had their immediate origin in a soccer match" (Cable 658). Even more perplexingly to one commentator at the time, "the two protagonists are participants in one of the very few examples of successful economic integration amongst developing countries, which as such, has been held up as a prototype of the kind of arrangement which could well be emulated by the large and growing number of very small states" (Cable

658). The war put this partnership on hold for several years. That a few soccer matches might interrupt a widely lauded example of successful regional economic integration seemed puzzling, at least from afar.

Closer to the border, however, the war's outbreak was less mysterious. Since 1958, the US-backed Central American Common Market (CACM) had been moving toward distributing labor and diversifying Central American economies. Yet each country struggled with its own domestic problems in the process. As Vincent Cable explains in his October 1969 analysis, the majority of Salvadoran land was in the hands of an infamously small elite, while much Honduran land was in the hands of US-owned fruit companies. El Salvador also had a much greater population density than its neighbor. The combination of relatively little land and its uneven distribution gave the country a large diaspora throughout Central America but especially in Honduras, where Salvadorans were drawn to fruit company jobs and unsettled tracts of land for farming (Anderson 71–73). Added to underlying demographic and economic pressures, the uneven process of integration created a pressure cooker of economic tensions primed to explode at the first sign of trouble—in this case, the World Cup qualifiers.

Combat was brief—earning the war its less sensational nickname, the Hundred Hours War—but in spite of its brevity, it claimed the lives of many and displaced many others, including tens of thousands of Salvadorans (Anderson 141). Prior to the war, the border was vaguely defined and laxly guarded. In its aftermath, the Honduran government expelled Salvadorans, and both sides increased border security. The CACM project ground to a halt, eventually paused for the remainder of the Cold War—over two decades—before being revived in the early 1990s. During that time, El Salvador descended into a bloody civil war between the state, right-wing paramilitaries, and left-wing militants. Writing in 1981, historian Thomas Anderson explains the 1969 war's effects: "The question remains as to how far the social and political deterioration of El Salvador over the last decade has been the product of the Soccer War, but certainly this much can be said: the war removed a major safety valve from a potentially explosive situation" (155). By removing the possibility of migration and equitable land distribution, the war worsened the already strained relationship between land and people.

With the benefit of hindsight, geographers could easily see how the expulsion of inhabitants, destruction of infrastructure, and severing of diplomatic ties created a sparsely inhabited stateless zone near the border that fed into the Salvadoran Civil War. Robert Thomas and Don Hoy describe how, from this no-man's-land, guerilla fighters carved out training areas for themselves after 1969 (fig. 3.1). Writing in the late

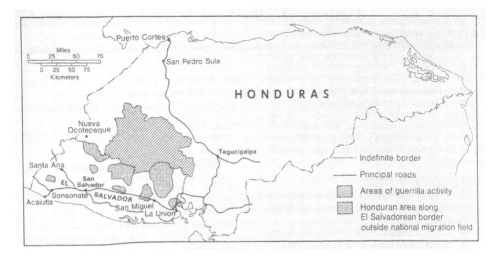

3.1. Map of the border between El Salvador and Honduras, including guerrilla training areas in the aftermath of the 1969 war. R. Thomas and D. Hoy, "A Demographic Perspective to El Salvador's Internal Struggle." *Yearbook* (Conference of Latin Americanist Geographers) 14 (1988).

1980s at the height of the civil war, the demographers comment on the state's inadvertent creation of a space from which to mount armed insurrection against it, where militants took advantage of areas previously traversed by migrants and government officials, now protected from prying eyes. The short 1969 war thus had a long, bloody afterlife in the civil war that lasted from 1980 to 1992.

The Soccer War has been dubbed a "demographic war" (Durham vii) because of the high population density of El Salvador compared to Honduras. However, as William Durham argues, the war was not solely demographic but also regional, emerging from uneven land distribution within the two countries as much as uneven population distribution among them. The border was the meeting point of these tensions. In contrast to the Chaco War, in which border areas were sparsely populated before the war and seen as sealed afterwards, these border areas were porous and overpopulated before the war and vacant after. This chapter focuses on how the El Salvador-Honduras border reflects and inflects internal tensions within each country and how these tensions ripple into the interstate system. The Soccer War only lasted about one hundred hours, but it consolidated preexisting economic disparities on both sides, manifested Cold War tensions, and established key conditions for the Salvadoran Civil War. As such, this was a war that showed an unrelenting back-and-forth between domestic and international pressures, between the *polemos* that informed anti-aggression pacts in the wake of the Second World War and the stasis of civil war that became all too common in Central America throughout the Cold War. It reflects a prototype of economic integration via labor and trade foiled by nationalism that resonates with contemporary disputes at the Mexico-US border.

As US political influence and expanding transnational capitalism interrupted the lines between domestic and foreign, regular citizens, military officers, and soccer fans began clinging to nationalist modes of belonging. They cut off ties from regional units. Theorists of globalization have noticed a similar trend in the present; as the world becomes more economically interconnected, there is often a backlash that Wendy Brown sees in building walls and fortifications; Giacomo Marramao sees in reversion to identity-based modes of belonging, such as nationalisms and fundamentalisms; and Mark Duffield sees as thwarting migratory flows.[1] In El Salvador in 1969, an early form of these reversions appeared at the outbreak of war. Polish journalist Ryszard Kapuściński documented Salvadorans' hearkening back to colonial politics, when from the front lines they called to colonize not only Honduras but also the traditionally colonizing powers of Europe: "The Salvadorans were moving to order: push through to the Atlantic, then to Europe and then the world!" (171). Instead of a Cold War mentality, the Salvadorans adopted an imperial one.

This call to colonize took place, perhaps most ironically, at the same time that the Apollo 11 crew made the first moon landing. Authors Roque Dalton and Horacio Castellanos Moya, whose works this chapter examines, cite the Salvadoran president's jibe in their writings on the Soccer War: "It's now safer to walk on the moon than through the streets of Honduras" (Dalton, *Las historias prohibidas* 222; Castellanos Moya, *Desmoronamiento* 99).[2] In the face of technological and economic progress, the Soccer War proved that nationalism was still a force to be reckoned with. Even as anti-aggression pacts and anti-communist policies infringed upon territorial integrity in the name of security, armed nationalism led to an extremely costly war that would feed the cycle of violence plaguing the region. The Soccer War is a key point on the continuum from internal to external war, here examined through Dalton's late poetry from the 1969 war until his untimely death in 1975 as well as Castellanos Moya's 2006 novel *Desmoronamiento* (Breakdown; Collapse). In these works, the relationship between territory and people shifts before, during, and after the war. This change also appears in the literary text's metareflection on representation in the face of crisis, while, as Dalton says, the dead become increasingly restless. In the works of these two authors, the Soccer War appears as part of the sedimentation of violence into society. It provides an early example of border conflict in the free-trade era while foreshadowing the twenty-first century's globally integrated stasis.

NAMING THE WAR

The name "Soccer War" has been attributed to Kapuściński, whose rich description of the war from the ground made it world-famous. In his account, Kapuściński draws parallels between the spectacles of sport and warfare. In spite of the war's spectacular portrayal in the media, however, he writes that the reality for the soldier on the ground was bleak: "War becomes a spectacle, a show, when it is seen from a distance and expertly re-shaped in the cutting room" (179–80). In war and sport, a territory or field is demarcated; spectators cheer one side or another. It can make compelling television, easily splitting into two sides like the Cold War division between capitalism and communism. But, Kapuściński insists, this division does not hold up in experience: "In reality a soldier sees no further than his own nose, has his eyes full of sand or sweat, shoots at random and clings to the ground like a mole. Above all, he is frightened" (180).[3] War is only a spectacle from afar.

The Soccer War frustrated the expansion of capitalism in the Americas under the forceful guidance of the United States. Unlike other wars in the region, especially the guerrilla conflicts of the 1970s and 1980s that mapped onto the division between left and right, this war was a conflict between two right-wing governments. Both sides struggled to balance landed elite and transnational business interests against the increasingly pressing claims of the landless. Consequently, small-scale conflicts over individual plots contributed to a larger tension between the oligarchy and the poor majority. In the face of expanding and increasingly diffuse power networks, soccer fans turned to immediate circumstances rather than overarching problems. Unlike the ongoing structural economic problems that led to migration and squatting, these conflicts played out in delimited spaces for set periods of time.

According to Carl von Clausewitz's famous aphorism, war is the continuation of policy by other means, and for Salvadoran poet and militant Dalton, the 1969 Soccer War was a continuation of the longstanding politics of demographic and economic repression in Central America. Dalton's collection *Las historias prohibidas del pulgarcito* (The little thumb's forbidden stories) tells the secret histories of El Salvador, using its nickname: "el pulgarcito de América" (America's little thumb). In the poem "La guerra es la continuación de la política por otros medios y la política es solamente la economía quintaesenciada (Materiales para un poema)" (War is the continuation of politics by other means, and politics is merely the quintessence of economics [materials for a poem]), Dalton shows that the war, while ridiculed in the international press, emerged from severe economic inequality. Dalton's title argues that the war represents the continuation of economic exploitation by other means. Unlike Kapuściński, Dalton sees the war as rooted in a history that extends much further back than the two World Cup qualifying matches. Dalton's poetry, especially *Las historias prohibidas*, illuminates a persistent tension in Salvadoran history: on one hand, violently imposed authority from the conquest of the Americas onward, and on the other, the indigenous and *campesino* populations that have historically challenged this authority.

"La guerra es la continuación" presents a collage of news fragments and pithy, sometimes ironic or mocking observations about the war. Among the poem's "materials" Dalton includes a clipping from a student newspaper that describes El Salvador's overpopulation problem succinctly: "For various reasons (the 1932 massacre, land evictions, chronic unemployment and hunger), an enormous wave of emigrants has left over-populated El Salvador for places abroad. . . . In Honduras, the Salvadoran population has risen to more than 350,000, the majority poor peasants, precarious occupants of virgin lands in under-populated Honduras" (*Las historias prohibidas* 210–11).[4] As Salvadorans squatted on underused lands over the border, Hondurans decided to enact land reform as a corrective to their own economic pressures. Dalton explains this move in another citation from a news clipping, quoting a Honduran official:

> To carry out the Agrarian Reform that the Alliance for Progress demands, we must distribute lands. The problem lies in *which* to distribute. Taking the holdings of the North American United Fruit Company is taboo. If we touched the property of the great old Honduran landed oligarchy, the Land Reform would be communist. Laying our hands on the national forests would be very costly. So, there's nothing left but the land being used by Salvadoran immigrants, which amounts to 370,000 hectares. If we kick out the Salvadorans, we'll show patriotic spirit, since we'll be recovering land in foreign hands for Hondurans. (*Las historias prohibidas* 214)[5]

Instead of depriving the United Fruit Company or wealthy oligarchs of their land, thus risking the accusation of communism, the government decided to enact reform by expelling Salvadorans without legal title to the lands they inhabited.[6] Officials began strategically applying previously unenforced laws on land ownership and citizenship. Dalton

repeatedly turns to the 1932 massacre of campesinos during an uprising that echoes through Salvadoran history. Throughout *Las historias
prohibidas*, the massacre shows that the people of El Salvador are never
fully taken into account.[7] Even in a news clipping from early June 1969,
Dalton cites a Honduran minister saying: "Illegal Salvadorans must leave
Honduras. Let El Salvador deal with its demography" (216).[8] The demographic problem is the problem of the relationship of people to territory
that has plagued the country for decades.

Following Dalton, the Soccer War is less about soccer and spectacle
and more about demography and history. It offers a privileged moment
for examining the relationship between people and territory, especially the logic of representation by which people correspond to national
territorial units and own property. Documentation of citizenship and
deeds to property proved contentious during the Soccer War and exposed how rocky the process of regional integration could be. In what
follows, I take a strongly etymological understanding of demography as
writing the *demos*. Through Dalton and Castellanos Moya, the Soccer
War portrays the slippage between territory and demos that continues
to challenge logics of representation even after the enclosure of frontiers
that we saw in the Chaco. This slippage presents an early clash between
economic integration on the one hand and demographic and migratory
suppression on the other. I follow Dalton's approach in *Las historias prohibidas* to suggest that there is a persistent low-level violence in Central
America with occasional flares. This view, in turn, challenges the widespread assertion that war causes "crises of representation" in literature,
philosophy, and politics. Instead, I argue that Dalton and Castellanos
Moya point to the failure of attempts to suppress warfare through integrated power networks, proper names, and national borders. More than
literature's representative failure, their work suggests that the destruction of war exposes an underlying stasis—ongoing, internecine conflict
at dynamic equilibrium, on the borders of literary and legal texts.

NAMING THE SOVEREIGN

Although the Soccer War manifested decades of political and economic
tension, it ended quickly thanks to forms of political organization developed in Europe after the Second World War. European and American
diplomats redoubled their efforts to ensure international cooperation and
anti-aggression more forcefully than the League of Nations had done.
The Soccer War proved such efforts successful, coming to a swift end
with the help of the Organización de Estados Americanos (OEA; Organization of American States, OAS). The organization was created as the

mechanism for Pan-American peacekeeping, beginning with the 1945 Act of Chapultepec and reinforced in the 1947 Inter-American Treaty of Reciprocal Assistance, unofficially called the Rio Treaty. It formed part of the international legal structures of "hemispheric defense," including security and cooperation pacts among member states, to quash the possibility of another war. Regional defense became a central tenet of trans-American anti-war doctrine in an attempt to prevent the recurring violence that had plagued Europe.

Anti-war policy also coincided with strengthening US influence in the Americas in general and in Central America in particular. US neo-imperialism saturated security policy and made it synonymous with anti-communism. Dalton points to this trend in the poem "O.E.A." from a collection published the same year as the Soccer War:

> The President of my country
> these days is called Colonel Fidel Sánchez Hernández.
> But General Somoza, President of Nicaragua,
> is also President of my country.
> And General Stroessner, President of Paraguay,
> is also a little bit President of my country, although less
> than the President of Honduras, which is to say
> General López Arellano, and more than the President of Haiti,
> Monsieur Duvalier.
> And the President of the United States is more President of my country,
> than the President of my country,
> the one that, as I said, these days,
> is called Colonel Fidel Sánchez Hernández. (*Taberna* 23)[9]

Dalton's poem makes the slippages from leader to leader visible as he runs down, one by one, their names and level of involvement in Salvadoran politics. He describes the laws of inter-American peacekeeping ironically, as they rely on a fluid arrangement of military personnel; all leaders are colonels and generals with the exception of the Haitian and US presidents. The US president remains unnamed; whether Dalton was referring to Lyndon Johnson or Richard Nixon matters little. The organization amounts to a many-headed hydra as the acts of international peacemaking in the wake of the Second World War fed into thinly veiled military control of the Americas. Between the proper names of each leader, Dalton points to power coalescing around the United States, which exerts more influence than the relatively weak, puppet-like presidents of El Salvador, Nicaragua, Paraguay, Honduras, and Haiti, whose disposability Dalton emphasizes in the repetition of *hoy por hoy* (these days, or for the time being). As Dalton makes the heads of state into transitive cogs in a US-run machine, he lays bare the link between war-making and peacekeeping.[10] Dalton's poetry pokes fun at this anti-aggression policy, especially the belief that the Euro-American cycle of destruction has to be stopped at the cost of democratic representation.

Dalton is not alone in observing a slippage in proper names associated with sovereignty during the post–Second World War period. Although his poem differs in format and tone from Theodor Adorno's famous remark—later recanted—that "to write poetry after Auschwitz is barbaric" (Adorno 34), both point to a peculiar and unique relationship between poetry and violence after the Second World War.[11] Structures of authority intended to control and delimit violence had already been undermined after the mass slaughter of the First World War in Europe and that of the Chaco War in Bolivia and Paraguay. After the Second World War in Europe and during the Cold War in Latin America, violence seemed more pervasive and less delimited in space and time.[12] For instance, Hannah Arendt's *Origins of Totalitarianism* argues that the supposed distinction between internal and external violence collapses under totalitarian regimes. Emmanuel Levinas goes a step further in the preface to his *Totality and Infinity*, identifying violence as the basis not just of certain governmental structures but of the unfolding of Western thought in general. Levinas sees the Greek polemos permeating the philosophical tradition and predisposing it to violence, a point taken up in decolonial critiques of continental philosophy. Polemos is the animating force behind everything from the struggle of the dialectic to the unfolding of ontological difference. According to this line of thought, the Second World War merely enacted what was already true philosophically.

For Levinas, it would not come as a surprise that Carl Schmitt and Martin Heidegger exchanged letters precisely about the role of polemos since the time of the ancient Greeks to the contemporary moment in 1933. Acknowledging receipt of the third edition of Schmitt's *Concept of the Political*, Heidegger writes to Schmitt that he also has a keen interest in Heraclitus's fragment 53, which reads: "War [polemos] is both father of all and king of all: it reveals the gods on the one hand and humans on the other, makes slaves on the one hand, the free on the other" (trans. and qtd. in Fried 21). Heraclitus names a sovereign—war—which confers structure and order on the world. In Heidegger's view, this war-king is critical to understanding polemos. He points out, "You [Schmitt] did not forget *basileus* [king], which gives definitive meaning to the whole [Heraclitean] maxim if one interprets it completely" (qtd. in Fried 28).

Heidegger does not elaborate. This king might be taken as damningly close to the Führer, or a more generous reading might interpret the war-king as the force responsible for the unfolding of the ontological difference, the encounter between Being and beings.[13] Heidegger adds a comment about the struggle he faced at the time: "But now I myself stand in the midst of the polemos [that is, in his role as Rector] and all literary projects must give way" (qtd. in Fried 28; brackets in the original).[14] His offhanded comment about his position as first Nazi Rector of the University of Freiburg draws the letter back to the immediate context but seems puzzling in light of Heidegger's insistence on the centrality of *basileus* and polemos. Why must polemos take precedence over literature?

Heidegger treats fragment 53 more extensively in *Introduction to Metaphysics*, first published in 1953 but based on lectures delivered in 1935: "The *polemos* named here is a strife that holds sway before everything divine and human, not war in the human sense. As Heraclitus thinks it, struggle first and foremost allows what essentially unfolds to step apart in opposition. . . . In con-frontation, world comes to be" (67). Heidegger sees the world unfolding through conflicts that form boundaries and delimit beings. Yet in the 1933 letter to Schmitt, the polemos consuming "all literary projects" seems to be war "in the human sense." This is not the polemos of ontological difference but a particular historical conflict. Heidegger's quick movement from the ontological to the everyday suggests that polemos pressures literature and philosophy into a confrontation that Heidegger leaves unexplored.

Dalton, writing during the Cold War, takes a different approach to the relationship between literature and philosophy via politics. Instead of focusing on how boundaries appear as Heidegger does, he mocks the *lack* of boundaries in organizations such as the OEA/OAS, pointing out that they effectively perpetuate US hegemony. Although the OEA/OAS aims to create diplomatic channels that suppress violence, in practice it conforms to US policy. From Dalton's perspective, the diplomatic suppression of warfare leads to violence in the form of a crisis of political representation in the Americas, signaling a growing divide between government and people. Dalton places these policies on display in another sphere that tends to get shunned during moments of crisis, as Heidegger showed: literature. Poetry *is* possible, Dalton seems to say, but under conditions of postwar anti-aggression pacts, each country's president slips easily into the other in a US-dominated ranking of power with little concern for the people. Poetry cannot declare polemos as sovereign. Instead, it points to the people's absence. For the people, naming runs the risk of appearing to power. For instance, Kapuściński asks one of the men he interviews why his country is at war. The man responds that he doesn't know what the war is about but wants to keep a low profile: "A man has to live in such a way that his name never reaches the ears of authorities" (180). This man demurs so that he can attend to his farm and so that he will pass unnoticed. Dalton, too, signals this aporia in the representative structures of politics and literature where the proper name fails. The people's distance from the sovereign exposes the growing chasm between transnational governance and the demos, especially during the Cold War. Poetry cannot name the sovereign or the poet; it cannot even classify the war as within or without.

NAMING AND FIDELITY

Las historias prohibidas shows the attempted erasure of the people's political agency in efforts to diffuse bellicose aggression. Dalton questions not only governmental authority but also the poet's voice in speaking for the people. His work blended his communist beliefs with literature. In an ars poetica dated 1962, for instance, Dalton ends by asking whom the poet should represent: "For whom shall the voice of the poet be?" (*El turno* 45).[15] The poet assumes responsibility for the people in spite of what he describes earlier in the poem as a world full of anxiety, desperation, crime, and hatred. By asking the question after detailing the world's ailments, he implies that the poet's voice serves as a conduit for the people's self-expression. In line with his militancy in the Ejército Revolucionario del Pueblo (ERP), Dalton sees the communist-poet's role as naming and representing the struggles of the people, at least in this phase of his career.

Dalton's approach resembles other communist poets of his generation, the aptly named Committed Generation, and politically engaged poets more generally. In the essay "Poetry and Communism," collected in *Age of the Poets* and focusing on the relationship between poetry and politics, Alain Badiou argues, "Poets are those who seek to create in language new names to name that which, before the poem, has no name. . . . The poem is a gift of the poet to language. But this gift, like language itself, is destined to the common—that is, to this anonymous point where what matters is not one person in particular but all, in the singular" (94). For Badiou, the poet names the common, and this is what makes poetry essentially communist. Yet Dalton has an uneasy relationship with naming, even if the name is singular and not particular. For him, the author eventually disappears among the people, no longer seeking to name or contribute to the "common" of language that Badiou defines. In "Alta hora de la noche" (In the dead of night) from the 1969 collection *El turno del ofendido*, Dalton moves explicitly toward anonymity, exhorting the reader: "When you learn that I have died, do not pronounce my name." Instead, he asks the reader to say other, more common words: "Flower, bee, teardrop, bread, storm." Saying his name—he describes it as pronouncing his eleven letters—would conjure him from the grave where he rests. And according to him, "I have earned silence" (119).[16] The word—poetry as naming—has the power to revive, but the poet prefers to remain unnamed and reserve the conjuring powers of the voice for daily necessities like bread.

In this poem, Dalton gives an eerie prediction of his own execution. His comrades accused him of being a CIA informant—an *oreja*, literally an "ear." As Kapuściński's poor farmer did not want his name to reach the ears of the authorities, so Dalton did not want to be a listening ear, spying on the ERP for the CIA. His comrades condemned him to death while he was fighting clandestinely in El Salvador, having returned from exile in Cuba and Czechoslovakia. The accusation eventually proved groundless, and Dalton's execution is still remembered as one of the dark moments of left-wing armed struggle in Central America. This early death meant that he would earn himself not silence but, instead, a place in interminable debates about the efficacy of militancy. Yet even before he returned to El Salvador to fight with the ERP, he was already transforming his name and identity. He underwent plastic surgery in Cuba and assumed a different name to disguise himself from the authorities.[17]

In this later period, during which he drafted *Las historias prohibidas*, he seemed to confer less authority to his name and his voice. Instead of intervening directly in the collection, Dalton curates the texts, organizing the national history of El Salvador into episodes and cycles in a compilation of news fragments and images. By this stage, Dalton no longer sees representation as the only criterion for evaluating art. The strong voice of the militant poet of the 1962 ars poetica disappears beneath a collage of facts, as *Las historias prohibidas* follows less the structure of a poetry collection and more one of an accumulation of primary sources through research. As this change takes place, both Dalton's voice and his name begin to recede in favor of staging historical resonance among seemingly unrelated pieces of information.

Critics consider the collection one of Dalton's most experimental and least accessible, representing a change in literary form that corresponds to a change in political circumstances. In their classic study of Central American revolutionary literature, John Beverley and Marc Zimmerman write that the collection "appear[s] at a time of crisis for the future of Latin American national liberation movements signaled by the general collapse of *foco* strategies after 1969, Allende's defeat in Chile, and—in Central America—the effects of the Soccer War and the repression of the UNO electoral coalition in El Salvador and the earthquake in Nicaragua. *Las historias* is written in response to and in a sense *on* the fault line of left fragmentation and debate over theory and strategy in this conjuncture" (133). Beverley and Zimmerman point to the fact that this compilation mirrors a broader sense of historical fragmentation in the late 1960s and early 1970s, and they contend that the collage represents constitutive silences within Salvadoran culture: "*Las historias*, as the plural suggests, also makes fun of the effort to construct a monolithic national narrative. 'Badly' made, ungainly, incoherent, it is an example of the fragmentation and silences of the national culture it seeks to represent, a world of unexpected contradictions and combinations, of multiple codes and temporalities" (132). The text fits this historical moment of fragmentation, which, in turn, mirrors Salvadoran national identity. Paradoxically, then, poetic fragmentation confers unity on the collection because El Salvador plays on the separation and unification of "el pulgarcito de América," an appendage to a larger unit, whether a hand or a continent.

While fragmentation certainly informs Dalton's portrayal of Salvadoran history, he radicalizes his approach to naming and history by creating constellations and repetitions within the collage. In this sense, Dalton interrupts "the orthodox Communist party stage theory of Latin American development" (Beverley and Zimmerman 132) that Beverley and Zimmerman accuse him of holding to. For instance, the 1932 massacre appears again and again, even out of historical time and in spite of the collection's broadly linear arc. In the poem "Todos" (All of us), Dalton identifies the massacre as a moment in which the Salvadoran people were born half dead: "We were all born half dead in 1932 / we survive but half alive" (*Las historias prohibidas* 128).[18] The "everyone" or "all of us" of the title democratizes, including the reader of the poem. Dalton points out that his reader is also half-dead and, by extension, contains the cadavers of others, unrepresented by proper names. This poem invokes Badiou's anonymous and singular point of the common, yet Dalton presses this anonymous point further, away from the naming and fidelity that are central to Badiou's philosophical system. As Badiou claims in the essay "Philosophy and Poetry from the Vantage Point of the Unnameable," also in *Age of the Poets*, the name is the fundamental connection between being and event: "Philosophy is the general theory of being and of the event, insofar as they are tied together by truth. For a truth is the work *upon* the being of a vanished event, of which

85

only the name remains" (57). Dalton's poetry seems to suggest that the name—whether of author or event—only half survives the catastrophe of history.

For Dalton, too, there is no longer a clear demarcation between within and without, living and dead. In her analysis, Yansi Pérez writes: "In order to find the other's word one has to move far away from what is one's own, far from property, far from the very concept of author and authorship" (179–80).[19] The masses of the demos become the unnameable others within. They are improper and unnamed to the reader and unauthorized and unauthored by the author. Dalton voices these unnamed without enclosing them under his poetic authority, much less a national identity. The uprising—stasis—of 1932 brought together the living and the dead, and the half-living, half-dead victims reappear when Dalton cites them as indicative of the land tensions that, unresolved, would spark the Soccer War and later civil war.[20]

Recalling a looming historical debt to his readers, Dalton interrupts the collection's chronology by burying the multiplying cadavers of generations past within each person. As history doubles back on itself in the text, the purportedly linear stages of communist development blur into one another. James Iffland sees Dalton's understanding of history as informed by Walter Benjamin. Like Benjamin, Dalton creates constellations that recall the forgotten victims of "progress," not melancholically but rather as "something completely contemporary" (Iffland 167). These dead do not belong but, without properly belonging, pass into the poem and into the present. Dalton points to the growing count of the dead in the ironically named "El descanso del guerrero" (The warrior's rest), from *Taberna y otros lugares*: "The dead become more unmanageable by the day / . . . / I think they're beginning to realize / that they are increasingly the majority" (6).[21] This silent majority gradually overtakes poetry, making it increasingly disobedient and unmanageable. Gone is poetry tied to sovereignty or truth, failing to adequately represent both. Gone, too, is the poet's vocation to name or call something into being. He now struggles to include voices that disobey his conjuring.

Dalton changes his approach to let these voices speak through the poem instead of through the poet. He gradually moves away from poetry as the privileged instrument for communicating a political message; as his career progresses, the relationship among voices within the poem becomes less hierarchical and more horizontal. As a result, his previously strong poetic voice diffuses into intertextuality in the penultimate poem of *Las historias prohibidas*, also cited above, "La guerra es la continuación de la política por otros medios y la política es solamente la economía quintaesenciada (Materiales para un poema)." Already from the title, the reader follows Dalton's leaps from Clausewitz to Marx, adapting his poetic materials to the multipart title. Dalton begins with one of those "raw materials," a news wire: "Tegucigalpa, May 25, 1969 (AP). The Honduran Ministry of Foreign Affairs, in a speech about the effects of Central American economic integration in the country, pointed to Salvadoran Colgate toothpaste as a factor in the increase of cavities among Honduran children" (197).[22] He drops the reader into a clipping about toothpaste. This first fragment ridicules the banality of cheap patriotism, ignores the transnational branding of Colgate, and mocks the gravity of a news story. Yet Dalton's only work in this ridicule comes in the fragment's frame. For the most part, the history of the war in "La guerra es la continuación" amounts to a collection of news wires, articles, and speeches. The poet rarely intervenes in his own voice, but he does build the fragments toward increasing intensity, from toothpaste toward landless peasants and the outbreak of hostilities and into a series of headlines about the war's effects.

The poetic voice seems to have disappeared completely, but Dalton has another trick waiting for his reader. Since *Las historias prohibidas* is such a thoroughly researched, almost academic collection, it includes a bibliography. At the end of the list, Dalton adds an important note: "Outside of the texts and original poems, three texts have been modified to achieve the author's desired effects and two texts that appear to be taken from other publications are apocryphal, also written originally by the author. It is the readers' responsibility to find them" (232).[23] Dalton writes two texts that he is not supposed to have written, texts that he attributes to other publications. He has worked his way around the proper names of presidents and poets in "O.E.A." and "Alta hora de la noche," and he has dispersed his poetic voice away from representation in "Todos." But he takes another step. He destroys the illusion of fidelity created in the thoroughly researched and carefully framed arrangement of texts. It becomes the reader's task to attribute truth or falsehood to the fragments. There is something improper and unaccounted for in this ostensibly national poetry collection about El Salvador. He introduces doubt and questions fidelity in a collection already defined by its forbidden stories.

The two texts that Dalton introduces do not represent anything but rather offer news articles written when no event took place. They are representations without presentation. These two apocryphal texts radically interrupt the type of bordering that happens around the names of the poet and sovereign as well as those around national culture. Until the last page of the collection, Dalton's false texts move, unnoticed, into the national narrative like unacknowledged migrants crossing the Salvadoran-Honduran border. They interrupt the propriety of the text, both in Dalton's poetic-academic exercise and in the state's texts on citizenship and property. Undocumented migrants and, more radically, squatters as undocumented land users introduce points where the texts of maps and deeds claim that there is nothing. This migration marks the nation's failure to represent its people as well as to contain and control movement. Like the false identification papers Dalton used to reenter El Salvador or the faked materials he used to construct his poems, these migrants do not belong from the state's perspective. Thus, in spite of its persistent reference to El Salvador, *Las historias prohibidas* disarticulates the national pretension to unity, moving instead toward an interruption of the smooth relationship between presentation and representation, an interruption of naming and placing. Dalton is not a faithful subject who names the demos to release it into the commonality of language; rather, he gradually becomes the subject who diffuses the poetic voice in disguise among the demos.[24] In this sense, Dalton's poetry aligns with a politics that pursues the anonymous and clandestine instead of advocating for a militant subject.

As migrants begin to populate the borderlands before the war, they expose the Soccer War's fundamental problem: the free market cosmo-polis, intended to emerge from regional integration, does not belong to the people, who appear as anarchic and improper. Central American integration had been intended to create a group of nations controlled by the heads of state listed in "O.E.A.," yet the integration project failed to represent life under a national or even regional frame. Instead, the Central American demos escapes, as Dalton's writing escapes the frame of truth. This same demos even escapes its own crisis in the name "Soccer War," which focuses more on spectacle and sport than on people. The headlines included in the final section of "La guerra es la continuación," "XXXVII. Some consequences of the conflict (to date)," include three worth particular mention: "REARMAMENT AND MODERNIZATION OF THE SALVADORAN ARMY UNDER NORTH AMERICAN DIRECTION," "REARMAMENT AND MODERNIZATION OF THE HONDURAN ARMY UNDER NORTH AMERICAN DIRECTION," and "DOZENS OF SALVADORANS WANDERING WITH THEIR HUNGER ON THEIR BACKS FROM HONDURAS TO EL SALVADOR AND FROM EL SALVADOR TO HONDURAS. IN HONDURAS THEY NO LONGER HAVE LAND. IN EL SALVADOR THEY HAVE NEITHER LAND NOR WORK. THEY ARE NEITHER SALVADORANS NOR HONDURANS: THEY ARE THE POOR" (227–29).[25] Dalton's *Las historias prohibidas* indexes this

looming and unrecognized conflict, belated product of the 1932 uprising continuing into the 1970s. Yet he does not aim at a fuller representation. Instead, he playfully dissolves the boundaries of authority,
naming, and fidelity, hinting at a dynamic that will become crucial in
the historical crisis coming to Central American history and literature:
the crisis of representation during the prolonged stasis of the civil wars.

Dalton's summary of the effects of the war suggests that poetry gradually builds toward self-destruction. From its improper names—demos
and *todos*—to its apocryphal materials to its exhortations that the reader
accuse the author of betrayal and infidelity, the poetic text enacts, even
encourages, its own undoing. Even before the outbreak of war, poetry
cannot name or enclose these materials, just as the state cannot close
the border to stem the tide of poor Salvadorans moving into Honduras.
Dalton points out that this gradual rise of tension from toothpaste to
mass displacement is part of a constellation of Central American history
that can be traced all the way back to the conquest. Toothpaste and cavity incidence, like the Soccer War, are merely ridiculous manifestations
of an extended pattern in which each episode elicits the violence of
the others. The Soccer War, then, becomes one of those constellations
around which literature reveals and represents stasis: uprising, internecine conflict, and revolt but also the continuity over time of the unrepresented majority. The civil war is unnamed but ongoing, even as the
event known as the Salvadoran Civil War has not yet begun.

WRITING THE DEMOS

Dalton emphasizes this continuity of violence when he returns to the
famous Clausewitz aphorism in one of the final fragments of "La guerra
es la continuación" about the Soccer War:

> The falsification of the history of that war
> is its continuation by other means
> the continuation of the true war carried out
> under the appearance of a war between El Salvador and Honduras:
> the imperialist-oligarchic-bourgeois-governmental war
> against the people of Honduras and El Salvador. (227)[26]

In the continuity between war and politics, historical war and fictionalized history, the Soccer War is only a symptom—or in Dalton's words,
"under the *appearance* of a war between El Salvador and Honduras" (227;
emphasis added). The true continuity of warfare in the region includes
both national and international exploitation: on one hand, the inability

to regulate private property because of oligarchic land ownership, and on the other, the inability to account for transnational labor in merging economies.

Dalton disarticulates national and literary frames and, as a consequence, challenges the relationship between politics and literature traditionally understood in Latin American cultural studies through testimonial, cosmopolitan, or realist approaches to literature. The first approach, through *testimonio*, considers literature an instrument of politics, especially in the tradition of engaged or committed art. A cursory glance might place Dalton as poet-militant in this camp, given that he sought political education and engagement through art. When critics describe Dalton's *Las historias prohibidas* as "difficult" or "inaccessible" (Beverley and Zimmerman), the implicit critique is that he has failed to be sufficiently democratic. It is a collection for the few, not the many. Cultural studies proposed to shift focus away from literature and toward testimonio, particularly in Central America during the 1970s to 1990s. John Beverley famously described testimonio as post-literature, which would stimulate political action. The oral histories recorded in testimonies came to represent the demos in an almost unmediated way, and those who gave testimony were placed within as literal and mimetic a frame as possible. In Beverley's words, this nonliterary literature "democratizes" the field of cultural studies because there are lower barriers to access (398).[27] Those who gave testimony replaced authors, not only because they created narratives around historical crises but also because they could frame themselves as subjects of history, as victims of a violent historical cycle and actors against its brutality.[28] However, testimonio also struggled to escape its legal origins. It was supposed to be a linguistic account of lived experience. Like Dalton, Rigoberta Menchú was emblematically accused of lying in her 1983 account *Me llamo Rigoberta Menchú y así me nació la conciencia*, which set off a regrettable episode in the US culture wars. Testimonial post-literature thus shared engaged literature's reliance on a true, faithful subject of history, expressed directly and accessibly. Yet, as we have seen, Dalton is not a faithful subject with accessible writing, nor is the demos he writes about easily captured.[29]

A second understanding of the relationship between literature and politics, through cosmopolitanism, sees testimonial post-literature as a critique of certain epistemologies and forms of knowledge. The self-styled decolonial school expands the critique of polemos in the wake of war, especially through Levinas's criticism of Heidegger, in order to consider how to remove the Western epistemic—even ontological—problem of oppression and recurring warfare. Decolonial scholars see themselves extending the historical moment of decolonization intellectually, as in Nelson Maldonado-Torres's *Against War*. The decolonial project generally sees itself building toward "critical cosmopolitanism," drawing on but taking distance from Kant's cosmopolitanism (Mignolo, "The Many Faces" 721).[30] And yet, the cosmo-polis is still a polis, as the Greek root reveals. It still implies conflict, not in the form of polemos but rather, as we have seen, in the form of stasis. In El Salvador, these conflicts included wars and uprisings which would become horrifically violent in the 1980s. Historical decolonization, after all, relied on the suppression of warfare in transnational organizations, which, as Dalton might be quick to point out, merely continued oppressive forms of violence through other mechanisms, especially as we will see below in more detail in the twin projects of fomenting the global circulation of capital and containing life, specifically by encouraging north–south economic relationships while preventing south–north migratory flows (Duffield, "Global Civil War"). For Dalton, decolonization might be an important historical process, but in "O.E.A.," it is clear that this process, whether political or epistemological, has not yet begun to unfold, if indeed it ever can.

A third approach to the relationship between literature and politics, based on a specific type of realism, makes literature secondary in the wake of historical devastation. After the Central American civil wars and the shortcomings of engaged art and testimonio, contemporary literature has been broadly seen as moving from portrayal of an authentic demos—whether to foment political consciousness or an ethical relationship with the other—toward portrayal of savage destruction. In particular since the 1992 Chapultepec Peace Accords that ended the Salvadoran Civil War, literature has been seen as indelibly marked by the experience of destruction implicit in surviving the cycle of armed insurgency. According to Sergio Villalobos-Ruminott, the descent into violence created a crisis of representation in literature and left-wing politics. Contemporary Central American narrative is a literature of destruction that has lost its emancipatory possibilities and utopian impulse. In authors such as Castellanos Moya and Rodrigo Rey Rosa, Villalobos-Ruminott sees "their distance from and suspicion with respect to magical realist and heroic narratives, which founded the utopia of the *hombre nuevo* [new man], and the liberationist ideologies that inspired popular fronts and their revolutionary armies" (134). Destruction characterizes Central American narrative, which in turn "has made explicit the naturalized character of violence, the deep crisis of a communitarian language to name a common history" (146). For Villalobos-Ruminott, the naturalization of violence in the wake of warfare has led to pared-down realism, which is not a disavowal of literature but rather literature's increasing approximation to historical reality.[31]

These three modes represent literary texts as responses to political and economic circumstances: testimony during Cold War insurgency, decolonial cosmopolitanism during neoliberal expansion, and a renewed realism after civil wars and during global financialization. Yet, as we have seen, war traverses each of these periods. Dalton's view of history—"The falsification of the history of that war / is its continuation by other means"—accounts for this war being referred to by different names and shifting into different forms. Hence, war is not an anomaly that literature reacts to or digests. Instead, it is the condition that reconfigures representative borders. When Dalton demonstrates the permeability of the literary text and its pretension to truth and representation, he illustrates that border formations, whether in linear history as the communist party stage theory or in spatial division, are nothing more than helpful delusions. Conflict is no longer clearly delimited as international or civil, bipolar or partisan. It is not temporally defined by the moment at which tension erupts into overt violence. It is both within and without, present before, during, and after the time-limited "war," with the Soccer War exceeding the timeframe of one hundred hours by decades. It is a continuous assimilation of violence.

This continuity of warfare appears just beyond the grasp of the state and just beyond the reach of the text. The Soccer War resulted in cleared tracts of Honduran land from which Salvadoran rebels could train for attacks against government forces years later. Figuratively, the border places citizens just as Dalton's authorial frame in *Las historias prohibidas* places texts. Neither is impermeable. In writing a "national" poetry collection for El Salvador, Dalton paradoxically unbinds this border, eliciting the slippage between demos and writing that takes place on the map in the anarchic spaces cleared of state presence. At the edge of testimonial truth and mimetic writing, the bordering functions of naming and fidelity come undone, and the poem becomes a staging ground for experimentation in which Dalton represents a type of warfare both partially contained and partially unbound. *Las historias prohibidas* thus accomplishes three things; it disrupts the proper name as the index of identity assumed in testimonio, interrupts the authority that an author might expect from cosmopolitanism, and questions the fidelity that realism assumes by admitting that the text itself may be apocryphal. Instead of writing an engagement with the demos or a response to the unfolding of history as war—polemos—Dalton writes about the interrupted identification between demos and territory, demos and author, and even the demos and itself. It becomes difficult, if not impossible, for him to name the history of violence. The resulting continuous warfare is a key part of Castellanos Moya's *Desmoronamiento*, where the themes of border, betrayal, and the destruction of literature take Dalton's approach to the Soccer War into the twenty-first century.

TRACING CENTRAL AMERICAN COLLAPSE

From the very first pages of Castellanos Moya's *Desmoronamiento*, the main character, doña Lena, accuses her daughter, husband, sister, and virtually everyone around her of being a traitor. She is particularly antagonistic toward Salvadorans and those that associate with them; her daughter's most egregious sin is marrying a Salvadoran. Doña Lena even goes so far as to say that the civil war is the result of the Salvadorans' aggressive temperament (193). Like Dalton, she casts the war as a continuation of the Soccer War turned inward: "[Doña Lena] used to say that we had done right to kick the Salvadorans out of Honduras, even though they came after us in a treacherous war. 'Those people are evil, and now that they don't have anyone to attack, they've decided to kill each other'" (193).[32] The continuation of the 1969 war, doña Lena points out, is merely its transferal and containment among the "barbaric" people who started it.

This continuity of warfare appears in Dalton's collection from a left-wing Salvadoran perspective, but in *Desmoronamiento*, it is mostly right-wing and Honduran. Castellanos Moya, like Dalton, compiles documents over a long period of time, revisiting some of the major historical events of the period, from a few years before the war to several decades after, through the daily lives of an upper-class family. The first part of the novel describes the wedding day of doña Lena and don Erasmo's daughter, Esther (Teti), coincidentally the same day as the assassination of John F. Kennedy in 1963. The second part includes letters between Teti, living with her husband in El Salvador, and her father don Erasmo Mira Brossa, living in Honduras—first during the 1969 Soccer War and then after Teti's husband's murder and a failed 1972 coup in El Salvador. These moments form some of the "fault lines" of leftist politics on which *Las historias prohibidas* rests in Beverley and Zimmerman's account. The third part takes place just after doña Lena suffers a stroke in late 1991 and continues through her death and the settling of her estate in 1992.

The last part of the novel focuses on inheritance, not only how the family divides up Lena's property but also, tangentially, the unexpected ways the Soccer War's legacy affected the family. We learn that Teti never returned to Honduras, even though she had planned to, and that Lena's favorite grandson, Eri, disappeared for several years during the civil war. While the family suspects that Eri joined the Salvadoran insurgency, they have no evidence. Ironically, Eri is the only actual traitor to doña Lena's political ideals, yet because of his close relationship with his grandmother, he is never accused of betrayal. Instead, Lena suspects that he has been either kidnapped or driven mad by Salvadorans. Eri later reappears but moves to Mexico. When he finally returns to Honduras, it is only to execute his grandmother's estate as quickly and efficiently as possible and move on with his life.

All of this information about Eri's later life filters through the first-person narrative of a character called Mateo in the final part of the novel. Officially, Mateo is Lena's gardener, but he also works as a handyman, chauffeur, and security guard. If Lena is characterized by her anger and accusations of betrayal and Eri by his reticence and mysteriousness, then Mateo seems the portrait of the common-sense campesino. He spends much of the final part of the novel securing the estate from real and imagined threats while Lena's condition slowly deteriorates. His typical tasks include things like "closing doors and windows" (158) and "repairing a stone fence that had been damaged by a strong gust of wind" (173).[33] Mateo has internalized his responsibility for closing and protecting the property to such an extent that he even has a nightmare that Lena is furious with him: "At some point in the night, I thought I heard the sound of doña Lena's cane hitting the floor tile, as if she were stomping around the house, as if I hadn't shut each and every one of the doors to the rooms and hallway, exactly as she did. Echoes remain in houses, even when no one lives in them" (161).[34] Lena's spirit inhabits the house, and so, throughout her illness and even when she is absent, Mateo makes an effort to protect the house as she would. He doesn't allow Lena's other grandson, Eri's brother Alfredito, into the house for fear that he might steal something.

The older, more mature Eri, on the other hand, gives the impression of a slightly jaded and worldly journalist. In one of his rare conversations—most of what we see of him comes through Lena's memories—Eri asks Mateo about some of his family's properties in Olancho, trying to determine if his inheritance might be larger than expected. Mateo responds, "I had heard doña Lena mention before that her family's lands had been lost to endless disputes among the heirs and that land reform had dealt them the final blow; I also told him that the lawyer Mira Brossa [doña Lena's husband and Eri's grandfather], when he was director of the National Agrarian Institute, twenty years ago, had had to distribute the last portions among campesino cooperatives, something that doña Lena never forgave him for and for which she accused him of being a 'useful idiot' of the communist priests" (201).[35] The family's patrimony has gradually been dismantled, in spite of doña Lena's lifelong efforts to protect it for her beloved Eri. They had to gradually sell off assets to diffuse the tension that came with an awareness of class struggle and resultant land reform. We learn that, since her husband died, doña Lena has lived from selling small parcels of land from her estate when the need arose. Very little remained by the time of her death.

In this final part of the novel, Castellanos Moya establishes a tension between doña Lena's obsession with property and territorialization and her grandson's desire to liquidate the property and move the money out of the country. The novel allegorizes the dematerialization of capital as financialization and speculation take over from landed and manufacturing modes of accumulation. This shift represents a significant change from the years immediately following the war, when Dalton saw class positions firmly entrenched with the oligarchy holding its land with an iron fist as the dispossessed moved between El Salvador to Honduras in a stateless, precarious existence. Land reform and migration have dissipated some of the territorial tension between the two countries. Now, lower-class Mateo is responsible for protecting Lena's property while upper-middle-class Eri moves from place to place, dismantling and distributing assets among the heirs. Mateo fixes fences and locks doors; Eri flies around Central America on mysterious and dubious political and journalistic missions. As nascent globalization reconfigures the relationship to capital accumulation, class-based relationships to property change. Likewise, the economic integration of the CACM, stalled for decades after the Soccer War, was gradually being reworked into the circuits of the 1994 North American Free Trade Agreement (NAFTA) and the later 2005 Central American Free Trade Agreement (CAFTA).[36]

Castellanos Moya depicts this shift through the generations. Doña Lena, for instance, viewed assets as physical property. With the rise of finance capitalism in the 1990s, Lena's view became outdated. Eri sees more value in assets that can easily move across borders. If Cold War anti-aggression treaties compressed the relationship of political leaders among themselves, causing the demos to disappear, more recent changes undermined the traditionally fixed relationship of sovereignty to territory. The closest Castellanos Moya gets to a sovereign in *Desmoronamiento* is doña Lena, and Lena's death is attributed to repeated cerebral hemorrhages, an overflow of blood outside of vessels and into the brain. Her hemorrhage makes her incoherent, so that she repeats her invective against traitors and malcontents but she loses the thread of her lifelong insults. As Mateo says, "It was strange listening to her because she repeated phrases that I knew by heart from hearing them over and over again through the years, but all mixed up, like she'd lost the thread" (185).[37] The connection between her invective and her cries of betrayal comes apart as more and more blood spills into her brain, making her death from excess liquidity symbolic. For this modern-day sovereign even the slippery nonnarrative connections that Dalton laid out in his poem "O.E.A." come unbound, invective and assets liquefying.

Doña Lena's death also recalls the medical definition of stasis: a stoppage of circulation. She served this function in the family, like a clot preventing the family's movement between Honduras and El Salvador, a bastion of private property and old, upper-class Honduran ways. She dies of the hemorrhage that finally overwhelms the clot, and her death precipitates the liquidation of her estate. Her assets escape national boundaries, when toward the end, Mateo accompanies Eri as he exchanges dollars on the black market before returning to Mexico with the cash. Mateo then has another nightmare in which he imagines Lena's desperation about the dismantling of her estate: "I woke up when she [doña Lena] screamed, beside herself, that that pair of traitors [her daughter Teti and grandson Eri] would pay dearly, that their curse would be to roam without homeland or possessions for the rest of their lives. Then I heard the energetic bang of her cane in the hallway, as if doña Lena had just gotten up, angry because I had forgotten to lock the doors of the house as was my job" (207–8).[38] Mateo's nightmare version of Lena insists on physical security despite the definitive deterritorialization of the landed oligarchy. According to Mateo, the spirit of doña Lena wants to dispossess her traitorous heirs, but her intention to release them from the property is precisely what they want. Cash has become much more valuable than land.

Mateo, however, has a different relationship to doña Lena's legacy. He had long been promised the deed to the converted shed where he lives and a small plot of land around it, and after Lena's death, the heirs comply with her intention to compensate him for his years of service. Upon receiving the deed, Mateo immediately and happily takes it to show his family. He and his sons sacrifice a suckling pig and build a fence on which they hang the name of the small plot: "Granja doña Lena" (209–10). Against the crisis of destruction, dispossession, and flight considered characteristic of contemporary Central American literature, Mateo celebrates the document that gives him ownership over the small parcel of land. Doña Lena's name survives in his inheritance more than

in the inheritance of her own family. This affirmation of property, ownership, and the secure legacy of the matriarch ensures Mateo's containment on the land but also his long-awaited self-sufficiency. Castellanos
Moya shows that finally the campesino who had been left out of agrarian
reform can have the land that he had needed since the 1960s, but only
when it is no longer useful to the upper classes. Moreover, in transferring
and documenting properties and borders in *Desmoronamiento*, Castellanos
Moya suggests that, from at least one perspective, writing is not in crisis.
In fact, it is stronger than ever. It instantiates the law. It allows the dispossessed to come into ownership.

On the other hand, Mateo is also responsible for burning documents
that affirm national and territorial belonging. Doña Lena instructed him
to destroy everything after her death, and just after the nightmare in
which Lena scolds him, he remembers his promise: "I remembered that
I hadn't fulfilled her wish to burn the folders that she had hidden under
the old typewriter and that I now had stored in the basement" (208).[39]
Before throwing them on the fire, he leafs through the documents and
finds some poems, probably Lena's early nationalist poetry from her time
as a journalist and young society lady. They also include folders full of
letters. As Mateo burns doña Lena's files, the reader comes to realize that
Mateo is simultaneously destroying all of the documents reprinted in
the novel's second part, "Del archivo de Erasmo Mira Brossa" (From the
files of Erasmo Mira Brossa). Castellanos Moya stages one of his characters burning out the middle section of the novel, which the reader has
just finished, enacting the destruction of his own writing and of poetry.
On one hand, it seems that Castellanos Moya affirms the strong connection between writing and representation in the law: the deed affirming
land ownership and the honorific matriarch's name on the property.
On the other hand, he oversees the dismantling of the estate and burns
nationalist poems and family records.

Mateo's nightmare about Lena is a version of the "nightmare of history," in which the past weighs as heavily on Dalton's engaged Marxist
poetry as on Castellanos Moya's reactionary characters. The nightmare
evokes Dalton's line, "The dead become more unmanageable by the
day" (*Taberna* 6), which in turn recalls Marx's *Eighteenth Brumaire*: "The
tradition of all dead generations weighs like a nightmare on the brains
of the living" (15).[40] Both Dalton and Castellanos Moya thus compile
documentary evidence of the Soccer War, including news, letters, and
poems. Both point to the fact that the archive includes pathological nationalism, property deeds, legal titles, proper names, and anti-aggression
pacts. The author can manipulate this archive, destroy it, or rework it

to include false testimony.[41] For both authors, there is an equivocal and potentially destructive relationship to writing.

Dalton and Castellanos Moya ask how to read and write in such a way that the resulting text is subject to betrayal or destruction. These texts treat warfare as containment—in Dalton through objective facts and doctrine and in Castellanos Moya through the character of doña Lena, the knot that keeps the family from unraveling. But they also signal warfare's seepage—in Dalton's apocryphal texts and in Castellanos Moya's hemorrhage, capital flight, and archival destruction. The writing of this war—once subject to alternations between internal and external conflicts within Central America—signals the perpetuation of conflict out of bounds. Writing is the trace of this violence. It contains and escapes. It is subject to betrayal, disruption, and destruction. The Soccer War complicates the use of writing as a technology of bordering. After the war, it becomes the trace of an interrupted border, crossed by landless peasants, refugees, soldiers, and guerilla fighters and marking the gradual collapse of the ordering schema of property and the state.

SOVEREIGNTY WITHOUT DEMOS

The disarticulation of writing and propriety in Castellanos Moya and Dalton illustrates the slippage between writing and demos. Their etymological demography combines captured with anarchic space, including documents establishing identity, ownership, and the law. This approach depicts a now-global tension that became visible in the 1969 Soccer War: the hazy border between within and without and the impossible task of disentangling politics, economics, and demography under regional and global economic integration. After all, the CACM project was an early example of this erosion of national sovereignty, met with virulent nationalism in a space that did not admit migration. Whether on the soccer field or as part of the national territory, Salvadorans and Hondurans felt threatened and sought a return to a clearly, though artificially, delimited sovereign state. Crisis accompanied the partial disarticulation of this border, and it became both the place from which war was planned and staged during the subsequent Salvadoran Civil War and the clot in the circulation of capital during the long suspension of the CACM. Writing this border in a demographic key, as Dalton and Castellanos Moya do, is critical to understanding the conflicting tensions at play in border conflicts that, although they may be less overt than the Soccer War, have increasingly demonstrated economic integration met with nationalist backlash.

Under contemporary globalization, people are more mobile and interconnected than ever, like Eri in *Desmoronamiento*. But governments also rely on regional legal structures and personal and group identities to fortify borders and create "secure" pockets within this more connected world. As Marramao writes, "It is said that the mobility of human beings, capital, commodities and information is irrevocably eroding the territorial logic on which our societies are founded. On the other hand, the end of the system of nation states is thought to trigger the compensatory phenomenon of the search for security and anchoring in an identity within homogeneous regional legal orders" (97). Marramao suggests that, in the face of these contradictory movements, it is helpful to take "the perspective of the *longue durée* . . . to track those constitutive conditions of sovereignty and of modern law whose disarticulation lies at the bottom of the confusion and the discomfort in which we find ourselves today" (98). Marramao's *longue durée*, in turn, picks up Dalton's continuity of warfare. *Las historias prohibidas* extends back to the Spanish conquest, picking up the 1932 massacre, then into ongoing US overreach in Central America. Through his method, Dalton makes clear that what is called internal or external conflict shifts over time. The classification of conflict as polemos is only ever temporary, and time is not linear in his poetic collage. The apparent disarticulation of sovereignty today merely manifests this temporal disjunction.

Castellanos Moya, in turn, points out the importance of time in the epigraph to *Desmoronamiento*, taken from Shakespeare's play *Pericles*, which names time the most arbitrary of sovereigns: "Whereby I see that Time's the king of men, / He's both their parent, and he is their grave, / And gives them what he will, not what they crave" (Shakespeare 253).[42] Castellanos Moya does not present an accumulation of facts, as in *Las historias prohibidas*. Instead, he simply points to time as a kind of motor in the slow unraveling of his plot.[43] He attributes the quote to Shakespeare, but it is more likely that the play was written in conjunction with lesser-known playwright George Wilkins. This confusion about the author's identity recalls Dalton's trick of reducing himself to anonymity in "Alta hora de la noche" and adding texts of dubious authorship to *Las historias prohibidas*. When considering the poem against the name of the poet, the play against the name of the playwright, literature does not serve as an extension of representation, fidelity, and testimony. Instead of being relegated to the mimicry of truth or king as in Plato's infamous condemnation of poetry, Castellanos Moya points to time disarticulating atemporal formulae. Neither god nor militant nor heir, time frustrates desire, or "what they crave." And as time exercises sovereignty, it is as slippery as the sovereigns in Dalton's "O.E.A." Compared to Heidegger and Schmitt who identify polemos as sovereign, here sovereignty cannot capture an unmanageable and unnamed people, only fleetingly represented in text. Once the limits of sovereignty disperse, as they do in Dalton and Castellanos Moya, the Soccer War definitively becomes stasis rather than polemos, infected with the apocryphal and improper.

The failure to capture the demos emerges—not from the warfare and generalized destruction of the twentieth century but rather, at least partially, from the well-intentioned attempt to suppress conflict without reconfiguring its terms. From transnational anti-aggression pacts to the philosophical critique of polemos to financialization, the partial breakdowns—to use Castellanos Moya's title—of sovereignty, property, and cosmopolitanism have increased the tension between clot and hemorrhage, containment and liquidation. Security analysts now "assert that the traditional dichotomy between the *national* and the *international* has collapsed" (Duffield, "Global Civil War" 149). At the same time, contemporary political theorists are developing frameworks to account for fundamentalisms and identity politics that feed into what Mary Kaldor calls "new wars" and Carlo Galli calls "global war" that produce what Marramao refers to as the confusion and discomfort of the present.[44]

The authors here posit demography, in the strongest sense, as the unaccounted-for tension between the containment and uncontainability of the demos. Their texts clear a path for a different perspective from which to view cultural production in the wake of warfare. This perspective does not valorize polemos as sovereign or motor of history, as Heidegger and Schmitt did in the 1930s. Instead, it questions the idea that history can be linear or divisible. It views sovereignty as slippery and differing from itself over time as boundaries shift, echoing Dalton and Castellanos Moya—or Shakespeare or Wilkins. The author's authority is not important. The author might even burn literature, as Mateo burns Lena's nationalist poems or as Castellanos Moya burns out the novel's second section. Viewing literature as a response to conflict places it in a necessarily secondary position and confines it to realism and mimicry. Taking a long and nonlinear view of integration, nationalism, migration, and betrayal, *Las historias prohibidas* and *Desmoronamiento* make the war part of a disputed inheritance of the past in which state bordering destroys the documents from which both states and literature are made. Both authors build on, with, and against these documents to extend the Soccer War into past and present. Instead of the idea of polemos as "king of all" since Heraclitus, they see multiple stories and histories, interrupting the temporal and spatial bounds of sovereignty and leading to collapse and destruction. Time is sovereign here, spinning off histories that are unequal to each other, stories that sometimes disappear in bibliographies and archives.[45]

Writing might, at times, return to its old modalities, in which conflict is both a precondition of literature and of its annihilation. In the same way, the demos might turn into a cohesive group, declaring traitors and anchoring itself in nations and properties. After all, as Marramao argues, the contemporary world seems to have loosened itself from some of the narrative threads, such as the nation, that emerge from the literary and legal archive.[46] Just as doña Lena's hemorrhage caused her to confuse one traitor with the next, the partial unbinding of the narrative of historical progress means that a ludicrous sovereign naming might emerge, returning older forms of governance, property, and identification. From the uprising in 1932 to international war in 1969 to the dozen years of civil war and into the post–Cold War era, the creation of a regional and globally connected Central American cosmo-polis has sought to contain violence. Yet it has been subject to an almost perpetual violence circumventing borders and working its way through the populace. Even now, migration within and from Central America is cast as anomalously high in the media. The Soccer War tells a different story; the relationship between demos and land has long been fraught.

Against those who view the Soccer War as a minor or insignificant scuffle, Dalton and Castellanos Moya depict the conflict as a flashpoint that illuminates a spatiotemporal structure based on perpetuating low-level violence in the name of order. Before, during, and after the brief war, the region was plagued by stasis, a prototype of the global civil war that would come after the end of the Cold War, inflicted upon it and within it in the names of different regimes of sovereignty. The reaction against polemos during the Cold War, later taken up in decolonial thought, inadvertently feeds this status quo of stasis. As overt war becomes the enemy, subtler forms of violence fade into the background, even as they remain pervasive. In destabilizing the border, the Soccer War exposed the failure of demographic containment, disturbing questions of testimonial truth and betrayal as well as the optics of the state and sovereign. If in the Chaco War, the border formed the skin of a self-consuming national body, the Soccer War takes the question of the border to the limits of propriety and documentation. It also offers a prototype of the economic integration and demographic containment that would appear at the Mexico-US border in the 1990s and continue into the present. The incomplete national hypostasis that the border represents, whether in the remote Chaco or in the emptied border zones between El Salvador and Honduras, transforms the border into a flash point of what political theorists increasingly refer to as global war; that is, contemporary stasis.

In the Soccer War, stasis appears as much by force as diplomacy. The war does not reveal a "crisis of representation" in which literature is unable to be faithful to the destruction of the world. Rather, literature about the Soccer War presents the growing breach between writing and demography, law and trace. At this intersection, Dalton and Castellanos Moya avoid the tired debates about the exhaustion of engaged, testimonial, and destructive aesthetics. They present the voices that interrupt the poem, burn the archive, and depict the stasis that has gone unrecognized for decades. The voices of the restless dead can be heard instead of suppressed in the name of anti-aggression. In the next chapter, a capacious understanding of stasis appears in the Falklands/Malvinas War through a series of spatial and temporal displacements that exclude the demos from the war into the neoliberal era. Like the Central American borderlands, the islands bear a complex relationship to sovereignty and bordering as the people's relationship to political and literary representation changes. The dead of the Falklands/Malvinas, too, are restless.

CHAPTER 4

THE FALKLANDS/ MALVINAS WAR AND NEOLIBERAL ECSTASY

La patria existe a nivel simbólico. Básicamente, es una metáfora. Si uno
trata de hacerla real toda de golpe se le evaporará de las manos.
—Carlos Gamerro, *Las Islas*

At the center of the Plaza Islas Malvinas in Argentina's southernmost city
of Ushuaia stands a large cast bronze wall with the cutout shape of the
two largest islands in the Falkland/Malvinas archipelago. Visitors can
see mountain and sky through the other side, and on a nice day with a
few clouds, it might look like the islands are draped in the sky-blue and
white Argentine flag. The bronze monument, designed by Vilma Natero, plays on the physical absence of the two islands in contrast to their
strong presence in Argentine history and memory in the wake of the
1982 war in which Argentina retook the islands only to lose them again
to the United Kingdom seventy-four days later. Cultural critic Vicente
Palermo writes that the monument frames national consciousness: "In
essence, it consists of a window to the sky through the silhouette of the
islands: we [Argentines] see the universe through Malvinas" (24). The
wall uses the shape of the islands to settle the sovereignty issue, filling in
the emptied geography with national meaning. During a 2012 expansion, town planners added a cenotaph—an empty tomb adorned with an
eternal flame—to commemorate the thirtieth anniversary of the war.

The Malvinas monument in Ushuaia reveals the islands as a vanishing point of Spanish and British empires in the Americas. Uninhabited for much of their recorded history, they have been subject to the laws of European empires since the French allegedly first sighted and named them. They had no known indigenous inhabitants, and European traders used the islands only sporadically. They remained unclaimed or vacant for long stretches at a time. At independence from Spain, there were few people living there. In accordance with the principle of *uti possidetis*, the islands transferred to the jurisdiction of the United Provinces of the Río de la Plata. But in 1833, the British expelled the existing inhabitants, mostly traders and mariners, and created the longest-lasting settlement in the islands' history. The British continue to exercise administrative power over the islands, which are officially considered an Overseas Territory of the United Kingdom. They maintain a military base, grant fishing privileges, and authorize and invest in oil exploration. During the twentieth century, the islands were only under effective Argentine control during the 1982 war.

The war itself was widely considered a diversionary tactic of the 1976–1983 Argentine military dictatorship—the euphemistically named Proceso de Reorganización Nacional, "Process of National Reorganization." The junta had made its most bloody impact in the early days of the infamous Dirty War, a campaign in which thousands of citizens were disappeared for being "subversives." After they had eradicated the most obvious dissent, the military government struggled with domestic issues—notably, uncontrolled inflation. They narrowly managed to avoid war with Chile in 1978 over the Beagle Channel as we saw in the introduction, and then seeing an opportunity to stoke nationalism in difficult domestic circumstances, they gradually increased the intensity and fervor of their focus on Malvinas in an effort to redirect attention away from problems at home.

Argentina mounted a surprise attack on the islands on April 2, 1982. They gambled, correctly, that the war would garner domestic support, and in an interview with Oriana Fallaci, de facto president Leopoldo Galtieri admitted that he thought the invasion was unlikely to draw a British response. Crowds rallied in the Plaza de Mayo in Buenos Aires in support of the invasion, but Galtieri had miscalculated. UK prime minister Margaret Thatcher sent the British fleet to roundly and handily defeat the Argentines. The Argentine government's well-oiled censorship and propaganda machine fooled civilians into believing that Argentina was winning until the bitter end. As a result, the loss came as a shock, and the frustrated citizenry rose to challenge the dictatorship. Those who had come to the Plaza de Mayo in support for the war pressured the junta to call elections immediately after their defeat. Electoral democracy was restored in 1983.

Given the highs and lows of the war, Malvinas occupies an ambivalent place in twentieth-century Argentine history. On one hand, the loss of the islands caused international embarrassment and national trauma. Those who returned from battle, mainly ill-trained and ill-equipped conscripts, were largely forgotten. Ex-combatants received little to no support, and veteran care reached a tipping point in the early twenty-first century, when there were more apparent deaths by suicide than in combat (Galak). On the other hand, the war finally put an end to dictatorship as a viable political model. The reinstatement of electoral democracy had a lasting positive effect, but the loss of the islands continues to haunt Argentina into the present. The recovery of Malvinas was stitched into the fabric of the Argentine state, appearing in the 1994 Constitution: "The recovery of said territories [the Malvinas, Sandwich, and South Georgia Islands] and full exercise of sovereignty, respecting the way of life of its inhabitants in conformity with the principles of international law, constitute a permanent and inalienable objective of the Argentine people" (*Constitución Nacional Argentina*). While the constitution ensures that Argentina will no longer break with international law and unilaterally invade the islands, it also refuses to give up on full territorial sovereignty.

Little wonder, then, that in the war's aftermath, the shapes of the islands have become floating signifiers, claimed by different groups at different times but consistently haunting Argentina. They are lost fragments of the nation, standing for the ghosts of forgotten and buried soldiers, the perceived irrevocable loss of a piece of the homeland, and violent British and Spanish imperial histories. At times they function metonymically as displaced parts of Argentina. As Carlos Gamerro writes in his novel *Las Islas*, "The homeland exists on a symbolic level. Basically, it's a metaphor. If you try to make it real all at once, it will evaporate right out of your hands" (132).[1] Similarly, if one tries to make Malvinas real all at once, the islands vanish into thin air. The border of the nation, including the bordered shapes of the islands, exists only symbolically as Gamerro takes the national metaphor a step further. The sovereignty conflict in Malvinas serves as an extreme example of the border as the spatial limit of sovereignty, displaced into the ocean and borne outside of time to a purely symbolic level. The emptied shapes represent Malvinas as a brutal, evaporating national metaphor.

This chapter examines Malvinas as metaphor, appearing and disappearing in culture during the war and into the late 1990s. Malvinas provides a clear example of the connection between stasis as unchanging border conflict and stasis as internal upheaval. Sovereignty issues that originated in the conquest continued under dictatorship and then democratic neoliberalism, even as the border remained spatially and temporally distant. This chapter takes each period in turn. Beginning with Susana Thénon's "Poema con traducción simultánea español-español" (Poem with simultaneous Spanish-Spanish translation), from 1987, there is a parallel between the Spanish empire and the Malvinas campaign through translation and imperial ontotheology. In Rodolfo Enrique Fogwill's canonical *Los pichiciegos: Visiones de una batalla subterránea* (The pichiciegos: visions of an underground battle; published in English as *Malvinas Requiem*), soldiers attempt to flee the dictatorship's authoritarian rule, but their group devolves into a repetition of hierarchical military authority. In Gamerro's *Las Islas* (The islands), history is repeated, mirrored, and mocked in the hyperbolic neoliberalism of the 1990s. Steeped in conspiracy theories and moving through digital and physical spaces, Gamerro's novel reinterprets the war's legacy using the recreational drug Ecstasy.

Taking a cue from Gamerro, the chapter plays with the range of meanings associated with the word *ecstasy*. *Ecstasy*, in its traditional sense, may seem an odd choice of terms given the anguish associated with Malvinas. The dictionary definition of *éxtasis* describes it as a "pleasurable emotional state of admiring exaltation" ("Éxtasis"), or "an overwhelming feeling of great happiness or joyful excitement" ("Ecstasy").[2] These definitions stand in stark contrast to the bloody conditions of war. Yet etymologically, the *ec-*, meaning "outside," also indicates displacement of *-stasis*, the process by which the Argentine state transferred its internal conflict outside of itself in the attempt to recover the islands. A stasis—internal conflict—within the Argentine state formed the basis of the external Malvinas conflict, which in turn has come to a kind of stasis—stagnation—in the intractable, ongoing sovereignty dispute. These definitions also place ecstasy squarely in line with the existential conflicts that Malvinas created in Argentina.

In the existential tradition, displacements, or *ecstases*, form the backdrop of the experience of temporality. Heidegger delineates three temporal ecstases: displacements into the past, the present, and the future. He describes temporality as outside of itself, with each of the temporal ecstases experienced as a displacement that connects to the overall experience of temporality. In Heidegger's words in *Being and Time*: "*Temporality is the primordial 'outside of itself' in and for itself.* Thus we call the phenomena of future, having-been, and present, the *ecstasies* of temporality. Temporality is not, prior to this, a being that first emerges from *itself*; rather, its essence is temporalizing in the unity of *ecstasies*" (314). This chapter explores temporalizing, especially as ecstasy that interrupts the monolithic time of sovereignty and the violence of bordering. Temporal ecstasy also describes the war's most important psychological consequence: post-traumatic stress disorder (PTSD). Veterans suffering from PTSD experience intense flashbacks to the battlefield, psychically transported into the past in explosive, destructive ecstasy. Ecstasy's historical association with religious trances and more recent use for MDMA also names the unusual displacements that Malvinas evokes during and after the war. The geographical shape of Malvinas, emptied of philosophical and material ground, serves as a brutal metaphor for these displacements, the stasis transported outside of Argentina and back again.

MISTRANSLATED METAPHORS OF CONQUEST

The Falklands/Malvinas War cannot be disentangled from the history of European imperialism in South America. The opening lines of Thénon's "Poema" make this apparent: "Cristóforo / (Bearer of Christ)" (152).[3] Given the title, the reader expects a translation and is immediately provided an etymological breakdown of the name Cristóforo. Yet the person the poet refers to—Christopher Columbus—would be called Cristóbal in Spanish. Thénon switches the Spanish name with the Italian one. This first misstep cues the reader that her "simultaneous translation" from Spanish to Spanish will be riddled with such misdirection both in the "original" text to be translated and in the parenthetical "translation." It also calls attention to the appropriateness of Columbus's given name, considering his task of carrying Christianity across the Atlantic; the Greek suffix *-foro* in the name Cristóforo indicates "bearing Christ." Likewise, the word *translation* means "carrying across," with meaning transferred from language to language. For the poet, translation of the proper name Christopher feeds into the "proper" religion and vice versa. Translation also serves as a go-between for the two historical events in the poem: the Spanish conquest and the Malvinas War. The *-foro* suffix in Cristóforo becomes a metaphor. Thénon draws a parallel between the two historical events and her own poetic devices.[4]

Throughout the poem, Thénon uses translation to disrupt, confuse, and amend the repetition of the conquest. Take, for instance, these lines:

alguno exclamó tierra
　(ninguno exclamó thálassa)

desembarcaron
en 1492 a.D.
  (pisaron
  en 1982 a.D.) (153)

***

someone proclaimed land
  (no one proclaimed thalassa)
they disembarked
in 1492 AD
  (they stepped
  into 1982 AD)

The translations are evidently no longer Spanish to Spanish but shift into other languages—here Greek, but elsewhere English and German. In these lines, Thénon layers the Malvinas conflict with an ancient Greek invocation of the sea goddess Thalassa, who famously choked on the bodies of the Trojan War dead. The substitution gives the impression of history as repeated disaster. Both war and anti-imperialism stretch back millennia, and this war resembles the many wars before it.

Mixing these three conflicts, the poem questions the nature of historical time. Thénon asserts that the years 1492 and 1982 are similar, and the poem promises to provide the reader a "simultaneous" translation. But just as in simultaneous interpreting, simultaneous translation arrives with a slight lag. Thénon records this in the poetic form, in which the reader cannot read both the text on the left and the indented text in the line below at the same time. To compensate for the delay, however, she plays with words, as in the poem's final lines in which the words *mundos* (worlds) and *inmundos* (brutes, barbarians, or swine) appear to be interchangeable. She also misuses the near-homonyms *missal* (missal) and *misil* (missile). The poem's final lines deepen the connection between the conquest and Malvinas in an appeal to God and Queen, connecting Isabella of Castile to Elizabeth II of Britain since both are called Isabel in Spanish. As Thénon compresses the historical events of conquest and invasion into a few lines, she indicates that the true link between them—the only line in which original and translation are the same—is violence in the name of God and crown: "por Dios y Nuestra Reina" (for God and Our Queen). Thénon suggests that war, repeated again and again, becomes a metaphor in which historical "truth" is meant to appear through an ontotheological chain. The comparison she makes between 1492 and 1982 aims to convince the reader of the simultaneity of the two wars—their copresence in a metaphysical view of history—while the misdirections and lags frustrate the reader and the ontotheological chain.

This pretended simultaneity is always interrupted. As we have seen, the poem's translations are riddled with errors. While the trauma of Malvinas recalls the historical trauma of conquest, drawing on similar narrative structures and vocabularies, the two events can never be exactly the same. To make this clear, the poem ends by substituting "A M É N," meaning "so be it," with "O M E N," a prophecy. The end becomes another beginning. While Thénon fosters repetition, she also interrupts the equivalence between one event and another as she interrupts the equivalence between one language and another. Such a smooth transfer would replicate the metaphor, "transferring" or "bearing across" imperialism and evangelization. It would make the poem another instrument of symbolic violence. By mistranslating and retranslating, she challenges the compression of meaning and time that make these events a metaphor. She parses and separates the compression of historical violence.

UNDERGROUND REPETITION

As Thénon's poem shows by tying Malvinas to Spanish imperialism, the 1982 campaign against the British resembled the Argentine struggle for independence from Spain, pitting a relatively young independent nation against an old colonial power. As such, it drew support from a coalition that ranged from the most ardent nationalists to the most ardent anti-imperialists. From the left, the Grupo de Discusión Socialista, "Socialist Discussion Group," which consisted of Argentine intellectuals living in exile in Mexico, issued a statement in support of the war and in common cause with anti-imperial struggles worldwide (Rozitchner 139–53). However, their statement against imperialism unwittingly fed into the much more recent Dirty War. After all, the junta's invasion of Malvinas created a galvanizing distraction from domestic problems. According to León Rozitchner in *Malvinas: de la guerra sucia a la guerra limpia* (Malvinas: From the dirty war to the clean war), the attitude that the Argentine populace needed to be "reorganized," which in practice meant repressed, before "maturing" into democracy takes an imperial attitude toward the Argentine people as a whole.[5] Rozitchner points out that the Argentine invasion is no less imperial than the initial British one. It merely demonstrates the similarity between strong-arm tactics used at home and those used abroad.

The war's most canonical novel, *Los pichiciegos*, taps into this critical but slippery distinction between challenging authority and reproducing it under different circumstances. Urban legend has it that the author, so-ciologist and ex-advertising executive Fogwill, wrote the novel during the last few days of the war, fueled by a healthy supply of cocaine and whiskey. *Los pichiciegos* started what would become an entire Malvinas genre characterized by dark satire that presented the antiheroic under-side of the war. The novel follows deserters from the Argentine military, who were largely conscripts, as they form an underground society. The subterranean colony takes its name from an armadillo—the *pichiciego*, or pink fairy armadillo—native to central Argentina that burrows into the ground when threatened. The deserters, *pichis* for short, have all abandoned their regiments and built an underground network of tunnels they refer to as the *pichicera*. They come from different regions of Argen-tina and are therefore sometimes seen as representative of a microcosm of the country's diversity. They survive by storing provisions and barter-ing with neighboring groups, leaving their tunnels only under cover of darkness for fear of being killed by the British as enemy combatants or by the Argentines as traitors.

Because of their flagrant disobedience of orders, the pichis are often cast as part of an inkling of the anti-government sentiment that, after defeat, led to the rapid fall of the dictatorship. For many, the pichis rep-resent the counterhegemonic movement that presaged the end of the dictatorship. Critical analyses of the novel are filled with examples of how it challenges literary and political convention. For instance, Julieta Vitullo describes *Los pichiciegos* as setting the stage for later portrayals of Malvinas as an inversion of the war epic (19; 72–78). Vitullo draws on earlier analyses, including Martín Kohan's article "El fin de una épica," which relates Fogwill's novel to the end of the hero's epic. Kohan points out that Fogwill clears the path for a focus on the farcical rather than the dramatic aspects of war in Gamerro's *Las Islas* (6). For Beatriz Sarlo, the erosion of nationalism has made it so that the pichis form an "un-derground colony where they take refuge in order to survive and where values are organized according to a single social mission: preserving life" (12).[6] The sovereignty conflict leads to escapism for survival. Sarlo espe-cially emphasizes that the pichis create a community based on life, rather than death, seeing the men as representative of survival against the state and the novel as a text that refuses to recognize war as politics.

Like many of those that read the novel through its counterhege-monic currents, Sarlo's analysis of *Los pichiciegos* functions in the interval between one type of sovereignty and another, in the period of inter-regnum between dictatorship and democracy. The pichis, freed from the obligation to kill or be killed, enter subterranean space in which they can escape the virulent nationalism that brought them to Malvinas. While traditionally power comes from above, the pichis invert this structure, presenting an underground current of survival and community; they have inverted the top–down logic of hierarchy and replaced it with a bottom–up model. From this perspective, it is easy to see them as presenting a counternarrative that feeds the anti-authoritarian impulse in the aftermath of the war. Bernard McGuirk writes that Fogwill's novel "performs a counter-foundational narrative of inverted values, an underground movement that whilst apparently refusing metaphor, exploits the metaphorical power of the literal" (21). This "counter-foundation" works against the state's military order, and by placing his characters underground, Fogwill makes their situation echo with those who rise from below to challenge the dictatorship.

However, *Los pichiciegos* also represents the transferal and continuation of the dictatorship's internal power dynamics to a different place. As Rozitchner describes the hidden connection between "dirty" and "clean" wars in policy and rhetoric, Fogwill's novel can be read as an exploration of the connection between dirty and clean wars in fiction. This interpretation does not suggest that previous readings such as Sarlo's and McGuirk's are unfounded; throughout the novel, Fogwill emphasizes survival in the face of constant threat. In particular, at the beginning, it seems uncertain whether the pichi community is horizontal or hierarchical. But this uncertainty gradually gives way to new rules imposed and habits defined. For example, Fogwill describes one of the earliest rules that the leaders—the *Reyes* or *Magos*, "Kings"—issue: the men are strictly forbidden from drinking potentially contaminated water and from defecating in the burrow. They must boil all water or drink maté, tea, or coffee to avoid getting uncontrollable diarrhea on pain of death. Having described the rule, Fogwill writes, "And even though nobody knew if the Kings were capable of killing a pichi or not, just in case they weren't going to test it: they obeyed" (34–35).[7] Obedience, rather than disobedience, quickly becomes the norm underground, as above.

Once the pichis have become accustomed to the control that the Kings exert, their leaders ensure power in ways that mimic the dictatorship. One evening, lubricated by a healthy dose of whiskey, the men discuss the thousands of disappearances and death flights under the dictatorship.[8] They wonder aloud whether Argentines will ever be allowed to vote again, and later that night, the scribe, Quique, and another of the Kings, el Turco, are fitfully trying to sleep. Suffering from a guilty conscience, Quique asks: "'Hey, Turco . . . do you think . . . ?' 'What?' 'That they could vote?' 'They can't do anything!' said el Turco, and, 'Go to sleep!'" (58).[9] The issue never arises again. The Kings have slipped from the state-sanctioned violence of war to the state-instantiating violence of centralized authority and a lack of popular sovereignty. Underground, they escape the war but reproduce the lack of democracy, turning their power against their own. Later, the Kings collectively decide which are the weakest of the bunch, and those select few never come back from a "mission" to the British encampment. When el Turco returns, he feels compelled to invent an explanation: "Since no one mentioned the pichis that were missing, el Turco brought up the subject and said that they'd stayed with the English, as a guarantee, and everyone believed or wanted to believe or make believe that they believed" (64).[10] Their disappearance without a trace bears the hallmarks of the arbitrary violence and utilitarian logic toward the populace that the dictatorship used to justify its actions. This parallel to the dictatorship is often unremarked in the novel's criticism, which tends to follow the story, wanting to believe or to feign belief in the pichis' anti-authoritarianism.

Fogwill also suggests a reason the pichis are unable to create a viable alternative: they are trapped by fear. They deserted their regiments out of fear and remain under threat. Their inability to escape the war completely forces them to try different ways of dealing with the stress. As the narrator describes el Turco, the King in charge of getting rid of the weak pichis: "It's fear that unleashes the instinct that everyone has inside, and just like some people who are afraid turn into assholes because they awaken something sleeping inside them, in him it awoke his inner Arab: that instinct to accumulate stuff and exchange it and take charge. . . . And it wouldn't occur to anyone who saw him ordering people around, trading, and storing stuff that behind all of that was fear. But it's fear that's behind it, controlling you, changing you" (103–4).[11] El Turco gathers the materials needed for survival, channeling his fear of death toward commerce. The underground economy emerges as a response to fear, part of the instinct to survive, in the racialized stereotype of el Turco's "inner Arab." This economy begins to function in line with the value placed on survival that drove the pichis underground in the first place.

As time goes by, the underground market begins to change as el Turco shrewdly manipulates resources: "If he had extra kerosene, he spread a rumor that he needed kerosene, he was running out of kerosene, anybody would give anything for kerosene. Afterwards he'd send a random pichi to the Commissary or to the town or to the English to offer kerosene and come back with tons of stuff in exchange for a watered-down barrel that was left over in the first place" (136).[12] The exaggerated scarcity of gas inflates its worth, and el Turco's market manipulation drives

the underground economy toward accumulation. In turn, the more resources the Kings acquire and control, the easier it is to assert their control over other pichis. Mimicking the shift from state sovereignty in its
traditional form—the four Kings—to more flexible economic forms, el
Turco depicts the early stages of the coming rampant neoliberalism and
artificially inflated market that would dominate post-dictatorship Argentina.[13] Paola Ehrmantraut sees this as a shift from a military model of
masculinity during the dictatorship to a business-dominated one in the
post-dictatorship. As Zac Zimmer points out, "The Pichis' desire and
willingness to surrender themselves to the unregulated, underground
market . . . lends the text its eerie sense of prediction" (145). Survival,
it seems, can escape neither the logic of protection nor the language of
value; it is survival at any cost.

Consequently, Fogwill's prescience does not lie in his prediction
of public disobedience. Instead, it lies in the final passages of the short
novel in which the pichis' fate is sealed. Faced with threats to their
survival—the choice of fight or flight—the pichis try to escape but unwittingly recreate the dictatorship's political conditions and the later,
chaotic turn toward minimally regulated neoliberalism. In the end,
carbon monoxide kills everyone in the burrow except Quique. He returns to Buenos Aires to tell their story, imagining that the small colony
will be frozen into the land: "The two English, twenty-three pichis,
and everything they had stored under there will become one single
thing, a new rock lodged in the old rock of the hill" (155).[14] Through
Quique, Fogwill shows that the pichis try to flee, only to get frozen in
the same state they had tried to escape.[15] The pichis' thwarted fight-or-
flight response sets the stage for a repetition of traumatic stress in the
vast fictional and nonfictional cultural production that would follow,
exhibiting a compulsion to repeat the survival response and escape the
twin traumas of dictatorship and war. The pichis form the cornerstone
of an emergent form of sociopolitical organization, replicating aspects
of the dictatorship and the neoliberal consensus to come. They follow
the shift in emphasis from state-sponsored death to a life controlled by
value—biopolitics and neoliberalization—in the post-dictatorship reconfiguration of politics.[16]

APHASIA AND CYBORG TRANSLATION

Gamerro's novel *Las Islas* adapts *Los pichiciegos* to developments in the
1990s. By the tenth anniversary of the war in 1992, when *Las Islas* is
set, powerful business interests in Buenos Aires appear to manipulate
ex-combatants and government figures alike as Gamerro brings the

war back to the home front. Instead of using an extended metaphor of the underground like Fogwill, he alternates between urban and virtual planes. In battle reenactments throughout Buenos Aires as well as video games, the war rages on. Gamerro rewrites the Malvinas genre as more than just a late imperial conflict; he uses irreverence and farce to portray and mock imperialism and capitalism.

Most importantly, Gamerro's cyberpunk version of the war engages in a series of repetitions in real and virtual space that modify traditional conceptions of trauma. Gamerro stages what used to be called "traumatic neuroses," now diagnosed as PTSD, among those who suffered repression during the dictatorship and those who returned from combat. Since Freud, such "neuroses" have been associated with the "compulsion to repeat" (Freud 19). Trauma, characterized by an inability to act or produce language at the time of the event, seems to defy logic by reactivating memories and causing unconscious repetition of the traumatic experience long after it has ended. As a consequence, trauma disrupts the linear understanding of past, present, and future—the subject's temporal self-understanding.[17] Throughout the novel, Gamerro's characters retell and reenact the war, apparently in order to master an event that exceeded their understanding. During these repetitions, the novel's protagonist, Felipe Félix, seems able to master different methods of communication, from hacking computer code to deciphering cryptic handwriting, and events, from the tenth anniversary of the war to the five-hundredth anniversary of Columbus's arrival in the Americas. He relies on parallels, fragments, and translations that disrupt the traditional arrow of time, mocking the seriousness of the war while participating in numerous temporal displacements, or ecstases.

Gamerro mocks the clichés of the war to simultaneously honor and deride his predecessors. Naturally, he references *Los pichiciegos* but spends little time revisiting the battlefield, except in a rare instance in which Félix describes how, like the *pichiciegos*, the men in his group came from different regions of Argentina and so represented a microcosm of the country. Although Félix and his comrades did not desert, they were extremely isolated in their positions on the battlefield. When not being bombarded, they searched for objects that might be valuable to trade with neighboring groups, or as the narrator describes it, "spending our evenings bartering with neighbouring clans (food, batteries, helicopter fuel, clothes, empty tin cans, dry peat; everything had a value, except money)" (343–44).[18] Much like the early stages of the pichi economy, before it turned to accumulation, Félix and his comrades create an economy based on barter.

Unlike in Fogwill, however, Gamerro explains that the men cannot desert.[19] One passage describes how Félix's group comes across a lost soldier, marked as a conscript from the class born in 1963, who seems to be trying, unsuccessfully, to leave his regiment:

> He'd turned up one day, asking for something to eat, and couldn't say which company or regiment he was from. He was a '63—you could see it in his eyes—and had apparently fled after being mistreated or picked on by some officer; changing position was the nearest thing to deserting you could hope for on these shitty Islands. There had been a debate at first about whether to keep him (they could have been court-martialled, and then there wasn't enough food to go round), but they adopted him as a mascot after Carlos forced the vote, and as he didn't say a word or have any identification, he was nicknamed "Hijitus." (342)[20]

Unlike in *Los pichiciegos*, in which the idea of voting is ludicrous, in *Las Islas* there is a vote about whether to keep or expel the newcomer, and in spite of insufficient provisions, they keep him. They name the new soldier after the cartoon character Hijitus, a poor boy with an innocent face who lives inside a pipe in the suburbs of Buenos Aires along with a dog and a magical hat. Here Gamerro filters Fogwill's pichiciegos through popular culture; Hijitus's pipes were the closest Gamerro could come to a pichicera. Gamerro's pichicera, then, is doubly fictional—a cartoon character with superpowers rewriting the classic Malvinas novel. The passage echoes Fogwill's when the pichis "want to believe" or "make believe they believe" that they will be freed from the pull of war some day. In the end, for Gamerro, Hijitus is just a scared kid living in a fantasy world.

Gamerro's citation of a popular cartoon is hardly his only mocking exaggeration of the war's key tropes. Elsewhere, he takes up the legacy of Spanish imperialism and the Viceroyalty of the Río de la Plata. Upon return from war, protagonist Félix joins a fictional ex-combatant organization called La Asociación Virreinal, "The Viceroyal Association," which, alongside its Malvinas advocacy, is intent on restoring *all* colonial borders of the Viceroyalty. The association advocates for an extremely strict interpretation of the principle of uti possidetis, "for which it proposes, among other things, the reconquest of Bolivia, Paraguay and Uruguay, and the invasion of Chile and Brazil" (52).[21] The newly reclaimed colonial borders would return the territory to its original Spanish mapping. Far from having popular support, this fringe group is penniless and tries to make money teaching courses on Argentine history, including anti-British and antisemitic conspiracy theories about the Islands. Their view that "las Malvinas son argentinas" (the Malvinas are Argentine) is merely a footnote to their desire to restore the Spanish Catholic empire to its former glory under an Argentine flag.

The Asociación Virreinal is just one of many examples of widespread nostalgia for the colonial period in *Las Islas*. Just as the novel rewrites Fogwill's story through popular culture, it also rewrites the history of the founding of Buenos Aires. The first European settlement there failed in 1541 after coming under attack by indigenous groups. The city was refounded in 1580. In Gamerro's novel, construction magnate Fausto Tamerlán is working on what he refers to as the Third Foundation of Buenos Aires.[22] He has built two imposing towers in the Buenos Aires neighborhood of Puerto Madero on land partially reclaimed from the Río de la Plata. According to Tamerlán, his towers are only the beginning of a more extensive new foundation that, in 1992, coincides with the five-hundredth anniversary of Columbus's first voyage to the Americas. The novel builds this anniversary into its setting and ridicules it. For instance, a company with an English name, Surprises from Spain, leases office space in one of Tamerlán's towers and decides to build a replica of one of Columbus's ships at the base of the towers. Tamerlán explains: "They've crossed the Atlantic for the Fifth Centenary Celebrations. A few days ago they started hammering away at that fucking caravel out there, for Expo América '92. . . . How the mighty are fallen! But we still have to raise the money for the Third Foundation, and I think it's only natural the Spaniards should chip in, like they did for the first two" (30).[23] Not only does Gamerro draw out Thénon's parallel with the conquest, he takes it to an extreme. He makes Tamerlán's company the post-Malvinas, post-dictatorship foundation of Argentina based on a new business boom, a profit-driven repetition of the old story. Ironies pile up as the caravel turns out to be a cheaply built imitation used to shelter homeless Malvinas veterans and Tamerlán's thugs. Gamerro later reveals that Surprises from Spain is a pyramid scheme based on exploiting social connections for the benefit of very few people at the top. If it were even possible to think of a counterfoundation in Fogwill's *Los pichiciegos*, Gamerro shows that these foundational gestures have been entirely appropriated by economic elites by the 1990s. They remain deeply rooted in the history of the exploitation of the Americas, now in a new gilded age.

The narrative also updates other historical figures. Gamerro names the businessman Fausto Tamerlán, invoking the German story of Faust, made immemorial by Goethe for his deal with the devil, and Tamerlán, the Mongolian conqueror Timur or Tamerlane, about whom Jorge Luis Borges begins a poem: "My kingdom is of this world" ("Tamerlán" 13).[24] The late twentieth-century amalgam of these mythical figures,

Fausto Tamerlán, has given everything for the success of his business, even betraying his business partner. These historical and mythical referents are woven into a complex whodunit story, which requires the reader to have patience untangling the threads of war and business to uncover how the seemingly endless recreations of Malvinas relate to an unsolved murder. At the beginning of the novel, Fausto Tamerlán contracts Félix to hack into a government database in order to find the list of people who were at a Surprises from Spain meeting. According to Tamerlán, the people are on an official list of witnesses to a crime that implicates his family. During the meeting, a man was thrown out of a window from Tamerlán's office in the opposite tower and into the void between the two. Tamerlán's son and heir César appears to be responsible, and so, as Tamerlán says, the witnesses from the other tower must be found and silenced. He trusts that Félix, a hacker, will be able to acquire the list of witnesses using his technical savvy and connections to the state intelligence agency, and Tamerlán's thugs will then hunt them down.

Gamerro then puts the cyberpunk genre to work to create one of his many replicas of Malvinas. Félix is still in contact with one of the officers he knew from the war, Verraco, who now works for the state intelligence agency, and Félix knows that Verraco wants to relive his experience in Malvinas as if he had never left. In order to access the list of witnesses, Félix creates a video game replica of the war and pairs it with a hidden virus—a Trojan horse, in another virtual reference to classical warfare. The game is designed to replicate the war as closely as possible. However, unable to locate the small war in the game's existing templates, Félix forges an eccentric mix of characters, settings, and weapons from conflicts as varied as the Shining Path and Desert Storm in order to approximate the war. The psychology of this move is clear. Since *Beyond the Pleasure Principle*, the repetition of trauma has been hypothesized as a way of gaining mastery in spite of helplessness, as in the famous description of the *fort/da* game: "At the outset he was in a passive situation—he was overpowered by the experience; but, by repeating it, unpleasurable though it was, as a game, he took on an active part. These efforts might be put down to an instinct for mastery that was acting independently of whether the memory was in itself pleasurable or not" (16).[25] Félix shows Verraco that he can gain mastery over the war by programming the game so that it is incredibly easy and the Argentines win every time. In this way, he ensures that Verraco gets hooked on reexperiencing the alternative virtual history as true. Yet the game also has a fatal flaw that Félix can exploit; he can change it so that the Argentines lose every time, retraumatizing Verraco but giving Félix another opportunity to return to the intelligence offices to "fix" it and retrieve the information the background virus has copied.

Félix successfully hacks the database and extracts the list, but his mysterious adversary is one step ahead of him and has already erased any useful information. Consequently, Félix has to leave the comfort of his virtual life to track down the witnesses in person. As he goes person-by-person looking for missing information, he realizes that his work for Tamerlán is somehow wrapped up in the Malvinas conflict, but he can't figure out exactly how. Félix suspects that one of the witnesses, who seems to have disappeared from the list and continues to elude him, might hold the answer. He thinks he might be able to find this missing witness through an old army friend, Emilio. The problem is that Emilio is permanently interned in a psychiatric hospital with aphasia, the result of a traumatic brain injury during the war. A desperate Félix goes to see Emilio anyway, hoping for even a glimpse of useful information. Inevitably, Emilio disappoints, and Félix thinks to himself: "There's all the data you need, the facts, the dates, the names; a tale told by an aphasic with a bullet in his brain who wasn't as lucky as you were—or maybe luckier. Who knows? *You* ask him" (*Las Islas* 409, emphasis added).[26] Emilio's words are an unintelligible mix of recognizable phonemes, or as Emilio himself says when he is trying to talk to Félix, "datos de babelidad" (data of babelity) (409). According to the doctors, Emilio perceives no problems with his own speech: "Someone once explained to me that his ears perceived his own speech flawlessly, that it was ours that had become an obscene blabbering. He hadn't lost his speech; everyone else had!" (421).[27] Emilio's injury makes language unintelligible to him. Malvinas was his Babel.[28]

The reader learns that Félix also suffered a traumatic brain injury; a piece of his helmet became lodged in his skull toward the end of the war. Upon his return to Buenos Aires, he was interned in the same hospital as Emilio for seemingly incurable amnesia, but he eventually recovered his memory. In fact, the injury increased rather than decreased his capacity for communication. Félix began to understand computer code perfectly: "I now got on with machines as if we belonged to the same species and the only possible explanation lay here, in this lump crisscrossed with scars that my hair in the mirror hadn't quite yet managed to cover, a piece of the machine that I'd taken into my body forever" (425).[29] The doctors explain that the shrapnel cannot be extracted from his skull because the bone has begun to heal around it. With the benefit of hindsight, Félix sees his injury as a blessing, giving him the tools for his true calling as a hacker after the war.

Mostly human but part machine, both Emilio and Félix fit Donna Haraway's definition of a cyborg from her seminal "Cyborg Manifesto" as "a hybrid of machine and organism, a creature of social reality as well as a creature of fiction" (149). They straddle this threshold between fiction and reality, human and machine, as they incorporate the instruments of warfare. However, their capacities for communication and translation stand at opposite extremes. Emilio's aphasia limits him to a sound-based language that, while reproducing certain identifiable phonemes and combining them into new words, seems virtually untranslatable. It is a linguistic code that has strayed from the objects it names, signifiers that do not correspond to comprehensible signifieds. In contrast, Félix's brain injury allows him to translate seamlessly between human and machine languages. In his communication with computers, Félix finds a language that approaches a code for information itself. Compared to the untranslatability of Emilio's speech, drifting toward the sonic and poetic, Félix approaches the universally translatable code of binary numbers without any poetic function. Gamerro presents Félix's translation as pure exchange without metaphorical slippage.

Dramatic plot twists break the translational impasse between Emilio and Félix. The elusive Major X, also known as Arturo Cuervo, arrives at the psychiatric ward. Félix finds him copying down Emilio's gibberish in an effort to crack the code. Connecting Cuervo's strange behavior with what he has learned from earlier encounters, Félix realizes that Cuervo is trying to access his own combat diary, which has been stored in Emilio's impressive memory but jumbled by the injury. Like Fogwill's character Quique, Emilio was the scribe to a phantom battalion lost in Malvinas, in which—as luck would have it—Tamerlán's older son, Fausto Jr., groomed to be heir, fought. Félix immediately connects the characters in his mind. He reasons that Tamerlán really wants to know whether his older son is still alive, and in order to find out, he needs access to any and all information about the lost battalion. Félix understands that, although Emilio lost his speech in the war, Major X's diary and all of the information it contained about the shadow Malvinas campaign remains in Emilio's memory, albeit improperly encoded. Major X is trying to translate it back into usable form. As a result, Gamerro must reconcile the extremes of aphasia and computer code in order to carry the plot ahead.

WRITING THE BODY

Emilio's bullet and Félix's shrapnel alter communication, but they are also forms of inscription on the body. As the plot thickens, Félix realizes that Cuervo is the estranged husband of another of the witnesses, Gloria, who has become Félix's love interest. In his first visit to Gloria before he knew anything about her ex-husband, Félix felt what he thought where tactile illusions on Gloria's body as they made love in the dark. In fact, when he turns on the light he discovers that they were actually marks of torture: "It was these shiny little scars that my fingers had detected, confusing them in the dark with some obscure tactile illusion produced by my enchantment; only now did the map I'd drawn by joining up these dots with my fingers begin to take shape" (Gamerro, *Las Islas* 307).[30] Once he sees the scars, an ashamed Gloria feels she has to explain the torture. The darker scars were from cigarette burns, she clarifies, the lighter ones from an electric probe, or *picana*. Cuervo had been her torturer. He had taken a liking to her, and they had eventually married.

The mysterious Cuervo thus leaves behind different types of writing: one in his diary, stored, although jumbled, in Emilio's mind and copied into the papers; another, the marks on Gloria's body. Cuervo's use of the popular Argentine notebook brand Cuadernos Gloria seals the connection between his two modes of writing. Gamerro moves the plot through connections between these different types of writing. And Félix can read them. He traces the marks on Gloria's skin as the machine in him senses an electrical impulse, as J. Andrew Brown points out in *Cyborgs in Latin America* (113–144). When Félix finally recovers Cuervo's journal, he connects the war story from the *cuadernos* to crazed businessman Tamerlán's quest to find his son. These writings bridge the major historical moments in the novel: the inscription of the dictatorship in torture, the war in bullets and shrapnel, and the post-dictatorship neoliberal consensus in Tamerlán's towers.

As *Las Islas* builds this historical arc through inscription, it challenges the idea, widespread in cultural criticism, that Malvinas elicited a stylistic break. Compared to the Dirty War stories of disappearances and torture, which were deadly serious, the war has been seen as irreverent and farcical. Kohan, for example, writes that Fogwill's *Los pichiciegos* marks the end of the Argentine war epic, setting the stage for Gamerro's wild experiments in *Las Islas* ("El fin de una épica" 6). Similarly, María Teresa Gramuglio argues that since Fogwill, Malvinas novels have been primarily about the picaresque. In her words, Fogwill "imagined the war as an underground picaresque of survival, that eroded any future epic in advance" (12). She argues that this approach does not apply to novels about the dictatorship: "There is no picaresque or grotesque or farce in the stories of kidnappings, disappearances, torture, concentration camps" (12). Yet I have argued that Fogwill's novel can also be read as an extension of the dictatorship's anti-democratic principles, where the underground cannot help but reproduce what happens above. Read in this way, differences in style or technique between dictatorship, war, and post-dictatorship fiction merely mask the extension and displacement of violence into different contexts and onto different bodies. Stylistic differences mark nothing more than the expansion and displacement of stasis in the cultural sphere.

Beyond the detectable wounds and inscriptions in Félix and Emilio's brains and on Gloria's skin, the psychic wounds from the dictatorship and war reshape temporality for the characters. For instance, Gloria explains her involvement in left-wing militancy in the early 1970s. At the end of a demonstration, someone killed her boyfriend by driving an axe into his head in the middle of the street. Her reaction was paralysis: "Me, I was paralysed, I couldn't even shout" (Gamerro, *Las Islas* 309).[31] Gloria says that the event split her life in two: "That day was like a revelation to me, you see? As if it had been my own head the axe had split in two. I stayed in the movement, even after the coup, but only as a reflex, on automatic pilot" (309).[32] The feelings of paralysis and her inability to verbalize make it clear that she suffers from traumatic stress. After her arrest, the repeated trauma of gang rape in detention made her black out to avoid knowing what was happening: "I know I just blanked out at some point, like they'd pulled the plug: it just disconnected" (310).[33] Gloria uses an electrical metaphor to explain how she stops inhabiting her own body, divorcing somatic experience from consciousness as she dissociates. Her corporal and psychic wounds divide the narrative timeline and create what Gloria describes in her dissociation as an ecstatic displacement from herself.[34]

Gloria's story matches the typical stories of the Dirty War that Gramuglio describes. They are heavy and serious, not at all farcical. Yet, Gamerro also takes a similar tone in the parts of the novel about war. Despite recreational drugs, video games, pastiche, and farcical exaggeration, Félix, for instance, acknowledges that the majority of the men sent to the islands came back damaged. While they did not necessarily suffer brain injuries like him, they were still traumatized in such a way that they were no longer able to lead normal lives after they returned. This trauma may not be detectable; after all, Freud wrote: "In the case of the war neuroses, the fact that the same symptoms sometimes came about without the intervention of any gross mechanical force seemed at once enlightening and bewildering" (12). Félix describes the bewildering part of "war neuroses" as a change of shape, not necessarily in the brain as a result of "gross mechanical force" but in the space the men occupy in society: "We left a precise space when we left, but we changed shape over there, and when we got back we didn't fit into the jigsaw any more, whichever way you turned us; ten thousand of us came back—enlightened, mad, damned prophets—and here we are, roaming free from one end of the country to the other, speaking a language no one understands, pretending we're working, playing football, screwing, but never quite here, always aware that there's a precious and indefinable part of ourselves buried over there" (Gamerro, *Las Islas* 413).[35] After leaving Argentina for the war, the men became others to themselves. They no longer fit in the space they had once occupied, even though they continued to go through the motions. Their language also shifts so that they end up "speaking a language no one understands." Emilio is only the most extreme example of how the ex-combatants have been cut off from communicating with those around them. They are not so dissimilar from victims of dictatorship repression.

Gamerro's seemingly interminable Malvinas stories, adaptations, miniatures, and commemorations are not merely picaresque or grotesque. Rather, they are repetitions of the traumatic event in pastiche and farce—a cyberpunk version of the repetition compulsion that attempts to recover the capacity for language and action that went missing during the traumatic event. Just as the transition from the Dirty War to Malvinas was ecstatic—the state projecting its internal conflict beyond its borders—the response of those affected by these events was likewise ecstatic: outside of their consciousness, dissociative. It brought about a fundamental change in form and self-identity. Following Freud, Catherine Malabou explains that physical or psychic trauma can create a new persona that inhabits the same body: "As a result of serious trauma, or sometimes for no reason at all, the path splits and a new, unprecedented persona comes to live with the former person, and eventually takes up all the room" (*Ontology of the Accident* 1). The event destroys one psychic form and creates another. *Las Islas* depicts this change in the nonidentity of the rape survivor with herself and the combat veteran with himself.

For Malabou, this unprecedented new persona is inexplicable based on the past and reveals "the psyche's ability . . . to survive the dislocation of its history" (*New Wounded* 60). The larger question facing Argentina in the wake of the Dirty War and Malvinas is how to "survive the dislocation of its history." The answer, as Palermo points out, has been to smooth over the disruption and make Malvinas an issue of national identity. But according to Félix, the ex-combatants cannot be reincorporated into the nation, even if they attempt a zombie-like assimilation. They just don't fit. The various forms of writing—on bodies, in memory, and in aphasic and computer code—reveal a more fundamental problem than fitting back into the nation. It is not that a Malvinas novel like *Las Islas* is not serious enough; it is that the novel interrupts the very premise of the war—namely, that something can be restored to its original state. It questions the very idea that, when people talk about "Las Malvinas," they are referring to the same place before, during, and after the war. In Gamerro's novel, there is no direct, self-evident relationship between the islands' name and their geography or the soldier's name and his consciousness.

Gamerro's *Las Islas* asks the reader to confront the terrifying thought that, as Malabou has it, "we might, one day, become someone else, an absolute other, someone who will never be reconciled with themselves again, someone who will be this form of us without redemption or atonement, without last wishes, this damned form, outside time" (Malabou, *Ontology of the Accident* 2–3). In the characters of Emilio, Félix, and Gloria, Gamerro shows this damning, irrevocable change. They cannot be the same people they were before. At the same time, the islands that Argentina claims now are not the same ones they invaded in 1982, at least on a symbolic level. This symbolic nonidentity does not mean that the islands should, by sheer inertia, remain British. It means that symbolic and narrative structures must change, recognizing that claims to sovereignty rely on an impossible self-identity. And in spite of what some critics have said, Malvinas does not lend itself to farce inherently but rather lends itself to the interruption of self-identity and linear temporality. For each of Gamerro's characters, the inscription of trauma provokes a proliferation of temporal splits. Only these damned forms remain.

MDMA, ECSTASY

The relationship between Gloria and Félix represents the intertwining of the traumatic histories of the Dirty War and Malvinas in the fictional present of 1990s Argentina. Yet while Félix often discusses the war's effects on his friends, Gamerro gives no indication that Félix suffers from PTSD until the end of *Las Islas*.[36] As the novel comes to its climax, Félix is trapped in Tamerlán's office, forced to witness the violent and charged confrontation between Tamerlán and his surviving son, César. César and the family psychoanalyst kill Tamerlán and torture Félix using a drug that supposedly blocks the body's natural pain inhibitors. As the effects of the drug become overwhelming, Félix has a vivid flashback to the war. Although Gamerro revealed Félix's injury and amnesia earlier in the novel, he concealed the fact that Félix became mute during the final battle at the end of the war. In the scene, he tries helplessly to translate his companions' surrender to the British, having served as a reliable Spanish–English interpreter throughout the novel, but no one can hear him. He thinks he must be dead (Gamerro, *Las Islas* 562). Félix describes the paralysis that accompanies his aphasia and vividly remembers the surrender as his body leaving the islands and floating back toward Buenos Aires. This uncanny self-separation recurs as Félix leaves Tamerlán's tower ten years later on the anniversary of the surrender: June 14, 1992.

Félix recovers consciousness somewhere at the base of the tower, near the replica of Columbus's ship but remains stunned. Meandering around, he finds comfort in the hospitality of the vagabond that lives in containers in and around the port and sometimes inside Columbus's ship. Félix learns that this man is also an ex-combatant from Malvinas. In the ironically titled chapter "The Recovery of the Islands," Félix leaves Tamerlán's towers in Puerto Madero and treks across Buenos Aires on Sunday night, headed home. Ten years have passed, but for him, the war is as real as it was a decade before, as he describes it: "Like the clocks of Hiroshima, time for us had stopped at an instant" (587).[37] The moment of surrender has become an eternal present of ruin and destruction. On his walk, he comes across the ghosts of his former comrades from one of the war's last battles at Mount Longdon. Félix talks vaguely of joining them in the afterlife, but the ghosts urge him not to commit suicide. If he dies, they say, no one will be able to invoke them together as a group. They will only be able to appear individually to their families. Félix's existence holds them together in the world of the living.

One of the ghosts of his friends asks Félix if he knows what hell is, and he responds, "You bet I do. I could write the book" (590).[38] The reader is left wondering if this is that book. Then the ghosts leave, and despite their exhortations, Félix wants to commit suicide. He walks toward Gloria's house, and when he arrives, he tells her everything, starting with the beginning of the story and following the same structure as the novel: "I started with the day I first entered Tamerlán's tower, or with the day the three cops brought me the draft to rejoin the army, there wasn't much difference. As I went on, I realised the two stories had ended up merging into one like two rivers that join to form a third; or perhaps there'd only been one river all along and it was me who had encountered two separate stretches of it at two moments in my life without realising the water was the same" (596).[39] Although a decade apart, Félix sees the two stories as part of the same timeline that folds back on itself, "another twist to the Möbius strip that, weaving between two worlds intertwined like two facing mirrors, had ended up merely finding its own tail" (597).[40] The characters, in the ecstatic flights of their own memories, can travel through this timeline, encountering places where their stories converge outside of linear time. Gamerro's temporality resists a single direction. In its serpentine twists and turns, it superimposes events upon each other, allowing them to split into different branches of the same story before converging again.

After Félix finishes telling his story, Gloria says that she agrees with his conclusion; they should commit suicide. They prepare everything and take cyanide pills that Gloria says she has left from her guerrilla days. Soon after they prepare the scene of their death, however, the reader discovers that she lied to him. The pill is actually MDMA, or Ecstasy. Initially, Félix does not realize that he has been tricked, and by the time he does, the effects have already taken hold. He no longer cares whether he lives or dies because of the pleasure and intensity of his bodily sensations. The attempted suicide becomes a confusion of death with pleasure. In that moment, Félix resembles Slavoj Žižek's version of the post-traumatic subject: the subject that has survived its own death (Žižek 28). Félix's near-death experience during the war caused a trauma response, but in attempting to cure himself of flashbacks by suicide ten years later, he modifies his reaction.[41] In *Las Islas*, Ecstasy helps Gloria and Félix overcome persistent and inevitable detours into their pasts. It also helps them commit suicide without killing themselves, allowing them to overcome the repetition compulsion.

Thanks to Ecstasy, Félix can symbolically reconfigure the events that have appeared throughout the novel. As Gloria and Félix talk about the pills, Gloria says, "Hey, I think these things are the real deal." Félix asks, "Where did you get them?" To which Gloria replies, "Manna from heaven. A friend from Spain." And Félix wonders, "Christopher Columbus?" (Gamerro, *Las Islas* 603).[42] Having just left the fake caravel and considering the imperial histories woven into the plot, Félix thinks that the pills must have come from Spain with Columbus. Yet this "discovery" is not one of conquest but rather a psychic experience that reshapes Félix's internal symbolic and temporal landscape.[43] Columbus's journey remains a presence but becomes utterly meaningless as a metaphor, a vessel of meaning. The connection to the conquest is merely a mental slip on Félix's part. Columbus's landing and the Spanish MDMA merge into the same temporal flow that is neither celebrated nor reviled. In that moment, the conquest has shed its emotional and symbolic weight.

As Félix says immediately after his question about Columbus, the high alters his relationship to his body. It changes his way of being in and relating to the world. Specifically, the "discovery" of the New

World, as both the Americas and a new psychic life reshapes his understanding of himself in the world: "A fresh gust of warm air blowing
from the new world extinguished the words in our mouths before we
could speak them and a drowsy sweetness gripped my limbs, holding
them fast, delivering me defenceless into her irreverent hands, which
began to knead the clay of my old body. A new identity was being born,
trembling as her fingers gradually drew out the forms of the new; the
hands of Rodin couldn't have breathed more life into my limbs" (603).[44]
He feels his body reshaped like clay in the capable hands of a sculp-
tor. MDMA likewise enhances the feeling of tactile connection, and
as Félix and Gloria touch each other, Félix describes how the contact
between their bodies lowers defenses that emerged as a result of their
past experience. Gamerro imagines the plasticity of clay, its ability to
take shape, at the same time that the neurons in Félix's brain fire together, altering the brain's established neurological patterns (Malabou, *New
Wounded*). Félix feels that his body is reborn as Ecstasy helps him work
through the past. Surviving his own death creates a material, formal
change in the body.

MDMA also changes the way Félix communicates with and through
symbols and bodies. Félix's communication resembles Emilio's sound-
based language, melting away the surface and distance between words
and things. Words no longer index objects but instead fuse with them:

> Our words had fallen away like our clothes and in this terrible, fearless
> nakedness the voice was nothing but breathing sounds, the same sound
> repeated again and again, equivalent to all of literature, the words poured
> into my ears nothing but prolongations of the lips that were kissing them.
> How wrong I'd always been: it wasn't things that were distanced from
> words, it was us. In the same way that, for the first time, I was touching
> what my greedy baby's hands were reaching for, for the first time I was
> saying the words I'd only repeated until now, saying them with my whole
> body, not just my tongue and throat and voice . . . the voice was the sense
> of touch turned inward. (603–4)[45]

Félix's ecstasy merges signifier and signified. No longer a process of
encoding or translation, the voice becomes the instrument for speaking things, as sound eliminates distance from the objects around him.
Likewise, the traditional barrier between subject and object, self and
other disappears. As a consequence, the contact with the other deforms
and reforms his identity. Gloria's care for Félix means not only that she
switches the pills so he cannot commit suicide but also that her contact
with him at this crucial moment destroys his attachment to the narrative

of what came before. His story becomes meaningless, and he can no longer retell it in the same way.

The ecstatic high presents a reinterpretation of Heidegger's temporal ecstases. The "discovery" becomes less colonial and more resonant with a passage in *Being and Time*, in which Heidegger connects temporality, spatiality, and taking care:

> The self-directed discovering of a region is grounded in an ecstatically retentive awaiting of the possible hither and whither. As a directed awaiting of region, making room is equiprimordially a bringing-near [*Nähern*] (or de-distancing) of things at hand and objectively present. De-distancing, taking care comes back out of the previously discovered region to what is nearest [*Nächste*]. . . . Because Dasein as temporality is ecstatic and horizontal in its being, it can factically and constantly take along space for which it has made room. With regard to this space ecstatically made room for, the here of its actual factical location or situation never signifies a position in space, but the leeway of the range of the totality of useful things taken care of nearby—a leeway that has been opened in directionality and de-distancing. (351)

While Heidegger's language certainly differs from Gamerro's, both remark on the shift in space and distance that accompanies ecstatic temporality as a kind of caretaking. Rather than the repetition compulsion of PTSD, forcing the subject ceaselessly into the past, Heidegger describes the ecstatic temporality in which Dasein takes care of what is nearby. During the high, MDMA likewise helps Félix connect to a different aspect of his temporal existence. As he comes down, he comes nearer to the objects around him, approaching what Heidegger refers to as de-distancing.

Félix's relationship to time also changes thanks to the high. Time, represented by the ticking clock, melts away for a while, he explains. It becomes multidimensional. Félix notices himself coming down, he says, because although he doesn't feel fear, anguish, guilt, or impotence, they become possible again; that is, the discomforts of past and future begin to creep in. He notices "the clocks had regained their authority over time, minutely slicing it up with their precise knives, objects were again clothing themselves in their surfaces and fingers no longer sank in when they touched things" (Gamerro, *Las Islas* 606).[46] The relationship between past and present becomes increasingly discordant, even violent, like knives slicing time to pieces. The barrier between self and other also reappears, and while Félix is disappointed, he is no longer suicidal. The traditional structure of temporality returns, but Félix is no longer captive to it.

Félix notes that something has changed. His understanding of the world is no longer ruled by mythical eternities playing off each other as in previous chapters. In his words: "First I fall into hell, then I emerge in paradise, and suddenly . . . here" (609).[47] He ends up somewhere entirely mundane: Gloria's house. Ecstasy is neither the hell of flashbacks and ghosts nor the heaven of the high. Gloria's house is not an extension of Malvinas, as Buenos Aires had been throughout the novel, nor is it meaningful in the way that Tamerlán's towers and Columbus's caravel were. Rather, the temporal ecstases of past, present, and future are outside themselves—discordant. It is impossible to cultivate harmony between them, but as he comes down from the high, Félix begins to experience time as the unity of these displacements.

The powers of the mythical, symbolic, and fantastic, which had ruled the plot until now, dissolve in these final pages. Gloria, whose body had been a site of violent inscription, finally tells a story of her own creation, inventing a fairy tale to help Félix sleep off his hangover. But from the beginning, she warns him that it will be a reverse fairy tale, where the expected happens—the glass shoe fits the stepsister and the ugly duckling becomes an ugly duck. There is no transformation for the sake of salvation. In Gloria's story, the princess's prince remains a frog and she plans to bear his tadpoles. In this final scene, Gloria and Félix experience the final element of temporal ecstasy: projection into the future. They plan to go to the cinema later with Gloria's daughters, as if this day were like any other. They arrive at a provisional treaty with the three components of ecstatic temporality: past, present, and future. Gamerro engages myth and epic while acknowledging that the lost islands will not return after some magical, storybook transformation. The hope lies not in the restoration of lost territory and imperial borders nor the charging of the nation with metaphorical meaning but instead in the possibility of overcoming the past in order to inhabit the everyday ecstasy that is past, present, and future, neither heaven nor hell.

MIRRORED ISLANDS, SPECULAR DEMOCRACY

During most of *Las Islas*, Félix conjures a symbolic universe as a filter for his life, moving in and out of models and recreations of the past, but Félix's experience also exceeds metaphorical assimilation. As Žižek writes, the post-traumatic subject "cannot be identified (does not fully overlap) with 'stories it is telling itself about itself,' with the narrative symbolic texture of its life" (29).[48] By the end of the novel, Félix's stories are relegated to the preceding pages. In Malabou's terms, he has become a being wholly unrecognizable to himself. He no longer strives for meaning, just as Gloria no longer plays the role of torture victim. The transformation of their bodies—their change of shape—changes the "narrative symbolic texture" of the characters' stories. *Las Islas* exhibits the repetition compulsion to exhaustion; Malvinas is associated with national identity and belonging in political discourse in a fort/da game—first here, then gone—ad infinitum. But the subject, in this case the heterogeneous national subject that goes by the monolithic name of Argentina, never achieves mastery. The nation merely casts away and brings back Malvinas over and over again.

Since the 1994 constitution's proclamation of the state's objective of recovery of the islands and full sovereignty in the South Atlantic, this dynamic of loss and restoration has been inscribed in the fabric of electoral democracy. *Las Islas* marks the transition into the post-dictatorship period and neoliberal consensus, in which Tamerlán begins to see that time has become more important than territory. In one of the novel's final chapters, he looks out of his office window to the heavy machinery reclaiming land from the Río de la Plata and remarks, "We're reclaiming land from the river. Reclaiming. Ha! So much effort to buy space when what I need is time" (506).[49] By the tenth anniversary of the war, the dictatorship has been replaced with ultra-rich businessmen. The manipulation of territory, critical to convincing left-wing intellectuals to support the war regardless of its political origin, has been replaced by the manipulation of time, vital for securing capital in the nepotistic business world. In the following pages, Tamerlán's prophecy is fulfilled. His company falls, and he falls with it, out of a broken window in one of his towers. He needed more time to secure his legacy. Fausto Jr., not César, was supposed to inherit the company.

The conflict between the two brothers recalls Borges's well-known prose poem about the war, "Juan López y John Ward," which claims that two men fighting in Malvinas, "might have been friends, but they saw each other face-to-face only once, on some islands that were too famous, and each one was Cain and each one was Abel" (95).[50] The Tamerlán brothers takes this aphorism away from the battlefield and back to Argentina, where the conflict continues to haunt the democratic period. The two sons are locked in a battle that takes place in their father's two towers.[51] The towers, like the since-fallen twin towers of the World Trade Center in New York, are supposed to represent beacons of financial power in the rising Global South. They also have an additional power structure built into them: double-sided mirrors that create a point of maximum visibility at the top and minimum visibility at the bottom. The lowest-level employees work on the lowest floors of the building, and supervisors can turn the mirrors to monitor any room below them. In turn, the supervisors on the next level up can make these subordinates appear, and so on up to Tamerlán himself. The building is a hierarchical adaptation of the panopticon.

As the plot comes to its climax, Tamerlán's enemies invert all of the mirrors so that the top of the tower becomes the point of minimum rather than maximum visibility in order to obscure their approach. To fend off the oncoming attack, Félix hacks the electronic system that flips the mirrors, making them rotate constantly to buy more time. He believes that an imminent attack must be part of César's spectacular final coup against his father, but he is wrong. As César explains when Félix asks if he will take over control of the business from his murdered father: "I'm going to flog [the company]. Control will be handed to a plc, and Canal [the psychoanalyst] and I will be shareholders. We've already sorted out the restructuring. We're going to rotate all the mirrors so nobody really knows where the boss is. It'll be a democracy. A democracy without the people. That whole personalised, hierarchic deal is too vulnerable. The spider's mistake" (Gamerro, *Las Islas* 543).[52] The final sentence hearkens back to the beginning of the novel, in which Félix feels himself becoming trapped in Tamerlán's web. Tamerlán is overthrown, but the coup does not invert the hierarchy or replace one despot with another. Instead, the power structure shifts to assume a truly neoliberal form in which power is dispersed among shareholders in the form of money and influence. There is no figurehead to hold accountable. This, in turn, is cast as democracy.

Profound organizational changes mask the fact that what is left after Tamerlán's fall is a democracy without a people, a democracy of shareholders. His death is merely a convenient excuse for a more efficient way of organizing profit, just as the fall of the junta fostered the conditions for someone like Tamerlán to rise. As a government employee explains earlier in the novel, bureaucracy under President Carlos Menem is "an anarchist utopia in reverse. An organisation without leaders where nobody's free" (143).[53] Malvinas precedes these changes in structure—the overthrow of the dictatorship in 1982 and the assassination of Tamerlán on the tenth anniversary of defeat in 1992. First with Fausto Jr., who fought in the war, and then with César, who dissolved his father's company, this modern Romulus and Remus of Buenos Aires shift from dictatorship to democracy via war. Gamerro shows that these changes, while apparently disruptive and ecstatic, are merely formal. They enact a restoration masquerading as a new order.[54]

In rewriting the end of the war in parallel with electoral democracy and a business boom ten years later, Gamerro's version of Malvinas challenges the story that the war caused the people to rise against the dictatorship. Gamerro shows that power merely flips the border between inside and outside, like a rotating mirror to obscure its machinations, showing one side, then the other. Mirrors quickly change structural appearances, making it difficult to locate a given concentration of power. As in the specular democracy that followed the war, Malvinas is the abiding node around which these shifts are reflected. The geography of the two islands, split across a channel, reflects Argentina's dictatorship and neoliberal democracy, Juan López and John Ward, Cain and Abel. The war marks a split within Argentina, in which the appearance of change and movement masks the actual stagnation between internalizing and externalizing the Malvinas question over the political divide. It is a repetition that somehow evokes but fails to represent a specular image of the people, the *demos*, in rotating mirrors.

Yet Gamerro also includes another set of siblings as a counterweight to César and Fausto Jr.: Gloria's twin daughters, Soledad and Malvina. The twins are a living legacy of the war. They are the product of Gloria's rape by Cuervo, and they were born prematurely on the day the war broke out: April 2, 1982. They bear the names that Cuervo instructed Gloria to use, taken from the two islands he had set out to take back from the British.[55] Symbolically, they seal a pact between the militants suppressed during the dictatorship—in this case Gloria—and the military elites in charge—Cuervo. The girls are the bond between them, a family built on sexual and emotional abuse. Their names seal the incarnation of the issue on which left and right, militants and military finally agreed, fostering patriotism in even the dictatorship's most ardent critics. Yet Gamerro does not make the girls a synthesis of opposing factions. They are female, a notable sexual difference from the military officers and businessmen that dominate the novel, and they have Down syndrome, a contingent excess, an extra copy of chromosome 21. This difference represents a code disruption, typical of Gamerro, only this time in the genetic rather than linguistic code. This genetic excess reshapes the legacy of the war. It frees the girls from assuming the role that Cuervo wanted for them: to represent the country overcoming the opposition between left and right through nationalism.

Unsurprisingly, upon return from Malvinas, Cuervo finds his newborn daughters intolerable and abandons the family. Soledad and Malvina thus ensure the symbolic and metaphorical destruction of Malvinas. Their corporal and genetic differences provide Gamerro with a more lasting version of the ecstasy of Félix's high, in which form and content are transformed. For Félix, MDMA makes the border between subject and object disappear. It fuses the world around him into a borderless transcendence that then settles into an ecstatic unity as he comes down. Identity becomes fundamentally malleable, changing in response to a violent temporality. Gamerro's portrayal of Soledad and Malvina goes one step further, leaving behind the post-traumatic subject entirely. The twins bear no relation to the symbolic resonance of their names, nor do they invoke their genealogy. Instead, they represent something like what Malabou describes as "an absolute existential improvisation" (*Ontology of the Accident* 2).[56] They exist in the wake of destruction as contingent excess, as children that do not seek the mastery of the fort/da game that their parents play. They were supposed to be the most emphatic metaphors of Malvinas, but they refuse. The metaphor has, at last, slipped through Gamerro's hands.

Las Islas thus presents a contrast between the neoliberal state's response to trauma—frantic repetition and projection; interiorization and exteriorization—and another, subjective and fictional way of treating the dispute as ecstatic transformation and displacement from the self. The novel shows that to inscribe Malvinas as a central metaphor for Argentine identity is to misunderstand the state's projection onto the islands. Malvinas marks the etymological definition of *ecstasy*—on one hand, as displaced internal conflict, and on the other, as nonidentity and temporal disjunction. Gamerro evokes an ecstatic, post-Malvinas Argentina beyond repetition. From Columbus's ship in Thénon to Tamerlán's twin towers, war—destruction—has been the norm. *Las Islas* seeks to finally empty Malvinas of its symbolic meaning, flipping the border like a mirror, so that the islands represent the specular democracy of contemporary stasis. The *polemos* of the past is gone, replaced with a conflict that shifts rapidly from physical to virtual and historic to philosophical planes. The lost border is repeated internally in metaphors and mirrors. The image of Malvinas as a lost piece of the homeland, appearing in monuments throughout Argentina, reminds the country not of a historical quest for restitution but of the ongoing stasis moving through cultural, political, and historical spheres. Against the nationalist understanding of Malvinas, this displacement reconfigures subjectivity and sovereignty in the present. Malvinas surpasses the polemos of sovereign conflict, repeats the legacy of dictatorship, protests the incomplete dismantling of imperialism, and denounces financial capitalism's stunted democracy all at once. At last, Malvinas represents nothing less than ecstasy. As the next chapter shows, the islands' reconfiguration of the spatial and symbolic limits of sovereignty is far from finished.

CHAPTER 5

THE FALKLANDS/ MALVINAS WAR AND BORDER METASTASIS

"¿Quiénes somos nosotros?", volví a preguntar, y tuve la impresión de que me había pasado toda la guerra haciéndome esa pregunta.
—**Patricio Pron**, *Nosotros caminamos en sueños*

In December 2001, Argentina suffered an acute financial and political crisis. The government froze assets in bank accounts, prohibiting withdrawals in the hope of reining in inflation. Argentina's crisis led to a rapid succession of presidents, eventually settling into the left-populist governments of Néstor Kirchner from 2003 to 2007 and Cristina Fernández de Kirchner from 2007 to 2015. Currency was more tightly controlled. Argentines could not easily access US dollars, and the peso was pegged to the US dollar at a fixed rate that was, at times, wildly different from the informal peso–dollar exchange. The unofficial "blue" rate was a better bet for foreign investors and tourists, giving Argentines access to dollars in cash that were otherwise tightly controlled, as regular people tried to protect decades of savings from economic turbulence.

A few months earlier in September 2001, there was a global reconfiguration of the practice and strategy of warfare, originating in the United States in response to the events of 9/11. War became increasingly detached from the sovereign state, turning into an ongoing standoff between a burgeoning military-industrial complex on one side and well-networked guerrillas on the other. The so-called War on Terror changed the logistic and political structure of armed conflict, challenging the long-held understanding of territory as the spatial extent of sovereignty, as Stuart Elden defines it in *Terror and Territory*, and consequently borders as limits to sovereign power. Conflict became increasingly deterritorialized, no longer bound to delimited national spaces and the border became more diffuse.

Both the United States and Argentina experienced the sharp growing pains of nascent globalization, as the relationship between territory, economics, and power shifted throughout the Americas in late 2001. Violence came unmoored from national borders and increasingly linked to resource extraction. Argentina was suffering financial hemorrhage, attempting to tie the currency back to its national territory with only marginal success. By asserting national control, both Kirchner administrations hoped to strengthen the country's insertion into the global economy and alleviate its debts, but these efforts were decidedly against the global trend toward financialization and would ultimately lead to the fall of Kirchnerism in a right-wing backlash during a reactionary cycle that brought various regional pink tide governments to an end. Although the processes were apparently opposite—the United States moved away from a state-based understanding of territory as Argentina attempted to reassert it economically—they reflect similar anxieties about the changing economic and political landscape after 2001, especially desuturing power from territory.

During the same period, the Malvinas conflict grew in the Argentine public eye. Against the willful oblivion and shame that prevailed immediately after the war, dubbed *desmalvinización*, there was a rising consciousness of a historical claim to justice, dubbed *remalvinización*. This process brought the conflict back to the forefront of collective consciousness around the time of its twenty-fifth and thirtieth anniversaries in 2007 and 2012, respectively. The war's legacy garnered political purchase among anti-imperialist and nationalist voters largely associated with the populist-left Kirchners and became a key part of their cultural and political agenda. The public reclamation of Argentina's sovereign rights to the islands meant that, in Vicente Palermo's view, the "causa Malvinas" became indistinguishable from Argentine identity in the twenty-first century (16–25). Signs dotting roads throughout the countryside remind motorists of the sovereignty claim and indicate the distance to the islands, even though it is, of course, impossible to cross the South Atlantic by car. A presidentially sponsored television ad ahead of the 2012 London Olympics showed an Argentine athlete training on the islands with the message: "To compete on English soil, we train on Argentine soil" (Presidencia de la Nación Argentina).[1] Two years later, FIFA fined the Argentine national soccer team for displaying a sign reading "Las Malvinas son argentinas" or "The Malvinas Are Argentine" ("FIFA"). British television show *Top Gear* took sports cars on a tour around Patagonia before fleeing the southern city of Ushuaia after being pelted with rocks ("*Top Gear* Crew"). In 2022, the song "Muchachos, ahora nos volvimos a ilusionar" (Guys, we've got our hopes up again), with an homage to "the Malvinas kids I'll never forget," went viral, accompanying Argentina all the way to their World Cup championship.[2] Global sports gatherings and minor diplomatic meetings have become stages on which to protest the ongoing lack of attention to Malvinas outside of Argentina.

The sovereignty claim has remained static, even though the terms under which it is defined and the circumstances in which it is negotiated have undergone significant change since 2001. Most notably, the role of the border has shifted in the twenty-first century. Sandro Mezzadra and Brett Neilson's *Border as Method* describes the "mobility and proliferation of borders" (24) under globalization. Mezzadra and Neilson chart bordering through labor and migration, culminating in a discussion of contemporary political subjectivity and border-crossing. As borders move and proliferate, citizenship becomes less important, and the citizen is replaced with a more diffuse transnational subject, in turn subjected to a more diffuse regime of labor and economics. In place of citizenship, international law tends to use the category of the person to refer to a subject endowed with human rights and not necessarily bound by national limits. This change is not merely legalistic but rather signals a fundamental shift in the organization of political space as the role of sovereignty changes.

The border conflicts in previous chapters have offered glimpses of some of the problems that emerge in contemporary globalization. For instance, while the Chaco War attempted to seal a border and fix a national essence through hypostasis, the border actually remained partially open. The impossibility of distinguishing whether the border was open or closed, permeable or impermeable, persisted for decades. Contemporary borders merely exacerbate this indistinction, adding layers of people and goods, movement and stoppage among modes of transportation. While the Soccer War exposed the potential weakness of forced economic integration, contemporary movement patterns reveal that north–south economic flows and south–north migratory flows have come to a crisis point. As people and goods cross borders with increasing frequency, sovereign limits have come partially unbound from national territory and, despite reactionary attempts to return to old borders, this change appears inexorable.

This chapter examines border changes accompanying globalization in post-2001 film, theater, and fiction about the Falklands/Malvinas War. While the sovereignty of the islands remained unchanged during this period, ideas and realities of bordering, violence, and subjectivity shifted, often creating a clash about the site of conflict and the meanings of political and social categories today. I analyze these changes through the figure of metastasis, which, while it appears to contain the word *stasis*, has its origin in a different Greek root, *methistanai*, meaning "change." Metastasis describes a "change of position, state, or form" ("Metastasis" [*Merriam-Webster*]). For instance, as a matter of national importance, Argentina seeks a change of state through which the islands would return to union with the mainland. In medicine, metastasis is associated with cancer's spread to a new site: "The spread of a disease-producing agency (such as cancer cells) from the initial or primary site of disease to another part of the body" ("Metastasis" [*Merriam-Webster*]).[3] Likewise, Malvinas appears as a disease in the body politic, materializing at incongruous sites throughout the country and at unexpected moments in history. This spread of disease to different sites encapsulates Mezzadra and Neilson's description of contemporary borders proliferating and changing location in the present. Finally, in rhetoric, metastasis indicates a "rapid transition from one point to the next, or a glossing over of some point as of too little importance to dwell upon" ("Metastasis" [*Oxford Dictionary of Literary Terms*]) but also "turning back an insult or objection against the person who made it" (Lanham 101). Such rhetorical moves are common when discussing Malvinas, tending to reinforce clearly defined and entrenched perspectives—for instance, deriding British imperialism while tacitly ignoring its Spanish counterpart. Similar quick argumentative moves facilitate rapid shifts in framework; for instance, moving from the nation to the person while skipping over the increasingly weakened category of the citizen. This chapter argues that border metastases reveal the breakdown of political categories, taking the Falklands/Malvinas as exemplary of contemporary changes in the politics and culture of the border.

After 2001, sovereignty faded and discourses of human rights and resource extraction began to dominate discussions of the Falklands/Malvinas. The islands' geographic limit began to appear at different—sometimes distant—sites, sometimes in tandem, sometimes in tension with evolving political categories. As a result, the upheaval that the conflict caused within Argentina changed—metastasized. This metastasis appears in the cultural sphere; for instance, in Tristán Bauer's celebrated 2005 film *Iluminados por el fuego* (Enlightened by fire; commercially released as *Blessed by Fire*). The film depicts a shift in focus from the discourse of national to human rights and collective to individual concerns. Moving past the uneasy ecstasy of the late 1990s, rhetoric about the islands reflected an increasingly emphatic assertion of sovereignty, against the rising tide of globalization. Given this weakened national sovereignty, however, a new generation of filmmakers, playwrights, and authors depict the Falklands/Malvinas as a distant and paradoxical site of conflict on a now-global stage. This generation has depersonalized the conflict by challenging models based on human rights and testimony and moving toward third-person forms of cultural expression. Lola Arias's play *Minefield/Campo minado* and film *Theatre of War/Teatro de guerra* use masking, reenactment, translation, and repetition to interrupt personal identity as well as attachment to ideas of testimony, rights, personhood, and sovereignty, centering the conflict while decentering the individual. Similarly, Patricio Pron's novella *Nosotros caminamos en sueños* (We walk in dreams; We sleepwalk) satirizes the war through espionage, technology, and market manipulation at incongruent sites and in surreal battles only vaguely reminiscent of the 1982 war. For Pron, changes in position, state, and form reveal the contours of global metastasis to comic effect. Beneath the satire, however, lies the intimation that previously stable categories such as border, war, and soldier have melded into meaninglessness. The stasis of the past metastasizes in the twenty-first-century Falklands/Malvinas.

ECONOMIC CRISIS AND FROZEN TIME

The 2001 economic crisis created the conditions for a national political reckoning with the past. Malvinas was not exempt, especially four years later after the commercial success of *Iluminados por el fuego*, which depicted a veteran cast out of a society that had largely forgotten the war. The film was based on Malvinas veteran Edgardo Esteban's testimonial account, published in 1993 under the same title. Bauer's film adaptation follows ex-combatants from the battlefields into the twenty-first century. It brought attention to abuses of power within the armed forces, especially officers' abuse of conscripts, increasing public pressure and encouraging accountability. In the years after the film's release, veterans would begin to benefit from social services aimed at healing long-discounted physical and psychic wounds, while officers who had abused their subordinates were prosecuted for human rights violations beginning in 2009.

In creating the film version, Bauer adapted Esteban's written testimony to the early 2000s. The first scene shows protests in the streets of Buenos Aires as the government was increasingly forced to respond to popular demands thanks to large-scale public protest.[4] The main character is called Esteban Leguizamón, a slight change from Edgardo Esteban. He walks through a large demonstration, reporting on protestors' demands to a live film crew. Bauer's choice to open with a handheld camera places the audience inside the upheaval of the early 2000s when protestors ousted the government. He inserts a shot of federal police officers smoking and watching the crowd through an out-of-focus fence, establishing a parallel to the anti-government sentiment in the immediate aftermath of the war when protestors finally ousted the junta. The uprisings stand in opposition to apathetic, brutish state forces. Bauer seals the comparison by focusing on a protestor holding a microphone and announcing, "Out with all of them! Let's go to the Plaza de Mayo!" (00:02:09–00:02:13).[5] Revolt against neoliberal policies in the 2000s then feeds into the main story about the legacy of Malvinas so the demands of human rights and democracy are yoked together from the opening scene.[6]

In contrast to the oversaturated colors and raucousness of the first scene, Bauer then shifts his attention to social isolation among veterans. Esteban gets a call late at night. His expression darkens, and he heads to the emergency room as the film cuts to a camera mounted on an ambulance, hurrying through the now-deserted streets of Buenos Aires. Alberto Vargas is arriving at the hospital, unconscious after an apparent suicide attempt. His ex-wife Marta is with him. The light is cool, with white and blue dominating, often casting Marta in shadow. Bauer uses a handheld camera again for verisimilitude, but now focuses on Alberto's helplessness and isolation rather than the crowd's call to action. After some flashbacks that establish Esteban and Alberto's relationship as comrades and friends during the war, the film cuts to the interior of a café. Marta explains what has happened to her ex in the years since he came back from Malvinas. Alberto had an auto shop that closed, then lost his job in a factory. He gradually became consumed by drink and jealousy, and Marta explains, "We started falling and falling and we didn't stop until now" (00:27:13–00:27:19).[7] They separated, and she explains that he gradually became more and more isolated, attempting suicide with a cocktail of drugs and alcohol. She feels guilty, saying that she knew he would do it but felt powerless to stop him. Marta's account of her ex-husband's gradual descent into depression stands in stark contrast to Esteban's ordinary middle-class life as a journalist with a stable home centered around a nuclear family. Even in the film's first few scenes, Esteban always appears around others, while Alberto is almost always in frame alone. Later, Esteban alludes to his relatively "normal" life after the war, and only rarely does the war intrude on his daily experience, as when memories, spurred by meeting Alberto again, keep him awake at night. In another scene, we see him working late at the TV studio, scanning through old footage of the war as if to immerse himself in these memories. Yet, apart from these brief moments, Esteban is cast as a functional bourgeois subject, capable of adaptively coping with trauma.

Esteban and Alberto's very different postwar experiences initiate the film's exploration of the past. Flashbacks aim to show the audience why Alberto had such a difficult time while Esteban seems to have reintegrated himself into civilian life seamlessly. During one of the flashbacks, Alberto suffers torture at the hands of his superiors. He is staked out in below-freezing temperatures for killing sheep to feed himself and his starving comrades. The audience infers that this additional cruelty must have played a role in Alberto's later decline. Yet, in Marta's account: "We had some wonderful years" (00:26:26).[8] According to Marta, the closure of Alberto's garage and ultimate long-term unemployment contributed to his downward spiral. In this way, Bauer suggests two possible causes of Alberto's despair: first, the cruelty he suffered in Malvinas finally caught up to him, which the audience is led to infer from his treatment during the film; and later, the audience is told that he was a victim of a larger structural problem, specifically Argentina's downward economic spiral, which Marta suggests and Esteban's relatively insulated middle-class life confirms. In both cases, Alberto serves as an emblematic victim of Argentina's historical blows since the war. Bauer creates an analogue between dictatorship torture and economic exploitation, between human rights violations and the neoliberal marketplace as oppressive forces in the lives of ex-combatants. The implication is that economic disparities under neoliberalism mirror human rights abuses under the dictatorship. The same victim might suffer under both regimes. This coincidence yokes the pro-democracy sentiment of 1982 with the left-populist turn of the early 2000s. Both take the victim's side and cast historical justice through the lens of the individual.

The two explanations that *Iluminados por el fuego* offers for Alberto's depression thus place his misfortune at the intersection of human rights and neoliberalism. While human rights had already become the dominant paradigm for prosecuting crimes that took place under the dictatorship, neoliberalism sought to pin success and failure on the individual. As Fernando Rosenberg remarks in *After Human Rights*, the increasing influence of human rights discourse around the turn of the twenty-first century coincided with rising exploitation of workers in the neoliberal marketplace: "Human rights and neoliberal common sense share common ground that neither exhausts the emancipatory possibilities of human rights nor exempts neoliberal politics of blatantly ignoring rights" (1). The discourse of rights dovetails with neoliberalism in individualism. Human rights and neoliberalism are not the same, but they coincide in that they both cast the individual as the primary locus of legal and economic experience, as is the case for Alberto.

Toward the end of the film, Esteban says to a still-unconscious Alberto that the two men need to "cerrar la historia" (close out their [hi]story; 00:54:46), by traveling to the islands again. Soon after that, Alberto dies without ever having woken from his coma. Esteban decides to visit Malvinas alone as part of his reckoning with the past. The audience sees Esteban tour former battlefields, find his old foxhole, and climb in, symbolically burying himself in the past.[9] While underground, he finds a photograph and a pocket watch that had been left behind. The audience has seen both items in earlier flashbacks, and their reappearance releases a normally impassive Esteban's catharsis. Symbolically, the photograph and the stopped watch capture the stoppage of time in death. They bring to mind Esteban's fallen comrades from the war as well as the psychic death that Alberto struggled with for the rest of his life. In the next scene, Esteban stands in the Argentine cemetery at Darwin. He finds a fallen comrade's headstone and pays his respects as the camera turns to the dates: 1963–1982. This bracketed interval reflects the deep loss that the Malvinas generation endured. The headstone dates also stop the progression of time. This stoppage of time feeds directly into the message projected onto the screen moments later: "Las Malvinas son argentinas."[10] Sovereignty is again asserted outside of the narrative time of the film, even outside of time altogether, in an eternal present tense. First the film symbolically freezes time in these three objects—stopped watch, photo, and headstone—then it endorses Argentina's perpetual claim to the islands.

These images of stasis conflict with the passage of time that distinguishes film from photography. Film is a temporal medium; the passage of time smoothing over perception of the stoppage between frames. Yet Bauer stops the film to repeat the sovereignty claim. In this final moment, Iluminados por el fuego seems to insist that nothing has changed, even at the expense of temporal superimpositions and excisions concealing a messier reality. The film rehearses the same argument about the sovereignty of Malvinas, frozen in the purportedly timeless edifice of international law. Hence, in order to claim Malvinas in the present, Bauer falls into a paradox. The superimposed historical layers of 1982 and 2001 grate against the ahistorical assertion of sovereignty. At the same time, however, the claim to Malvinas is a protest, seeking to redress imperial dispossession and the loss of hundreds of lives. There is no historical or symbolic frame in which restitution, either of the national dispossession or of the loss of life, is possible. The discourse of sovereignty props up the film's final call to action, but everything that comes before reveals that what is actually at stake is how to mourn when a loss engendered by sovereignty can no longer be easily understood through sovereignty. This is Alberto's predicament. His suicide is presented as a consequence of the war, but it is also the result of his economic and social marginalization, the vicissitudes of a neoliberal regime of rights that left him behind. Rather than the film being seen as a justification of sovereignty or veterans' rights, it can be interpreted against the grain as asking how to mourn the loss of people like Alberto, a loss in danger of becoming inexplicable as time passes and sovereignty weakens.

Alberto's death is not the only one that undergoes resignification as sovereignty discourse gives way to the language of human rights and the individual in the twenty-first century. Families seeking to visit the graves of fallen Argentine soldiers on the islands have had strongly opposing views about how to properly mourn the dead as time goes by. They have argued in private and in public about whether the bodies of Argentines buried on the islands should be identified or repatriated to the mainland. If the bodies were identified, ex-combatants' families feared that they would automatically be moved to the continent, leaving no Argentine presence on the islands. The fallen soldiers were, in fact, affirming Argentine sovereignty with their bones. Leila Guerriero's *La otra guerra* (The other war) documents the struggle over whether to identify the bodies buried in the Argentine cemetery at Darwin, citing three reasons given by families of missing soldiers: "I opposed the identification because they said they wanted to bring the bodies back to the continent. I opposed the identification because I thought there was nothing left of my son. I opposed the identification because everyone else did" (14).[11] The identification of the body elicits these varied responses because it has the potential to change the relationship between Malvinas and the continent, the body and its grave, the families of the fallen and the state. Does the body need to be associated with the soldier's name? Is the final resting place a site of personal mourning or national loss? Is it important, in the wake of dictatorship-era political violence, to have a place to remember the missing family member, or is the family mem-

5.1. Portion of the frontispiece of *Leviathan* representing the sovereign body

ber's presence on the island a statement of national right? Does the fallen soldier symbolically represent Argentina, even in death?

Official discourse has tended to confine the conscript to the limited, primarily political role of citizen representing the sovereign body. The classic example of this sovereign figuration appears in the famous frontispiece of Thomas Hobbes's *Leviathan,* in which the sovereign's body is composed of his citizens. The image represents the unification of the commonwealth, and this unification is independent of the face or identity of the sovereign (fig. 5.1). Similarly, the identity of any individual citizen fades in comparison to their identification in the national body. As Guerriero's chronicle demonstrates, the families' belief that their deceased belong to this sovereign body coexists with, and often comes into conflict with, the more recent definitions of the person under the framework of human rights. One of the major points of contention in the repatriation debate involved how to refer to the soldiers. On their headstones they are identified as *soldado argentino sólo conocido por Dios* (Argentine soldier known only to God), but during repatriation they were

142

referred to as NN, *ningún nombre* (no name), resonant with how human rights activists referred to the disappeared during the dictatorship. As a result, families' decisions to support identification of the bodies would mean identifying their war dead with those that disappeared during the dictatorship, a political misalignment for more conservative families. In order to dissuade families from participating, opponents circulated a rumor that the only reason to identify the bodies was to relocate the remains to the continent. The conflict brewed into a perfect storm in which the spiritual dimension named by God in the headstone, the sovereign sense of the cemetery as national outpost, and the personal dimensions of biography and kinship came to form a hopeless knot around the remains of the fallen at Darwin. Ultimately, as Guerriero chronicles, the bodies in the cemetery were identified by a team of forensic scientists and reinterred as promised.

The conflict over the unidentified bodies in Darwin is by no means isolated. Spiritual, legal, and biological personhood continues to animate the legacy of Malvinas in the twenty-first century, and their conjunction in the figure of the "person" sits at the fraught center. As Roberto Esposito writes in *Third Person*:

> The new semantic epicenter, shifting away from the revolutionary emphasis on citizenship, is the unconditional demand for the dignity and worth of the human person. The reason for this substitution lies partly in the need to remove rights from the necessarily restricted limits of the nation; but the substitution also reflects the peculiar ability of the term 'person' to summarize, in a single word, elements and echoes deriving both from the culture of the Enlightenment and from theological language. One would be hard put to come up with a concept in the corpus of the Western tradition that has an equally dual character, simultaneously secular and religious. (70)

In both the film *Iluminados por el fuego* and the chronicle *La otra guerra*, Malvinas is trapped between static ideas of sovereignty and mutable ideas of personhood, between the reason for the war and its tragic aftermath. The film relies on rapid shifts from one to another, from the language of human rights to a static affirmation of sovereignty without calling attention to the swift transition. In this way, the film enacts a rhetorical metastasis that Guerriero points out is not quite so simple in lived experience. Mourners cling to the past and anchor themselves in sovereignty even as they acknowledge that political conditions have changed. As a result, Malvinas continues to anchor conflicting demands in Argentina.

5.2. An actor wearing a mask of Margaret Thatcher in front of the Union flag in *Minefield/Campo minado*. © Eugenia Kais

5.3. An actor wearing a mask of Leopoldo Galtieri in front of the Argentine flag in *Minefield/Campo minado*. © Eugenia Kais

MASKING AND SUPERFICIAL VIOLENCE

The 2016 play *Minefield/Campo minado*, directed by Arias, shows the Hobbesian sovereign mask coming apart. The play is an amalgamation of testimonies from six war veterans, three from each side.[12] In one scene, two of the actors wear masks, one of British prime minister Margaret Thatcher and one of Argentine de facto president Leopoldo Galtieri. The leaders sit on opposite sides of the stage in front of a flag, miming to nationally broadcast messages while archival recordings play for the audience (figs. 5.2 and 5.3). Arias invokes the Hobbesian trope of the sovereign face encapsulating the citizens, since an Argentine wears the Galtieri mask and a Brit the Thatcher mask. These masked actors portray sovereignty as a political force grafted onto citizens' bodies.

Yet Arias also distances the actors from the Hobbesian mask of sovereignty. After all, neither of the leaders is sovereign in the traditional sense. The British sovereign, Queen Elizabeth II, only appears through her elected emissary, Thatcher. The Argentine government lacked any claim to legitimacy, having come to power in a brutal coup and ruling by force. In Arias's staging, the masks do not sit flush with the actors' faces. As a result of this slight distance, the eye holes cut in each mask appear to be empty sockets, and the leader seems blind. This depthless gaze indicates a lack of vision, both literal and metaphorical, drawing the audience's attention to faces that, uncannily, fail to move even though their words can be heard. The distance between the actor's face and his mask is obvious, even though the audience is encouraged to bridge the gap by relying on archival audio and gestures. This gap between mask and face reveals that the quick and easy unification both sides achieved in 1982 has come apart in the twenty-first century. In spite of efforts to recover traditional sovereignty, the mask has delaminated from the face, and there is a vacancy underneath.

Arias indicates that, under contemporary geopolitical conditions, the fusion of leader with people is nothing more than a performance. Latex masks dramatize this thin, performative edge of power. Classically, the idea that the sovereign's face synthesizes the people depends on a cycle in which civil war gives way to the fusion of people with king, as Giorgio Agamben describes in his book on *stasis*. This unity then dissolves, leading back to civil war, and the cycle repeats (Agamben 46). In Arias's play, however, the cycle has come undone. When one of the actors, Lou, holds the Thatcher mask off to one side, it appears as though the prime minister has been decapitated, her head emptied and deformed (fig. 5.4). The scene evokes a bloodless revolution, which would have

145

5.4. British actor and veteran Lou with an empty Thatcher mask in *Minefield/ Campo minado*. Photograph by Tristram Kenton

been impossible at the time of the war with its galvanized nationalism. The temporal gap between the Falklands/Malvinas War and the performance has made the mask just a mask, no longer an emblem of unity nor part of a cycle of civil war and reunification. The war is now a spectacle displaced in space and time, and sovereignty is as blind and brainless as the misshapen mask.[13]

The traditional fusion of the sovereign mask weds the political with the theatrical tradition through the Latin *persona* and *dramatis personae*.

As Esposito points out: "Originally understood as a stage garment or theatrical costume, *persona* also began to designate the individual who wore it. The character played by the actor constituted the intermediate segment between the two meanings: it was through the interpretation of a role, by molding an individual, that, little by little, the mask was imprinted on the face of the wearer, until they corresponded in every detail" (74). The costume fuses with the actor until they are perceived as a single being, merging in the character. The masked persona obscures the difference between the actor's body and the character portrayed. As Esposito writes, drawing on Siegmund Schlossmann, "Person corresponds . . . to the irreducible difference that separates the living being from itself" (76). Person names the performative edge of being. Mezzadra and Neilson point to a similar fusion when Marx uses the term *Charaktermaske* to describe the relationship between "the owner of money and the possessor of labor power" (260) as persons in economic relation to one another. They are defined by the roles they play rather than any inherent identity.

Arias's innovation in *Minefield/Campo minado* is to foreground the use of persona and relationality over identity.[14] Throughout the play, the six veterans recount their stories using a variety of materials like photos, models, and other memorabilia to recreate war stories for the audience. These materials, some of which the actors had kept since 1982 and some of which were added for the play, supplement the testimonial accounts delivered directly to the audience. Staging these six separate accounts together shifts the roles of witnessing and testimony as Arias emphasizes that the actors play characters, even when portraying themselves in the past. As Jan Mieszkowski writes in *Watching War*, "At best, firsthand witness is incomplete and must be supplemented by some sort of inventive reconstruction or projection. At worst, seeing something in person . . . becomes a challenge to the claim that anything happened at all" (69). For Mieszkowski, image and imagination play a key role in witnessing. Likewise, the actors communicate with the audience through images and by invoking the imagination. Sometimes the audience hears emotional first-hand testimonial accounts of battle or sees written letters that have been preserved for decades. Other times the audience bears witness to scenes that seem, at best, tangentially connected to the war, such as an Argentine Beatles tribute band. In disrupting the expectation of a first-hand testimonial catharsis, an expectation fulfilled in the film *Iluminados por el fuego*, Arias shows that witnessing is only ever partial. It is enmeshed in other systems of meaning and performance. Masks, videos, photographs, newspapers, and news reels supplement the spectacle of war, but like the theatrical persona, they are only ever a supplement that feeds the audience's imagination of a character. As the latex mask and theatrical persona come apart, the spectacle of sovereign violence is rounded out with this imagination, filling gaps where the mask delaminates from the face, where sovereignty and identity come unbound.

Arias cultivates her exploration of persona through the set's surfaces. Even in scenes in which the actors do not use masks, she lingers on their faces using live video feeds. The images of the actors' faces are then projected, larger-than-life, onto the surface of a blank screen in the background. The audience sees the actors' faces as well as two-dimensional, enlarged projections, making the surface of the set into another type of flattened mask. The actors recount their own experiences, but their aged faces contrast to the pictures and videos of themselves as younger men. Their faces have been masked by time. As a result, even when the actors are portraying themselves in the past, Arias's use of video evokes a subtle theatrical masking. The flat screen on the set is described in the Spanish script as "un sinfín blanco en medio del escenario" (Arias 1; a white infinity/endlessness in the middle of the stage).[15] The *sinfín*, in turn, alludes to famous Austrian-American architect and theater designer Frederick Kiesler's conception of an "endless theatre" of curved and continuous space, enveloping the spectator in the happening (Philips 29–38). The war, of course, was this fully immersive and seemingly endless experience: the theater of war. On Arias's set, the blank space is where actors project photos, maps, diaries, and toy soldiers. The potential uses of the sinfín seem, fittingly, endless. Although the stories and objects the actors use to talk about the war allow them to rehearse, sometimes vehemently, their arguments about the sovereignty of the islands, the actors cannot make a sovereignty claim on the shared and blank territory of the sinfín; it is spatially and temporally unbound.

Throughout the play, there is a marked contrast between the surface of the sinfín and an explosive minefield. Arias describes traumatic memories as a minefield, potentially explosive at any moment (Gardner). Yet the boundless space of the sinfín empties that minefield. It is inert. Argentine veterans cannot form an attachment to the ground, even though they sing the famous "Marcha de las Malvinas," the chorus of which runs: "¡Ningún suelo más querido / de la patria en la extensión!" (No ground more beloved / in the whole of the country!). This ground, or *suelo*, is blank. Clare Finburgh's analysis of *Minefield/Campo minado* foregrounds this difference between surface and depth. Finburgh draws on Jean-Luc Nancy's essay "Image and Violence," which distinguishes two types of violence: one that seeks to uncover truth and one that does

5.5. Argentine actor and veteran Marcelo and British actor and veteran David in a staged therapy session in *Minefield/Campo minado*. Photograph by Tristram Kenton

not. The first is metaphysical violence that attempts to secure a ground. While Nancy focuses on images rather than wars and war reenactment, the 1982 war certainly enacted this type of violence. Nancy describes the other type of violence as an external force that intervenes in a system, deforming it. This type of violence, which Nancy calls "violence without violence" ("Image and Violence" 26), does not seek to reveal a truth or secure a ground. It is groundless, bottomless, and unfathomable: *sans-fond* (26). It forms the basis of many images, or what Nancy, quoting Borges, calls the "aesthetic fact" of an imminent revelation that does not take place (26). For Finburgh, Arias's play represents this type of aesthetic violence. Taking Finburgh's analysis a step further, the violence in *Minefield/Campo minado* is sans-fond and takes place temporally on the sinfin. The set of *Minefield/Campo minado* places war in a bottomless, endless space–time. Even though the actors rehearse their conflicting arguments about the islands, there is nowhere to anchor sovereignty claims on the set.

Arias uses the set as another type of mask when she stages a brief therapy session in which David, a British veteran and psychotherapist who works with veterans and their families, talks to Argentine veteran Marcelo about the war and its aftermath. As they talk, cameras project the men's faces onto the sinfín, creating a visual representation of the psychic scars that loom larger than their bodies (fig. 5.5). Here, the set enacts psychological projection and therapeutic transference. Yet in contrast to post-traumatic subjectivity isolated in an individual psyche (Berlant), the mise-en-scène connects the men in a therapeutic setting. Their dialogue is triangulated in video projection, distancing each man from himself and from his past. The set thus empties memory of its explosive power, replacing it with distance and passivity. Arias disarms her own minefield of memory as actors and audience encounter a conflict that never explodes. Additional layers of each actor-veteran's many personae open up through masking and surfacing, and the war becomes gradually neutralized. As a result of the delaminated masks and theatrical sinfín, Arias's play opens the gap between surface and depth, story and persona, image and violence. She distances the actors from the single testimonial truth that proved so evocative in the film *Iluminados por el fuego*, instead using the mask and projection to cultivate distance from testimonial and teleological modes of memory. The Falklands/Malvinas War moves into the impersonal interval between face and mask in Arias's globalized spectacle.

THIRD PERSON, THIRD LANGUAGE

These narrow spaces between face and mask, screen and image form thin borders that neutralize rather than enflame conflict. In these liminal spaces, Arias represents the impersonal interval between actor and character in plain sight. At the same time, the dramatic chorus traditionally represents a third-person presence on stage, as in Greek tragedy, in which the chorus establishes and frames the course of events, observing and commenting on them but never intervening. During the stasimon, the chorus sings in place, introducing motifs resonant with the main conflict while the actors are off stage. As Dimitris Vardoulakis describes in an analysis of *Antigone*, the chorus frames the political upheaval of *stasis* in their stasimon (*Sovereignty* 63–68).[16] While Arias does not use a chorus, she introduces a technical feature that mediates between lines of dialogue: supertitles. These projected translations serve as an analogue of the chorus. Actors deliver lines in their native languages, even when speaking to someone who speaks the other language. Supertitles translate for the audience, making it clear that Arias endeavors to foster fluid communication. From the beginning of the play, actor-veteran Marcelo Vallejo says, in Spanish: "The Brits don't speak Spanish, we Argentines don't speak English. But somehow we understood each other." (Arias 1).[17] At times, conversation flows easily, for instance in a mock daytime talk show in which former enemies meet and reconcile in front of a studio audience piped in through canned sound effects (30–33). This banal, made-for-TV moment offers a false panacea for war wounds. Other times, however, communication is difficult, as in a scene in which the actors scream over each other in a "history lesson" meant to settle the sovereignty dispute once and for all (61–64). Throughout the performance, supertitles propose to reach monolingual Spanish- and English-speaking audiences so that the audience does not miss a single line of dialogue. As the production traveled to different countries, the supertitles also contributed to its global translatability.

Arias's supertitles establish that, although the 1982 war was a liminal historical event, it can be translated onto the global stage. In this sense, Finburgh suggests that Arias solidifies "visual-culture theorist Nicholas Mirzoeff's claim that two of the most urgent issues to emerge since the start of the new millennium are the globalization of war and the globalization of spectacle" (164). In *Minefield/Campo minado*, translation brings a peripheral conflict to a global audience. As Arias presents contested borders on the set, translation articulates local with global, past with present. Translation also forms a core part of the concluding chapters of *Border as Method*. Mezzadra and Neilson argue that linguistic border crossing articulates inclusion and exclusion, playing a critical role in increasingly frequent contemporary border crossings. They even go so far as to "argue that in this context translation can play a key role in the invention of new forms of organization and new social institutions" (21). They draw on Naoki Sakai, who "locates translation in the very center of the semantic field of the border, arguing that it serves as both a bridging and a separating device between languages, cultures, and indeed subjectivities" (Mezzadra and Neilson 272). In mixing languages in *Minefield/Campo minado*, Arias tests this theory.

Although most of the play is easily translatable between Spanish and English, actor-veteran Sukrim, a Nepali Gurkha who fought for Britain, complicates matters. He occasionally speaks or sings in Nepali, which Arias leaves untranslated in the supertitles. In the written edition of the play, his untranslated dialogue and song lyrics are only referenced as "Sukrim sings a Nepali song and then exits" (Arias 33). But the lyrics are not written out in the original Nepali in the published script. In line with the play's bilingual title, the script was published in a bilingual edition, split down the middle, half in English and half in Spanish in a north–south orientation. By rotating the book, both versions open on the right-hand side presenting a monolingual text, in turn mimicking the north–south geopolitical tensions on display in the play's movement from London to Buenos Aires. However, the written text does not code-switch as it does during the performance nor does it reproduce any Nepali. In spite of Arias's efforts at presenting fully transparent written and supertitled translation, Sukrim's words in Nepali never appear.

This unexpected third language and its purposeful nontranslation suggests that translation serves a role beyond communication, mediation, or border-crossing. As theater critic Jean Graham-Jones writes, "Despite, or perhaps because of, the production's commitment to spoken and supertitled bilinguality, its moments of untranslated performance are all the more striking" (125). Nepali interrupts a history assumed to be bilateral and static, complicating the conflict between Britain and Argentina by recalling another imperial history. Gurkhas like Sukrim have fought for Britain since colonial times. They were British subjects who, even though they helped build and preserve the empire, did not qualify for UK citizenship until 2006 (Arias 58). Gurkha history traverses the periods of empire, decolonization, and globalization. According to Graham-Jones: "Sukrim's physical presence and linguistic-cultural untranslatability disturb the Malvinas/Falklands binational archive" (127). At the same time, Arias perplexingly limits translation to major imperial languages, reinforcing the binational structure of the war.

From one perspective, Sukrim's Nepali emphasizes the incongruous and untranslatable elements of the 1982 war. Untranslated Nepali illustrates the persistence of colonial repression. The exclusion of Nepali from the performance's supertitles and published script reveals Nepali as untranslatable difference. In her analysis, Graham-Jones employs Aníbal Quijano's "coloniality of power" (Graham-Jones 127) to describe the Gurkhas' confinement to the edges of empire. Given that Sukrim acts on behalf of empire while speaking a nonimperial language, she asks whether untranslated Nepali reaffirms colonialism or disrupts it. She also raises the ethical question of whether nontranslation deprives him of agency, ultimately concluding, "Sukrim's untranslatability and his untranslatable alterity possess a political dimension that troubles any presumed lack of agency on his part" (127). For Graham-Jones, Nepali indexes Sukrim's status as an outsider. Sukrim may be crossing borders, but he is not translating them. Graham-Jones celebrates this nontranslation as an index of a subject shaped by empire but not beholden to it.

From another perspective, Nepali interrupts a monolithic understanding of sovereignty. Arias's use of three native languages creates a heterogenous community of actors. In Sakai's definition of heterolingual address, translation builds a community united in difference: "In a nonaggregate community, . . . we are together and can address ourselves as 'we' because we are distant from one another and because our togetherness is not grounded on any common homogeneity" (7). The actors in *Minefield/Campo minado*, likewise, are not grounded in homogeneity. In this sense, they form a heterolingual community, defining itself in the first-person plural "we," *through* and *in spite of* differences in language and identity. Mezzadra and Neilson theorize that capital prefers homolingual address that creates equivalence through the commodity form. Akin to smooth translation, homolingual address flattens difference. For Mezzadra and Neilson, Sakai's heterolingual address—a community defined by linguistic diversity—is critical for defying the pull of capitalism in contemporary border crossing: "Precisely in this grappling with borders, translation, in the political understanding of its heterolingual modality that we are proposing, always implies a transformation of subjectivity" (310). For them, crossing languages and borders constitutes subjectivity under globalization, adopting and radicalizing Sakai's idea: "Far from appealing to a sovereign machine of mediation or to a transcendental scheme, the workings of this kind of translation remain immanent to the constitution and proliferation of struggles" (310). As a result, untranslated Nepali has the potential to interrupt sovereignty claims, at least partially, by signaling another unacknowledged struggle. Sukrim's untranslated song and speech might be productively used as a test case questioning sovereign transcendence. In this sense, Sukrim helps depict what Mezzadra and Neilson call "border as method," whereby a community founded on difference produces a subjectivity capable of challenging contemporary financial globalization.

Both Graham-Jones and Mezzadra and Neilson celebrate nontranslation as a political tool that produces a resistant form of subjectivity. For Graham-Jones, Sukrim's Nepali challenges imperialism, while for Mezzadra and Neilson, linguistic diversity presents the potential for an alternative, collective political subject. Yet, in the life story Sukrim presents in the play, there is no resistance to imperialism. Instead, there is an embrace of its permutations over the course of decades. The audience learns that after the war, Sukrim traveled the world performing odd jobs, ranging from exercises with the US military to working for private security forces in Iraq and at a gold mine in Ghana (Arias 58). He also worked for the multinational security firm G4S, headquartered in London and subject to numerous investigations—not mentioned in the play—regarding migrant rights, labor, and the use of force in detention. He has been an agent of capitalist globalization in many different forms. Sukrim's peripatetic existence as a transnational employee of the military-industrial complex also stands in contrast to his preservation of Gurkha traditions—for instance, he speaks Nepali and performs the traditional *kukri* knife dance during the play. Sukrim's story is as polyvocal as he is. It traverses colonial and capitalist global violence, laying bare the continuity between imperial, national, and global forms of war and throwing into question the proposal of nontranslation as inherently productive of resistant subjectivity.

Sukrim's biography exposes the fact that a member of the border-crossing, heterolingual "we" can also function as a cog in the military-industrial machine. After all, translation and nontranslation can be a vehicle for warmongering, peacemaking, or border crossing and support assimilation, acculturation, hybridization, diversification, or exoticization. Translation or nontranslation cannot sustain a cultural politics alone. Taken in context, Sukrim's story disarticulates the connection between heterolingual address and the formation of a collective subject as Mezzadra and Neilson posit. Gurkhas did not emerge as subjects thanks to their heterolingual inclusion in a broader community but were repeatedly excluded. Gurkhas became UK citizens long after their work as foot soldiers of empire. That is, they became eligible for citizenship after the knot of territorial, linguistic, and racial formations had been at least partially unraveled in the fabric of the nation. Sukrim's eligibility for citizenship, in turn, facilitated his work as a deterritorialized soldier of global capital rather than a resistant global subject.

Globalization diminished the legal importance of national frameworks as *person* took the place of *citizen*. As Esposito writes, the term *person* served as a point of confluence between philosophy, theology, law, and bioethics: "Because of its universal applicability, personhood is seen as the only semantic field that can possibly overlap the two spheres of law and humanity, separated as they are by the national ideology of citizenship. This means that a concept like that of human rights is only conceivable and viable through the lexicon of personhood" (3). The 1948 Universal Declaration of Human Rights established the primacy of personhood; yet, as Esposito remarks, the declaration has not cut down on victims of violence, plague, and famine. Nor have appeals to human rights put a stop to the growth of the security industry that is increasingly taking the place of national militaries. Esposito goes as far as to argue that "the essential failure of human rights, their inability to restore the broken connection between rights and life, does not take place in spite of the affirmation of the ideology of the person but rather *because* of it" (5). Personhood is an essentially weak point of convergence between biological, legal, and spiritual dimensions of the individual. And in *Minefield/*

Campo minado, identifications forged in personhood or resistant, untranslated essence obscure a more sinister dynamic: the symbiotic coexistence of human rights discourse with the military-industrial complex. In this way, *Minefield/Campo minado* challenges Mezzadra and Neilson's view of translation, offering a darker picture of border-crossing and subject formation under globalization.

In short, if Mezzadra and Neilson advocate a third-language, first-person model in the heterolingual "we," *Minefield/Campo minado* proposes a third-language, third-person model. Instead of linguistic difference blending into coherent subjectivity, the play shows a third language that does not become part of any collective. Sukrim's untranslated Nepali resembles a chorus's version of the third-person presence on stage. Yet this third person is not a person at all, merely indexing something beyond first and second persons. As Esposito writes of Maurice Blanchot: "The third person is not actually another person—with respect to the first and second—but rather something that extends out of the logic of the person, in favor of a different regime of meaning. When Maurice Blanchot identifies the third person with the enigmatic figure of the neuter, or neutral, he is seeking to remove it, preventively, from any undue personalization. The neuter is not another person to be added to the first two, but rather what is *neither* one *nor* the other and what defies all dichotomies founded on, or presupposed by, the language of the person" (16). The third person resembles the neuter, a figure that does not index the biological-legal being known as the person. Likewise, Sukrim's Nepali functions as a third person, evoking presence and absence, signification and nonsignification simultaneously. It is not a person but rather a neutral point of reference like the sinfín. Like a chorus invoking forces that influence the action yet do not participate in it, Sukrim's Nepali represents something beyond the war that nevertheless frames it. It indexes imperialism even as globalization has undermined the rigidity and centrality of the border, changing border-crossing, sovereignty, citizenship, and rights. This change raises questions about structures of representation, literary and cultural, linguistic and legal. It also requires us to reconsider the role that conflict plays in democracy, a question Arias continues investigating in the film adaptation of the play. As sovereignty undergoes metastasis, border conflicts become progressively removed from identity and subjectivity.

THIRD-PERSON SPECTACLE

Arias's film *Theatre of War/Teatro de guerra* radicalizes and further depersonalizes the war stories from *Minefield/Campo minado*. If in *Minefield/*

Campo minado Arias depicted the delamination of mask from face, emphasizing third-person and impersonal elements over first-person testimony, in *Theatre of War/Teatro de guerra*, she further separates persona from person. As the material undergoes its own formal change—its own metastasis—Arias emphasizes war as both drama and entertainment. Although she continues to follow the same actor-veterans playing themselves, she alters the narrative structure to repeat a single anecdote several times. While episodic conflicts were central in the play, now the conflict is circular. There is no progress, merely different versions of the same story. She changes the narrative structure and medium, exploring a final release to a third-person spectacle to round out her Malvinas cycle.

The repeated story is simple. As he was clearing the battlefield, British actor and veteran Lou remembers coming across a severely wounded Argentine soldier who started speaking to him in English. The man recounted a trip to Oxford before dying in Lou's arms. The story, which is told only once in the play, appears four times in the film: beginning and end, as well as twice in the middle. In contrast to Sukrim's untranslated Nepali, Lou's enemy uses a common language to communicate with his captor. This common language provided the men an instant connection that made the young Argentine's death more painful. Lou says that he wishes the man hadn't spoken English. In repeating an incident that hinges on the pain of clear communication in the film adaptation, Arias seems to be retreating from her exploration of linguistic difference in the play. As a result, while Sukrim seems to index exclusion from imperial Europe, Lou seems to reveal a desire to reinforce linguistic difference, to not speak the same language as one's enemy. Yet both use language to index absence. Sukrim shows the erasure of Gurkha tradition while Lou shows death as irreparable loss, even of his enemy.

The film opens with the first version of Lou's story before the audience even understands what is happening. Lou recounts the experience by enlisting the others to reenact the young man's death. Lou then tells the story four times, clarifying that he has different reactions—enacts different personae—each time. The story has now been reduced to a series of spectacles, sometimes simple recounting, sometimes more technically sophisticated. With each repetition, Lou's story shifts shape even though the events narrated change very little. At times, the story is central, and Lou explains that remembering the incident is not always painful or emotional but more like storytelling (*Theatre of War/Teatro de guerra* 00:54:00). Other times, Arias enlists other actors to retell the story, rehearsing and recreating the action, sometimes in minute detail. The third time Lou tells the story during the film, Arias creates a disconnect between the actor and himself. In this scene, Lou is alone, speaking directly to the camera. He neither reenacts what happened nor directs others to do so. After a while, his lips stop moving but his voice can still be heard (00:52:28). The audience's confusion lasts a moment before Arias cuts to old footage of a much younger Lou telling the same story on camera. The audience realizes that he had been lip syncing to old audio. The older Lou then explains that he had been filmed telling the story for a 1984 documentary. He felt ashamed for crying on television, especially for an enemy. He explains: "An actor would be proud of being able to cry in front of the camera, but I was a Royal Marine. And for the last thirty years I've felt guilty for grieving for a dead Argentine instead of one of our own. I've been worried that my lads would be ashamed of me. That's why I've not been to any reunions" (00:53:37–00:53:51). Arias creates distance between Lou and himself as he recounts his shame. By combining the younger Lou's voice with the older Lou's face, she interrupts his self-identity before finally making the older Lou's face and voice coincide. His shame, in turn, inhabits the interval between one recording and the other, after weeping for the enemy and before finally admitting his embarrassment publicly.

In Lou's story, as in all war stories, the witness's authority cannot be absolute. Indeed, by staging and restaging the same scene, Arias brings into question not only witnessing and memory but also directing. After all, she controls the actors' stories and movements as well as what footage makes the final cut. She shapes the form around the content, yet there would be no content without their experience. Like commanding officers in 1982, Arias manipulates the men, who then become like toy soldiers, and under her direction, the actor-veterans create the theater of war. The film takes the critique of direction more seriously than the play. In one scene, the actors sit in a bar, divided by nationality. The two English men complain that they are constantly told what to do during rehearsals, remarking that they are former Royal Marines, not professional actors (00:40:52–00:42:23). They complain that the whole production is fundamentally biased toward the Argentines. The camera then moves to the three Argentine men, drinking together and commenting on their irritations and annoyances with the Brits. The scene airs pent-up resentment on both sides, foregrounding grievances rather than the reconciliation the play tended toward. The actors retreat to their factions while Arias appears to chastise herself in front of her audience for her overbearing direction, perhaps even for placing her name as director and author over the stories of the veterans. She indicates that the director's authority, like the witness's, is not absolute. Much more than in *Minefield/Campo minado*, she cedes her authority to the men, who stage their own partial and supplemented Falklands/Malvinas spectacle.

Once the space between actor and director, narrative content and form, has been wedged open, the war stories appear more obviously as spectacle. They have clearly been staged for an audience, even in this film version.[18] The film develops a technique from the play in which testimonial anecdotes are recounted using toy soldiers. In one scene, the toys move around a basic papier-mâché set as Gabriel recounts an expedition across a minefield to get supplies. The miniatures capture the optics of war-made-play and war-made-spectacle, reflecting the violence of childhood play. The actors' manipulation of the toys on camera likewise conveys the power hierarchy at work. As the actor-veterans move the toys around the set, they assume the role of officers moving soldiers around the battlefield. At the same time, the toy soldiers represent the becoming-thing of the soldiers, especially Argentine conscripts treated like cannon fodder. The spectacle of soldiers that can be moved, manipulated, and destroyed lays bare their replaceability, replicating the power dynamics inherent in the theaters of war and drama.

Toward the end of the film, Lou tells his story one last time. In preparation, the actor-veterans from the original cast share memories with a younger group of actors. These Argentine actors, in turn, use the information to get into character in order to assume the role of the older ex-combatants. At times, the conversations are tense, and some of the younger Argentines' questions seem to irritate the older British men. Lou even admits that he's not sure about the young man taking his role. This time, as the reenactment of Lou's story unfolds, the original actor-veterans are retired to the role of spectators as, one by one, they are replaced on the staged battlefield. This incremental replacement creates distance from the firsthand memories that served as the bedrock of the play and film. The experience is transferred to an actor with no personal experience of the war. At last, it is depersonalized.

In preparation for this moment, the original cast directs. Lou, for instance, explains to the makeup artist what the dying soldier's wounds looked like. Instead of focusing on the wounds, however, the camera stays on Lou's face and leaves the younger man's face out of focus (01:12:38). This cinematographic choice plays with the audience's gaze, blending directorial and observational roles (fig. 5.6). From witnesses to directors, the actor-veterans of Arias's original cast finally become mere observers of the theater of war, spectators, third persons, outside the action. While they cannot stop watching their past play out again and again, they become increasingly distanced from the experience. The

5.8. British actor and veteran Lou behind the Argentine actor who will portray his enemy in a reenactment in *Theatre of War/Teatro de guerra*. © Gema Films SRL

more often they reach back for these memories or try to master them, the more the memories recede into a spectacle. They become merely a persona on display.

In *Theatre of War/Teatro de guerra*, Arias progressively decenters the person. From witness to director to observer, the stories that created the script of *Minefield/Campo minado* are gradually separated from the veterans. Arias withdraws as director, creating space for the actors to become directors. As a result, she opens the impersonal interval between the actor and his own experience. Her withdrawal from a position of authority leads to the actors' replacement by other actors. In this final staging of depersonalization, the Falklands/Malvinas experience becomes mere spectacle. This supplemented spectacle gestures toward the incremental separation—taking leave of narrative and person—that has taken place through Arias's series on the Falkland/Malvinas Islands, moving away from subjectivity and indexing the third person.

The theater of war is by no means incidental to the negotiation of the personal and personhood at global borders. Under globalization, border conflict—stasis rather than *polemos*—multiplies and takes different forms. As a result, the question of the enemy necessarily shifts. The enemy is no longer even necessarily a person. Conflict does not rely on a subject or identity. Instead, Arias suggests that in releasing such attachments, the nature of representation and spectacle changes. Likewise, in analyzing a stasimon from *Antigone*, Vardoulakis points out that the chorus uses the word *metastasis* to describe a change of circumstance. Changing winds are used as a metaphor for changing one's mind, a readjustment of conflict (*Sovereignty* 67). The chorus describes the change but never intervenes. Like Arias's actor-veterans when they finally retire to their places as spectators, the chorus indexes a presence with no place in the action. Opening a third-person perspective creates the possibility of changing one's mind. For Vardoulakis, such a change, such a metastasis, makes democracy possible: "This democratic conflict is the condition of the possibility of the political and hence of sovereignty. It is a conflict that has to be continuously enacted for the political to exist" (*Sovereignty* 68). As a result, metastasis conditions the political. Rather than deciding who is a friend or an enemy, as Carl Schmitt would, Arias asks that, within the impersonal, metastatic displacements of globalization, we consider releasing past stories and identities and changing our minds.

TRANSHISTORICAL AND TRANSNATIONAL SURFACING

Arias's theater of war becomes Pron's theater of the absurd in *Nosotros caminamos en sueños*. The novel uproots the Falklands/Malvinas conflict completely and makes it a joke. If for Arias the metastatic change of "position, state, or form" was part of the artistic evolution of her work from play to film, for Pron there is a literal change of position. According to the commanding officers in *Nosotros caminamos en sueños*, the location of the islands is a military secret. Their subordinates are largely apathetic about the war effort, and there is no obvious enemy. The soldiers move quickly from one site to another, sometimes defying the laws of physics, and they struggle to distinguish themselves from their enemies. And no wonder; the soldiers come from different ethnic backgrounds and have little shared identity or reason to fight. For them, the war is an absurd combination of waiting around and navigating bureaucracy, sometimes surreal but most often mundane.

Much of the humor in *Nosotros caminamos en sueños* comes from the fact that the soldiers do not understand or abide by the traditional rules of engagement. One soldier, Sorgenfrei, keeps standing in the middle of the battlefield, considering himself immune to danger. Sorgenfrei, after all, is German for "carefree" or "worry free." He lacks the quality of *Sorge*—"care," "concern," and even "anxiety"—essential in Martin Heidegger's *Being and Time*. Pron's Sorgenfrei explains that the enemy does not know him personally and therefore could not bear him any ill will. When his comrades tell him to get down, Sorgenfrei says frankly, "They're not shooting at me. They're shooting at everybody" (13).[19] He refuses to accept that he belongs to one side or the other and so does not see himself as representative of a larger group or cause. He even refuses to include himself in the "everybody." In the words of one of his comrades, "He's such an idiot, he could even pass for a hero!" (13).[20]

For Sorgenfrei, the violence of war is fundamentally impersonal. Indeed, its impersonality—the fact that, as Nancy has it, this "other violence" affirms nothing, reveals nothing, unites no one, and can be attributed to no one in particular—marks Pron's contribution to the literature of warfare in the contemporary period. By introducing Sorgenfrei in the early pages of the novel as not belonging to any particular side, Pron acknowledges the breakdown of nation-state borders under globalization. The rules of engagement have changed, and violence has come unmoored from the nation-state. As such, Pron's characters have trouble defining the categories of first, second, and third persons. They often ask who the first-person plural "we" is: "'Who are we?' I asked again, and I had the impression that I'd spent the whole war asking myself the same question" (106).[21] Pron denotes the absurd inability to define a collective self against an enemy. He describes this as a critical omission by the higher-ups: "Look, the problem here is that we've turned our friend into an enemy, but we've forgotten to turn our enemy into a friend. . . . Or turn our enemy's friend into an enemy, or ask our enemy's friend to say that he's our friend" (73).[22] The army has failed to organize groups into their usual configurations, and as a result, it is fighting without a clear picture of why or against whom. There is a total disarticulation of the first-person plural "we."

In another scene, the men try to distinguish the third-person plural *ustedes* from *nosotros*: "'Excuse me, sir, but who are we?' asked Whitelocke taking a step forward. 'I mean, are you talking about all of you [*ustedes*] or us [*nosotros*]?' Whitelocke insisted. 'All of you who? [*¿Qué ustedes?*]' asked the Colonel. 'Us who? [*¿Qué nosotros?*]' replied Whitelocke. 'Just forget about it,' sighed the Colonel Major. 'Forget who? You all or us? [*¿A ustedes o a nosotros?*]' asked Sorgenfrei" (77).[23] Throughout the novel, the soldiers try to find common traits or a shared cause, but they fail over and over again. In this way, Pron satirizes the grammatical structures of inclusion and exclusion, structures that are necessary for the nation-state to go to war. In the volley between *ustedes* and *nosotros*, Pron points out that armed conflict rests on the fusion of grammatical and political categories. Although in his introduction to the novel, Pron describes his inspiration as his childhood perception of the Malvinas War, what emerges is entirely displaced from any particular conflict or identity. The characters are a group of atomized, self-interested individuals—the neoliberal subject taken to an extreme. The group has become disarticulated and its cohesion fragmented. The plurality of a heterolingual "we," the condition of political subject formation in Mezzadra and Neilson, is gone. Likewise, Schmitt's definition of the political depends on the distinction between friend and enemy, implicitly dependent on a plurality of individuals forming groups. Both of those conditions have vanished. War is a bind not just between first and second persons but between first- and second-person *plurals*. This distinction separates war from the duel, but the characters' individualism keeps them from engaging in the state's pointless and disorganized campaign. Grammar is no longer an agglutinating force.

Once the group's cohesion has broken down, duels are all that is left. One soldier, O'Brien, wants to avenge his father's murder, which took place when O'Brien was only four years old. The murderer is an officer in the enemy army, possibly now a lieutenant colonel or colonel, called Graichen. O'Brien applies to the Office of Affronts and Questions of Honor to get permission to kill Graichen (Pron, *Nosotros caminamos en sueños* 86). The clerk takes O'Brien's information but explains that unfortunately someone else has already claimed the right to kill Graichen and offers two lieutenants in exchange (87). O'Brien refuses to accept because, naturally, a personal vendetta depends on the specific identities of those in question rather than their rough military equivalents. The clerk explains that O'Brien is getting a good deal because lieutenants are currently very highly valued, but, because O'Brien seems likable enough, the bureaucrat offers two lieutenants *and* a major. The negotiation reveals that army bureaucracy fails to understand the core of enmity. The clerk could have attempted to generalize O'Brien's animosity toward Graichen into broader accusations against the enemy. Instead, he tries to exchange them like cogs in a machine.

The clerk's misunderstanding is rooted in the belief that war obeys the logic of market forces. One official can be exchanged for another or others of roughly equivalent value. As the novel progresses, it becomes obvious that the bloated military-industrial complex is, in fact, responsible for numerous logistical challenges, surpluses, and shortages on the islands. In one passage, the reader learns that the government attempted to build a bridge to the islands but outsourced construction to a private company that would charge tolls. Mismanagement rendered the bridge completely dysfunctional (86). In some passages of the novel, officials buy, sell, and exchange soldiers. The narrator says he did not realize this was even possible, and he views it as suspiciously close to slavery (86). Exchanges are skewed and the troops are undersupplied because they have borrowed against the assets that would serve them best in combat, ending up with a surplus of lentils and a lack of anesthesia, for example (47–49). The military-industrial complex controls a flawed supply chain of off-kilter exchanges, existing in a purely hypothetical market that chases an ever-thinner profit margin rather than considering the necessities of combat.

Pron also shows how this new era of warfare builds on past forms of military engagement, so that, for instance, we see traditional forms of combat like trenches and tanks, grenades and tactical maps juxtaposed against more modern developments, such as a parody of Edward Snowden with his hand stuck in a grenade pin. Between the trench warfare of the First World War and the espionage of Wikileaks, Pron adds another ambiguous character: a sort of man-machine hybrid called el Tanquista. He is a space- and time-defying rebel who drives a hijacked tank around the islands sending messages to command about the war's progress. He seems to have been affiliated with the narrator's group at the initial disembarkation but has since gone rogue and now questions the validity of the war effort. El Tanquista resembles what Gilles Deleuze and Félix Guattari might call a war-machine-turned-nomad (419–21). He appears in different parts of the island, apparently simultaneously, but as an inveterate lone wolf, he refuses to associate himself with one side.[24] El Tanquista is a cyborg partisan, observing the war whose edges he skirts while sending back occasional communiqués, updating and satirizing tropes of war literature for the twenty-first century.

Toward the end of the novel, Pron finally comes back to the older forms of sovereignty and warfare associated with Malvinas. Still confused about who exactly the "nosotros" is, the narrator writes about his puzzling discovery that Argentines have started emerging from underground: "Sorgenfrei, Snowden, and the others were huddled around a hole from which Argentine soldiers kept coming up, surrendering as soon as they reached the surface. . . . They got all serious and insisted that the islands were Argentine, even though we hadn't seen a single Argentine there and we didn't have a clue if our enemy was Argentine or not: we were pretty sure that we weren't Argentine and that we had some right to the islands and we started asking ourselves if from that moment on we'd have to fight against two enemies instead of one" (*Nosotros caminamos en sueños* 114).[25] The Argentines begin surfacing to nominally lay claim to the islands, but they seem as foreign as everyone else. Their nationalism and sense of entitlement confuse Pron's characters, who do not understand group identities, their own or otherwise, as Pron takes aim at the now hackneyed "Las Malvinas son argentinas." While ground and depth are traditionally associated with ownership and legitimacy, in Pron's world they are meaningless. The metaphysical union of the nation-state form has been emptied out, becoming purely superficial. Contemporary sovereignty has nowhere to dig.

Like the surfaces that Arias employs in *Minefield/Campo minado*, Pron describes a topology that holds the soldiers together at a distance, with various ethnicities and nationalities sharing physical space but with no shared goals. The surface of the ground forms a point of assembly for dissimilar characters with the connection between them presupposed, yet often tenuous and easily disarticulated. On this surface, contemporary sovereignty comes to a limit characterized not by sovereignty but rather by the fragmentation and multiplication of bordering processes layered with bureaucratic priorities and responding to the transfer of matériel and personnel. These processes mostly take place in line with commodity flows yet have no pretension to depth or meaning. Pron's surface metastasis slips from site to site with the border following resources and exchanges. In the words of one official: "This isn't the bureaucratic army of your grandfather's days. This is a modern army that seeks to optimize its resources but avoids any kind of bureaucratic hurdle: we're a capitalist enterprise of massive extermination that cannot avoid the need to optimize its resources like any other business" (89).[26] The disintegration of group identification helps the army optimize flows, often in comically useless ways. Soldiers and nations—forms of identity-based subjectivity—are no longer important, replaced with profit and individuals who only encounter each other haphazardly and superficially.

The instruments of warfare also change. Pron, like Arias, moves toward impersonal destruction. The wholly inanimate presence of force appears in the figure of a bomb suspended over the battlefield for most of the novel. At first, the narrator is perplexed by it: "A bomb had been hanging over our heads and we had all been asking each other if that was normal in this war or new, unknown to those—like us—that had no previous experience with that type of thing" (23).[27] The bomb shows the ongoing potential for imminent and wholly impersonal destruction. Toward the end of the novel, the bomb starts swaying back and forth. The narrator remarks: "We all watched the bomb oscillate, expectant and convinced that this was the end, that it was time to say goodbye" (118).[28] He describes the bomb as "terrible and magnificent like the Voice of God or Judgment Day" (118).[29] But the bomb does not explode on impact. Instead, it bounces off the ground with a pathetic "Bop! Bop!" (118), crushing the character of the Teniente Perdido (Lost Lieutenant) before rolling off to one side. And yet the end—whether the narrator's death or the anticipated apocalyptic end of judgment day—does not arrive. The action continues, and the impersonal threat of violence again reveals nothing. The violence of war is just another event in a long string of absurdity. It is not teleological or metaphysical violence. Just after the fall of this terrible and magnificent bomb, the narrator writes that "time began to pass again, as if it had really stopped a moment ago" (119).[30] The suspension of time gives way to the course of battle as usual, a return to normal patterns of war and ultimately the revelation that, as Nancy writes, "there is nothing to reveal" ("Image and Violence" 26). For a moment, the battlefield had been configured around the impersonal weapon, but its excision from the agglutinating forces of identity makes it suddenly laughable.

Pron adds a final representation of the impersonal to his contemporary battlefield: an unidentified voice. The voice repeats the same phrase over and over again: "Stop stealing!" (*Nosotros caminamos en sueños* 13).[31] The phrase becomes a modern cry in the wilderness, attributed to no character in particular but rather the injunction of the battlefield. It serves as a counterweight to the officials' pursuit of resource optimization through bureaucracy and outright theft. As the novel progresses, it becomes more imploring: "Stop fucking stealing!" (95).[32] Not coincidentally, the command appears in the second-person informal singular. The voice speaks to a specific individual, even though it does not belong to any specific individual but represents a kind of late-capitalist plea with the forces of profit and expropriation. Evidently, faced with repeated disobedience, the still-unidentified voice gives up toward the end. The narrator describes himself ignoring the now feeble injunction: "I also paid no attention to the voice in the wilderness that cried, 'I'm tired of saying it now, so I won't anymore!'" (113).[33] Soon afterwards, the soldiers learn, via a message from el Tanquista, that they are attacking their own positions. The war effort has doubled back on itself, and the conflict is now the epitome of the absurd.

The novel's final pages depict the collapse of the categories of self and other, singular and plural. O'Brien, who had sworn to avenge his father's death by killing Graichen, dies before he can achieve his goal. His dying wish is that the narrator carry the burden of killing his father's murderer, but it seems as though the narrator has completely forgotten this feud. Toward the end of the novel, the narrator comes across a soldier who seems confused and hesitant to fight but happens to be his doppelgänger: "The soldier approached me as if to study me more closely and in that moment I noticed, and I think he did too, that there was a certain similarity between us: the same lock of hair that fell down our foreheads, a similar nose, the same eye color, similar scars on our cheeks and cheekbones from the cold, the same furrows and the same wrinkles that made us look alike" (119).[34] Looking at the enemy's face is like looking into a mirror. As the first- and second-person perspectives meld, self and other are intertwined, unable to differentiate themselves. In this final scene, they fuse in narcissism.

During the exchange, the narrator accepts an offer to drink from a hip flask before the other man extends a photograph toward him:

> Upon seeing the photo he handed to me, I wanted to show him that I too had a photo that I'd found in my uniform, show him that he and whoever had worn the uniform before me had loved the same woman, but reaching into my inside jacket pocket I only felt the butt of a pistol. So I took it out and shot the soldier twice in the face and he fell back; looking over his body and that face that didn't look like mine anymore I noticed that embroidered on his uniform was a name and that that name could still be read even though blood had started to spread all over his chest. I read 'Graichen' and I thought of O'Brien's request and I had the impression that everything was finally in order and fit into place. (120)[35]

Everything falls into place.[36] The vendetta has been settled; the war makes sense, at least to the narrator.

The reader, on the other hand, has some lingering questions: Did the narrator stumble upon Graichen purely by chance, or was he a hallucination? Is the narrator simply experiencing a prolonged episode of narcissism? Is Graichen's face no longer similar to the narrator's because of his injuries or because he had never really been the narrator's doppelgänger in the first place? Does he represent the self as enemy, or the zone of indistinction between friend and enemy? Is the narrator both O'Brien's friend and his long-lost enemy? Perhaps Pron is telling the reader that conflict is unnecessary; it is only between different sides of the self, the illusion of the self as a wholly coherent person. Perhaps Pron shows that the final battle is always a matter of chance. The enemy is whoever happens to be standing there rather than a defined person or group. The ambiguous ending of *Nosotros caminamos en sueños* collapses the boundaries between self and other, friend and enemy, reality and fantasy, first and second persons. Even the faintest illusion of true conflict—polemos—can no longer survive. Internal war—stasis—expands indefinitely as war proliferates out of bounds that are ever more superficial thanks to contemporary metastasis.

In Pron's final, obvious critique, feces bubble up from the surface of the ground with increasing frequency as the war draws to a close. Since the very beginning of the novel, the narrator had referred to the war itself as shit—"among all the shitty fucking things [*todas las putas mierdas*] in the world, this war was without a doubt the worst" (12)—and *Una puta mierda* had been Pron's title for the first version of the novel published in 2007.[37] The feces rising to the surface of the islands is an impersonal presence, just like the bomb and the voice in the wilderness. It is surreal and disgusting, a scatological reminder of the waste upon which societies found themselves. The shit on the surface is the only indication of someone passing through, as one man's dying cry is silenced by a sergeant and he complains, "But it's my only line!" (13).[38] Excrement obscures the soldiers on the islands as well as the ground and borders crossing it. The soldiers merely play a part. They understand that the rules of engagement are now mere performance rather than truth. The rules of engagement have changed. The military-industrial complex has transformed warfare in the present.

METASTATIC BORDERS

Since 2001, violence has metastasized, spreading into political, social, and cultural structures that are increasingly displaced from multiplying borders, increasingly individualized and yoked to the military-industrial complex. Although it may seem simpler to ignore these changes by clinging to past forms of sovereignty, as *Iluminados por el fuego* does, time only ever stops artificially. Establishing a sovereign border involves violence; specifically, the type of violating violence that, Nancy writes, seeks metaphysical truth over aesthetic revelation. Rather than engage in violating violence, Arias and Pron pick at the seams of fictive, anachronistic sovereignty, setting up revelations that never come to pass. The mask never fuses completely with an actor's face nor will a community's diversity map evenly onto its linguistic heterogeneity. Narratives that seek complexity beyond good and evil, conflict and reconciliation must be distanced, reshaped, and, in due time, released to third persons. For Pron, the absurd binds people together on the earth's surface while violence reveals nothing. Arias's and Pron's theatrical, cinematic, and fictional works enact iterative separations from the personal and toward the impersonal, acknowledging that borders are difficult to define and place in the present. These borders proliferate under globalization, whether on stages throughout the world, in airports or free-trade zones, at borders or on ships. The conflicts and contradictions inherent in modern metastatic borders indicate that the stasis of the past has become general.

The complete closure of the border was always a fiction, as in the Chaco, and now, at last, this closure has been exposed as impossible. The change in the shape of warfare has meant that the nation, already

weakened, no longer exerts the same force; the border no longer organizes violence as it once did. The clearly delimited territorial warfare of
1982 has given way to scattered and far-flung violence. These large-scale
changes after 2001 have had ambivalent effects in Argentina. On one
hand, the increasing emphasis on the person under the legal framework
of human rights has fueled lasting electoral democracy in Argentina and
helped veterans make justified demands for restitution. On the other
hand, these systems align with the individualistic tendencies of neoliberalism, increasingly beholden to the market rather than the social sphere.
While the grip of God and king has loosened in contemporary political
discourse, the new shape of sovereignty still comes from political theology. As Vardoulakis writes, "Globalization's justification and legitimacy
is accomplished through theological categories. The appeal to a univer-
salized individual whose *right* it is to act freely—indeed, as freed from the
hold of the state—is a reinscription of the religious sphere of the private
at the very core of the most emphatically, or presumptuously, secular"
("Stasis" 137). Recognizing vestiges of political theology prompts the
question of what might escape as borders undergo reconfiguration. The
stasis undergirding the political order is changing, metastasizing.

The changes since 2001 are at once terrifying and liberating. They
are terrifying because there is no narrative of cause and effect, no clearly
defined actors, and no clear code of right and wrong. The rules of engagement are unclear. Border conflicts continue to manifest the internal
tensions of stasis, such as those at the Mexico-US border, even as the
post-2001 world resembles a bizarre version of a Hobbesian war of all
against all, now with semiautonomous drones. The hallmark of contemporary political life is this imprecise and impersonal fear: an irruption of
violence aimed at no one in particular and everyone at the same time.
It is a miscalculation of enmity—Sorgenfrei's "They're not shooting at
me. They're shooting at everybody" (Pron, *Nosotros caminamos en sueños*
13)—on a grand scale. Yet the changes in the rules of engagement can
also be liberating. If violence is impersonal, then responses to it can be
impersonal too. If the territorial bounds of the nation have come undone, held together only on the surface, then there is no need to defend
codes of property and the proper nor narratives of progress that sediment
and obscure violence.

The readjustment of conflict—metastasis—offers another approach
to the political not defined by a decision on enmity. Instead, the condition of the political is the ability to change one's mind about the enemy
and the friend or even to withdraw from this structure and cultivate
third-person forms of engagement. Previous chapters have proposed that

stasis defines Latin American border conflicts. I have argued that since borders are constitutively mutable and permeable, this has always been the case. But it has become more visible over time through different instantiations and configurations of border conflict. Now, as the stasis visible at the edges of political groupings becomes generalized, it becomes possible to take distance from the conflict and change one's mind. It is possible to shift with the conflict or, to use a metaphor from *Antigone*, to adjust the sails to changing winds. In this sense, metastasis is "the condition of the possibility of the political" (Vardoulakis, *Sovereignty* 68). Under contemporary metastasis, political and cultural life, increasingly unmoored from the sovereign state, might become something altogether different. Metastasis suggests that conflict need not be rigid: "The prefix [*meta*] gives rise to the image of moving along, not remaining static in the inflexible intransigence that characterized the sovereign logic or the antidemocratic impulse. . . . Metastasis indicates an adjustment of the metaphorics of the invincible attitude in conflict" (Vardoulakis, *Sovereignty* 67). As the winds of globalization shift, contemporary borders become more diffuse. Border as stasis fractures and multiplies as border becomes metastasis.

CONCLUSION

BORDERLESS TEXTS, BORDERLESS POLITICS

The Other Border Wars has argued that border war can be seen as stasis rather than *polemos*. This is at once a theoretical and historical proposal. Borders purportedly enclosed independent Latin American nations, even besieging the idea of the nation. In reality, the border has never been closed, as chapters 1 and 2 reveal in the embodied and later cannibal nation-state. It has never been disconnected from domestic conflict and the exclusion of the *demos*, as chapter 3 shows. It has never been a site of static political conflict but rather been subject to ecstatic and meta-static displacements in time and space, as seen in chapters 4 and 5. These theoretical arguments challenge traditional concepts of sovereignty and bordering, foregrounding stasis. While similar ideas might be applied to a variety of border conflicts worldwide, the evolution of this structure of bordering becomes apparent in the Latin American context of European imperialism and US neo-imperialism. Through Latin America's border wars, it becomes clear that the border is not the key organizing force in cultural and political life that it purports to be in regionalist, nationalist, and identitarian formations.

At the same time, the idea of border war as stasis would not be possible without the cultural texts that have been analyzed here, interpellated as political and theoretical texts in their own right that speak to the fantasies and realities of borders. Latin American borders come into stark relief in literature and film about conflict, revealing both the border's haphazard construction and its life-or-death importance. The paradoxical tensions that meet at the border emerge forcefully in the 1930s, as soldiers in the Chaco rehearsed conquest-era myths and legal claims that sought to cover the region's immensity. Euro-American legal and philosophical systems of enclosure left a vacancy at the heart of the South American continent, leading to an unfounded belief in a firm border in the Chaco. After the war, border closure was exposed as nothing more than a useful fiction. The incomplete national hypostasis visible in the Chaco reveals how Latin American nations only partially fit into European political theological models of sovereignty. The decades after the war heightened the sense of a state of siege in landlocked Bolivia and Paraguay. The siege, foreshadowed in the Battle of Boquerón, has continued figuratively into the present in ongoing consumption of resources and questions of status, encouraging political and aesthetic programs based on manifestos but foreclosing a more open and less programmatic relationship to the future.

In 1969, demographic crisis and a porous border revealed that the Cold War push for Central American economic integration, backed by the United States, was undercut by stasis, even among politically aligned, right-wing governments. The Soccer War presents a stasis that, far from stagnant, involved perpetual movement as undocumented migrants and squatters crossed borders unannounced, redistributing conflict, propriety, and property. After the war, the cleared border zones between El Salvador and Honduras inadvertently created a training ground for guerilla fighters, ultimately contributing to the continuation of this short war into the dozen years of civil war in El Salvador. Honduran domestic conflict fed an international conflict, which led back to a Salvadoran domestic conflict. Ongoing internecine conflict, rooted in US-backed policies, has contributed to migration and capital flight to the Global North, causing tensions at Mexico's southern and northern borders in the twenty-first century. In the process, the demos in demography has been eclipsed. Demography is now little more than a number used for migration quotas. The expansive sense that Roque Dalton lent to the term has been lost in favor of simple counting.

In 1982, Argentina's invasion of the Falkland/Malvinas Islands shifted attention from the internal Dirty War to an external "clean" one.

Decrying British imperial presence, the Argentine state clung to Spanish territorial divisions and, after defeat, continued to claim the islands. As a result of the war, the 1994 Argentine constitution claims sovereignty over a territory it does not control in practice. Legally, the state stands outside of itself in an ecstasis, and ex-combatants symbolically reconfigure the war as existential ecstasy. Against the neoliberal model of a democracy of shareholders, this type of ecstasy acknowledges the islands not as a territory to reclaim but as the absence that binds dictatorship to electoral democracy. After 2001, sovereignty—and borders as spatial limits of sovereignty—became increasingly fraught. In line with this change, contemporary approaches to the Falklands/Malvinas unmask the sovereign as a forceful fiction by depicting the impersonal interval between mask and face. Testimonial truth and group identification fade as borders metastasize, and the impersonal and absurd take their place. Momentary disruptions of political theology provide a glimpse of a future in which, outside of the military-industrial complex, another perspective is possible.

Each of the border wars examined here emerges from particular internal and external tensions. Yet, as the film *Mi mejor enemigo* cited in the introduction recalls, the border is nothing more than a convenient way to organize space and time. It serves as a matrix that classifies bodies, politics, and culture—a matrix perpetually undermined by stasis. In the film, soldiers arbitrarily decide on the border between Chile and Argentina as the audience watches. The border simply differentiates them. While the scene in which the soldiers burn a line in the grass is surely fictional and exaggerated, it replicates many of the approaches to the border that rely on polemos. The line of fire attempts to clarify the conflict by deciding on and delimiting the enemy while simultaneously obscuring past conflicts—the Spanish empire and nineteenth-century wars—and ignoring current ones—illegitimate military governments and neo-imperial pressures from the Global North. The border fabricates a spatial difference that immediately becomes an article of faith for the soldiers. It is the only thing worth protecting. The film condenses into a few minutes a process that might take decades or even centuries to unfold, but because of this compression, the audience sees that the border is wholly artificial. The line did not exist prior to their agreement on its existence, and the rest of the land remains wide open.

In the film's climax, both sides prepare to go to war. The Chileans are outnumbered and thus will be easily overpowered. Certain of their imminent demise, they write letters to their families and deliver them to the Argentine officer to send afterwards, seeking to leave a mark of their passage on this earth. While they write, they envision their own deaths as the temporal limit to their existence. They miss the pope's offer to mediate the dispute because of a broken radio, and so tension builds and a brief skirmish ensues. Once the conflict resolves, however, the men are astounded at how quickly it is forgotten. The border appears in stark relief only in those few moments before the attack when they are confronted with the spatial and temporal limits of border and death. Afterwards, without the full ideological weight of a true enemy or a quest for historical truth, the border's importance dissipates. It served merely as a tool for visualizing the violence of sovereignty that imposes spatial limits on territory and temporal, existential limits on subjects. Before and after this moment, there is a zone of indistinction marked as stasis. Stasis opens the question of conflict and democracy that might otherwise be closed off by sovereignty and the border. It allows us to investigate the border as a limit without affirming its existence or conceding its importance.

Where does stasis leave the border in the present? Beyond specific historical disputes, *The Other Border Wars* has argued that the assumption of the border has hampered border studies. When left unquestioned, the border becomes politically, historically, and theoretically stronger, leading border studies to an unintentional and implicit reinforcement of bordering processes. For this reason, I have argued that it is important to disarticulate, piece by piece, articles of political, cultural, and regional faith: Latin American border closure has long been complete; civil and international conflicts can be easily distinguished; and sovereignty conflicts are immutable.

In addition to challenging these ideas, Latin America's paradoxically violent yet peaceful borders also force a new perspective on legal and cultural texts that seek to establish order. Typically, these texts have favored the border-as-polemos approach, useful for fomenting nationalism and xenophobia while making identity-based claims of fraternity that exclude racial and sexual minorities. Border-as-polemos simplifies political and aesthetic praxis, forcing political and cultural narratives to conform to conventions of inside versus outside, good versus evil, or conflict followed by reconciliation. However, if "stasis underlies all political praxis" (Vardoulakis, *Stasis* 121), a more complex picture appears. Stasis describes how people come together in relation to one another, in conflict or in harmony, whether sitting together in a hammock or claiming a parcel of land without any proof of ownership. These moments of political and aesthetic praxis are only tangentially related to bordering, but they, too, skirt the edges of political order. Unhampered by a sovereign limit, stasis allows difference-in-relation and relation-in-difference to appear without a plan for the future. Instead of telling the same tired tales with easy enemies and predictable endings, stories of stasis take unexpected turns, inspired by the spirit of borderless texts and borderless politics.

NOTES

INTRODUCTION: BORDER WAR AS STASIS

1. "Ni tú ni yo sabemos dónde está la frontera."

2. "Está invadiendo mi territorio."

3. "Dos pasos *chiquitos* hacia el Atlántico"; "Hacia allá, hombre."

4. Mares, along with many of the theorists cited below from Thucydides to Schmitt, are all grouped as political realists, meaning that they see the international order as essentially anarchic and believe states to be the main actors. One of the arguments that Mares's book makes that does *not* form part of his initial realist assumptions discounts the US role in inter–Latin American relations in his chapter "The Myth of Hegemonic Management" (55–83).

5. The Beagle Conflict hinged on the interpretation of two key issues. The first, *uti possidetis juris*, is an international law principle that provides for the transfer of territorial limits from colony to nation-state when a colony becomes independent. In this case, whatever territory had been administered by the Viceroyalty of the Río de la Plata would pass to independent Argentina and whatever had been under the Captaincy General of Chile would pass to independent Chile. The second principle presented to the courts was the bi-oceanic principle, which came from agreements made during the War of the Pacific in 1879–1883 between Chile, Peru, and Bolivia. In exchange for Argentine neutrality in the dispute, Chile agreed to preserve Argentine dominance in the Atlantic while maintaining its own dominance in the Pacific. Argentina argued that if the court agreed that the Beagle Channel flowed east past

the three islands, Chile would have an outlet to the South Atlantic in violation of this principle. Argentina risked losing the established equilibrium: one nation, one ocean. Independence-era treaties and peace agreements after nineteenth-century wars made promises that suddenly buckled under the weight of neo-imperialism.

6. Meticulously documented in over four hundred maps and other documents submitted to the courts of arbitration, the collection *Relaciones chileno-argentinas* provides beautiful documentary evidence of the claims over the years from cartographers of Spanish, German, Argentine, and Chilean origin.

7. Throughout this book, I use *stasis* in italics to refer to the ancient Greek definition; "stasis" without italics indicates the range of meanings I advance here.

8. Thucydides's Melian dialogue presents an early model for the oral arguments to reach an agreement, similar to the stasis procedure in rhetoric. In the Melian case, negotiations failed. Scholars of international relations often consider the Melian dialogue the foundation of political realism (see more in this introduction and chapter 1).

9. For a more detailed examination of the development of the term *stasis* in ancient Greece, see Kalimtzis, particularly chs. 1–2, 1–31.

10. The theorists of *stasis* cited above all explicitly draw from and reinterpret Aristotle or Plato. In readings of Aristotle, *stasis* seems to be valorized as something like an agon, poised between its disruptive model and the public space in which the disagreements of democracy appear (Vardoulakis, "Ends of Stasis" 155). In *Politics of Friendship*, Derrida meditates on inconsistencies in a politics of Aristotelian friendship as well as Schmittian enmity. The text *Political Theology II* in which Schmitt mentions *stasis* is subtitled *The Myth of the Closure of Any Political Theology*.

11. The two Heraclitean fragments in question are 53 ("War is the father of all and the king of all; and some he has made gods and some men, some bond and some free") and 80 ("We must know that war is common to all and strife is justice, and that all things come into being and pass away through strife"). The translations and interpretations are subject to dispute; see, especially, Fried 21–42.

12. Jean Bodin offers an early formulation of the state founded on "force and violence" (18) in his *Six Books of the Commonwealth*. Max Weber later popularized this idea, defining the state as a "monopoly on the legitimated use of physical force" (136). Brown's *Walled States* discusses the erosion of Westphalian sovereignty under globalization. Elden's *Birth* historicizes the idea of the "bordered power-container."

13. Moreiras's *Exhaustion* argues against hybridity, contending that the assertion of difference traps both hegemonic and subaltern subjects in an identity-based dialectic (see, especially, 264–300). Moreiras presents "savage hybridity" as exceeding the dialectic between hegemonic and counterhegemonic orders. For a related exploration in the wake of subaltern studies, see Williams, *Other Side*.

14. Throughout this book, I refer to the islands as "Falklands/Malvinas," the slash preserving the contested nature of the territory, rather than a hyphen, which suggests a supplement. When referring to the British perspective, I use "Falklands," and when referring to the Argentine perspective, I use "Malvinas." I place Falklands before Malvinas in accordance with the status quo, in which the islands are a British overseas territory. Note also that the two largest islands are part of an archipelago, and the 1982 attack was mounted against all British possessions in the South Atlantic, including the Sandwich and South Georgia Islands.

15. The conceptual development of the formless in Rodríguez Matos's *Writing of the Formless* serves as a key reference.

1. THE CHACO WAR AND ARCHIVAL HYPOSTASIS

Roa Bastos, *Hijo de hombre* 237 [2012]. Translation: "An old vice, this writing. A vicious circle that becomes virtuous when it closes itself outward. A way of fleeing from the non-place toward the stable space of signs."

1. "Los días transcurren monótonos, iguales. . . . Estamos fondeados en medio de la lenta y atigrada corriente, de más de un kilómetro de anchura. . . . Cuando se la mira fijamente, a ciertas horas, parece también detenida, inmóvil, muerta." All references to *Hijo de hombre* are from the revised edition (2012) unless otherwise noted.

2. "En mitad del Chaco, todavía estamos en sus latifundias. Ahora tendremos que pedirle permiso para ir a morir por sus tierras."

3. "¡Vamos a pelear y morir por patriotismo!"

4. "Pero nuestro patriotismo va a acabar teniendo olor a petróleo. . . . Las grandes empresas tienen buen olfato. Huelen de lejos el mar mineral enterrado en el Chaco."

5. "Evidentemente, la irrupción boliviana cierra sus dispositivos para cortar el río Paraguay, nuestro vulnerable espinazo de agua. Si llegan a tener su control, podrán doblar en dos al país y metérselo en el bolsillo."

6. "Esos bichos [las polillas] agujearon las Cédulas Reales. Se

NOTES TO PAGES 19–22

comieron las demarcaciones primitivas, la línea de hitos, el *uti possidetis*, se bebieron los ríos. Todo. Ahora nadie entiende nada. Ni nuestros doctores en límites. Ni los de ellos . . .”

7. Research suggests that even before the war the presence of exploitable petroleum was somewhat dubious, perhaps embellished by warmongers. For historical perspectives on this question, see Cote on Bolivia and Chesterton on Paraguay.

8. The League would soon meet its own demise when it failed to keep Europe from another bloody war. Costa du Rels, one of the Bolivian authors discussed in this chapter, served as a diplomat in the League of Nations until its final session.

9. In using the word *form*, I refer broadly to the metaphysical tradition extending from ancient Greek philosophy, especially Plato's theory of forms and Aristotle's division between form and matter.

10. “Éstas serían las cenizas del Edén, incinerado por el Castigo, sobre las cuales los hijos de Caín peregrinan ahora trajeados de kaki y verdeolivo. . . . De aquellos lodos salieron estos polvos.”

11. “Del otro lado está Kundt, el mercenario teutón. Dos escuelas europeas van a enfrentarse en un salvaje desierto americano, con medios primitivos, por intereses no tan primitivos. Es también una manera de actuar la civilización sobre un contorno inculto, encallado en el atraso del primer día del Génesis.”

12. In Thucydides's Melian dialogue, the origin of political realism, the Athenians presented the Melians with an ultimatum, and when they failed to capitulate, the Athenians killed and enslaved them.

13. Schmitt writes, “In a declaration dated August 3, 1932, 19 states in the Americas declared with respect to the Chaco War between Bolivia and Paraguay that they ‘would no more recognize a territorial regulation of the present (Chaco) conflict that was not brought about by peaceful means than they would the validity of territorial acquisitions brought about through occupation by armed conquest’” (Nomos 307).

14. The relationship between realism and the vanguard is explored further in chapter 2. Roa Bastos is often classified as a Boom author and associated with magical realism. Readings of Roa Bastos later in this chapter focus on ontological questions in his treatment of incarnation instead of the widely debated issue of magical realism as a category or technique.

15. David Harvey redefines primitive accumulation more broadly as accumulation by dispossession to indicate that it can happen at moments other than the earliest stages of capitalist accumulation (137–82). For more on primitive accumulation in *Hijo de hombre*, see Pous, ch. 1.

16. For more on this process, see Klein.

17. Siles Salinas analyzes Céspedes's fiction in detail in this section (*La literatura* 29–30).

18. Loraux also finds the displacement of xenophobia, associated with *polemos*, onto the family, associated with *stasis* (*Divided City* 212–13). Overcoming *stasis* depends on amnesty, the necessity of forgetting (245–64). Amnesia and aphasia are explored further in the next chapter alongside the threshold between city and family in the twenty-first-century legacy of the Chaco War.

19. The city here might well be fruitfully linked to Ángel Rama's lettered city, especially given the intersection between intellectual and political work in the biographies of the major figures of politics and letters studied in this chapter.

20. Son of the Bolivian president in power just before the outbreak of open hostilities—Hernando Siles, in office 1926–1930—Siles Salinas was also a longtime diplomat who worked extensively on brokering a deal for a seaport with Chile approximately twenty years after publishing his Chaco War compendium. His father was president during the initial Bolivian push into the Chaco. The fort at Vanguardia, discussed in the next chapter, was the site of an initial skirmish in 1928 during his tenure. Nevertheless, the dedication to *La literatura boliviana* reads, "A la memoria de mi padre, el Presidente Hernando Siles, quien supo evitar, con resolución y energía, una guerra que nunca debió haberse producido" (n.p.; To the memory of my father, President Hernando Siles, who knew how to avoid, with conviction and vigor, a war that never should have happened). Later in his diplomatic career, Siles Salinas wrote the book *Sí, el mar*, documenting the failed negotiation process between Bolivia and Chile in 1986–1987.

21. "Con más sed que odio."

22. "Siempre nada, igual que la guerra . . . ¡Esta nada no acabará jamás!"

23. In Heidegger's words: "*The essence of ground is the transcendental springing forth of grounding, strewn threefold into projection of world, absorption within beings, and ontological grounding of beings.* And it is for this reason alone that even the earliest questioning concerning the essence of *ground* shows itself to be entwined with the task of shedding light upon the essence of *being* and *truth*" ("On the Essence of Ground" 132).

24. To borrow an image from Lacanian psychoanalysis, the *points de capiton* are the points of convergence of signified and signifier that structure systems of linguistic meaning. They confer the stability that Roa Bastos mentions in the epigraph and to which I return at the end of the chapter.

25. Heidegger returns to the principle of sufficient reason in his 1955–1956 lecture course, *Principle*. The historical context changed drastically since the interwar anxiety expressed in "On the Essence of Ground" to preoccupation with the principle of sufficient reason as the rational foundation of modernity and hence of the atomic age. Heidegger urges a rethinking of the principle in light of the increasingly lethal advance of technology in modern times.

26. "Suceden cosas raras. Esa cámara obscura aprisionada en el fondo del pozo va revelando imágenes del agua, con el reactivo de los sueños. La obsesión del agua está creando un mundo particular y fantástico que se ha originado a los 41 metros, manifestándose en un curioso suceso acontecido en ese nivel.

"El Cosñi Herbozo . . . se había quedado adormecido en el fondo de la cisterna, cuando vio encenderse una serpiente de plata. La cogió y se deshizo en sus manos, pero aparecieron otras que comenzaron a bullir en el fondo del pozo hasta formar un manantial de borbollones blancos y sonoros que crecían, animando al cilindro tenebroso como a una serpiente encantada que perdió su rigidez para adquirir la flexibilidad de una columna de agua, sobre la que el Cosñi se sintió elevado hasta salir al haz alucinante de la tierra."

27. Especially in his early writings, Levinas also uses the term hypostasis to describe what Heidegger refers to as the ontological difference. These approaches are discussed in further detail in this chapter.

28. See also Sontag's classic essay "In Plato's Cave" from *On Photography*.

29. "He procurado trabajar, dando furiosos golpes con el pico, en la esperanza de acelerar con la actividad veloz el transcurso del tiempo. Pero el tiempo es fijo e invariable en ese recinto. Al no revelarse el cambio de las horas con la luz, el tiempo se estanca en el subsuelo con la negra uniformidad de una cámara obscura. Esta es la muerte de la luz."

30. The photographs of the Chaco War dead are, as might be expected, particularly brutal, depicting emaciated bodies, ripped open and consumed by animals and the elements. Numerous archival photos have been recently compiled in military historical collections. See, for instance, Sapienza.

31. "¿Tanto dolor, tanta búsqueda, tanto deseo, tanta alma sedienta acumulados en el profundo hueco originan esta floración de manantiales?"

32. The "devouring mother" metaphor resonates with Lacan's analysis of anxiety (Evans 10–12). As Evans writes, Lacan describes anxiety as arising from a fear of fragmentation in earlier seminars. This fear is

analogous to the sovereign state fearing disintegration as it approaches its border in my argument. However, in later seminars, Evans describes Lacan connecting anxiety to being swallowed up, ingested, and buried, as when the soldiers arrive at the well and fear being devoured by the earth.

33. "Creció el tiroteo de los pilas y se oía en medio de las detonaciones su alarido salvaje, concentrándose la furia del ataque sobre el pozo. Pero nosotros no cedíamos un metro, defendiéndolo ¡como si realmente tuviese agua!"

34. "Engullidos por sombra."

35. The versions differ substantially, especially toward the end. Here, I refer to the Spanish edition, published in La Paz in 1967. Unfortunately, it has a number of typographical errors.

36. "Bórlagui sintió el primer pinchazo de la duda. Sometido desde el comienzo de su carrera a la existencia precaria de los fortines, en territorios despoblados y malsanos, montando guardia entre fronteras inexistentes, causa de futuros conflictos, Bórlagui se había revestido de deza [sic] e impasibilidad." Note: Borlagui's surname is sometimes written with an accent and sometimes without.

37. "Mi autoridad, aquí, no proviene de dones ni grado, sino de mi saber y de la confianza que él inspira. Pues bien, toda mi ciencia consiste en esta ilusoria brújula. Al precio de una . . . superchería, ella ha podido mantener la disciplina, la cohesión y cristalizar la esperanza de cada uno. Ante la inminencia del peligro, todo ser busca el objeto o la imagen que fijan [sic] y retiene el destino."

38. There is an undeniable opposition between indigenous and European epistemologies. Costa du Rels portrays the indigenous characters as understanding the unpredictable landscape more clearly and calmly, whereas Borlagui goes on to explain that the fake compass provides him with a scientific, paternalistic superiority: "Aquellos pícaros no me perdonarían nunca el no saber más que ellos. La autoridad no dura sino cuando deriva de cierta superioridad reconocida por todos. . . . Yo no puedo destruir esta verdad. . . . Ella es fundamental. . . . Nuestra superioridad sobre ellos es indispensable a su salvación. Y a la nuestra" (Costa du Rels, *La laguna* 67; Those soundrels would never forgive me for not knowing more than them. Authority only lasts when it comes from a certain superiority everyone recognizes. . . . I can't undo this truth. . . . It's fundamental. . . . Our superiority over them is indispensable for their salvation. And ours.).

39. "[Contreras] Se apresuró a bajar, pero se detuvo en una de las últimas ramas. Allí recuperó fuerzas y, haciendo de su mano, una bocina, gritó, como los marineros de Colón, en vez de tierra:—Agua! Agua!"

40. In another strange story on the frustrated legacy of diplomacy in the Chaco War, Argentine diplomat Carlos Saavedra Lamas was awarded the 1936 Nobel Peace Prize for his role negotiating an end to the conflict and creating a South American anti-war pact. His medal surfaced years after his death in a pawnshop, apparently sold for its weight in gold because the owner did not recognize its symbolic import. It was later sold at public auction (Withnall).

41. Testimonials and histories of Mennonite settler colonialism just before the outbreak of war proves that the Chaco, while a latecomer to some European modes of colonization elsewhere in the continent, was very much inhabited at the time of the war by both indigenous and European groups. For a collection of documents related to the Chaco before, during, and after the war, see Lambert and Nickson.

42. Costa du Rels would also suffer the death of his son, fighting for the French resistance. The French edition, *Lagune H.3*, published in Buenos Aires in 1944, is dedicated to the memory of this deceased son.

43. "Hacía una hora que tenía la mirada fija, entre sus pupilas semicerradas, sobre el viejo árbol hierático, preguntándose por el origen de aquella extraña herida. Le hallaba un aire de tristeza majestuosa. Un rey destronado, tal vez humillado por la vejez y la ingratitud de los más jóvenes. Contreras le habló con tono compadecido, queriendo conocer las razones de un [*sic*] infortunio."

44. "Da dos vueltas el [*sic*] *toborochi*, como si esperara el momento propicio para hacerle una pregunta o asestarle un golpe. ¿Posee toda su razón, esta razón de la que siempre hizo el árbitro de sus pensamientos y de sus actos? Bruscamente, se pega al árbol y, con sus dos manos crispadas, en un esfuerzo del que ya no parecía capaz, se obstina en transformar esa cavidad en una inmensa boca entreabierta. Poco le falta para dejar allí todas sus uñas."

45. "Todo vibra. Todo resplandece en la fantasmagoría del amanecer. Contreras se siente como proyectado fuera de sí, al ver que por fin, la bocaza, la horrible bocaza, obra de sus manos, toda chorreante de luz,—¡ríe!"

46. In the second edition, Contreras eventually dies after risking his life to give water to a thirsty man in the no-man's-land between the trenches.

47. It should be noted that this interpretation attempts to open Costa du Rels's text to ambiguity, at times willfully and explicitly resisting the text. For example, Siles Salinas's reading of the novel fits very well with passages such as the one in which Borlagui dies and his last word is "fraternity" (Costa du Rels, *La laguna* 187) as well as a final passage:

"Tornadizo, el viento llevaba y traía aires de ambos países, tan semejantes los unos a los otros, que la guerra parecía más bien pendencia de familia, por una cuestión de linderos" (Costa du Rels, *La laguna* 212; The fickle wind brought and carried away the air of both countries, so similar to each other that the war seemed more like a family quarrel over a matter of boundaries). Yet there are also moments when the text opens itself to the difficulty of understanding this war, and I prefer to focus on these moments.

48. Elsewhere in the novel, this phenomenon is described as an indigeneity that inheres in the landscape: "Contreras ignoraba que existen aún en América meridional ciertos lugares secretos donde hallan refugio los grandes mitos incaicos, sustraídos a la voracidad de los conquistadores" (Costa du Rels, *La laguna* 36; Contreras did not know that in South America there still exist secret places where the great Incan myths find refuge, having avoided the voracity of the conquistadors).

49. In *Captives*, Havercroft analyzes the ways modern political theory seeks to undo the model of sovereignty without ever fully escaping it. Havercroft admits that his portrait takes broad strokes, clarifying: "Despite numerous attempts to move beyond sovereignty or re-imagine political community, . . . scholars of politics remain captivated by this picture of politics because it continues to set the terms according to which we debate our political ontology" (1). Havercroft also writes that, in spite of globalization, there is a tendency to look for some type of international sovereign. He uses skepticism to undo the bind between sovereignty and captivity.

50. On peripheral modernity and the photographic aura alongside a reading of "La paraguaya," see Paz Soldán, "La imagen."

51. "Aquella fotografía de mujer pertenecía a un paraguayo muerto."

52. "Linda, la mujer del bolí."

53. "Y siguieron la marcha por el bosque, llevándose el retrato de la 'viuda'."

54. To take the most obvious case of the state's intentional exclusion of gendered difference, women achieved full enfranchisement in Bolivia in 1952 and in Paraguay in 1961.

55. "Cabellos densos, negros y sueltos . . . rostro ligeramente redondeado . . . ojos inmensos"

56. "Su vida en incendio admitió, sin sentirlo, el hecho de su romántica relación con esa mujer incógnita y muda, con la lejana paraguaya alojada en la intimidad de su cartera como única mujer en el vacío que las otras no habían ocupado."

57. Agamben writes, "It is no coincidence that the 'terror' should

coincide with the moment in which life as such—the nation (which is to say, birth)—became the principle of sovereignty. The sole form in which life as such can be politicised is its unconditional exposure to death—that is, bare life" (24). Historically, the Chaco serves the function of immediate politicization after the exposure to death. Authors like Céspedes and especially Cerruto with *Aluvión de fuego* fomented political awareness and action based on the inequality they witnessed in the Chaco, as documented, if somewhat disparagingly, in Siles Salinas.

58. In Cristóbal Jara's segment of *Hijo de hombre* discussed in this chapter, Salu'í, a nurse, decides to abandon the camp and join Jara's suicide mission to bring water to the lost regiment behind Bolivian lines. She is not recognized when she approaches the water truck in the dark: "'*Mävaiko-nde?*' gritó Aquino el clásico santo y seña guaraní, repitiéndoselo de inmediato en castellano" (Roa Bastos, *Hijo de hombre* 292; *Mävaiko-nde?* Aquino shouted the classic Guaraní call for a password, repeating it immediately in Spanish). To this question, which Roa Bastos then offers in Spanish as "amigo o enemigo" (friend or foe), there is no response. Salu'í is another of the women who escapes Schmitt's axiomatic political divide. She is a friend, Paraguayan, but also a deserter and traitor, having abandoned her post as a nurse without permission. It is important to note that these women who confound the political divide do not cling to some other type of signification, such as a feminine essence; instead, they vacate the binary altogether. For more, see Malabou, *Changing Difference*.

59. In broad strokes, while both Heidegger and Levinas place emphasis on time, Heidegger sees Being in relation to death while Levinas relates it to the encounter with the Other. Using Levinas as a source in the first part of *Against War*, Maldonado-Torres discards ontology and largely ignores temporality in favor of fraternity and fecundity against which my interpretation argues.

60. The critique of fraternity in Siles Salinas might be extended to Levinas's much more developed and subtle understanding of the term, which nevertheless relies on this "work of identity" (Levinas, *Time* 52) emptied out in the Chaco literature as I present it here and echoed in the reading of "La paraguaya."

61. "Cierta importancia operativa."

62. "Sin poder destruir ese monstruo de mi propio delirio."

63. "Pensando quizá que toda la tierra muerta del Chaco no iba a alcanzar a cubrirlos, a tapar esos agujeros del tamaño de un hombre."

64. This passage echoes the broader motif of holes and craters throughout *Hijo de hombre*, recalling the holes made from an exploded

train carrying revolutionaries, intercepted by another train packed with bombs. In that instance, too, the earth seemed insufficient to cover the hole ripped into the railways, which served as a mass grave.

65. In the two main characters, Roa Bastos presents a battle story (Miguel Vera) and a travel story (Cristóbal Jara), invoking the epic poems *The Iliad* and *The Odyssey* as well as suggesting a Schmittian concern with the conflict between land and water, now displaced into the desert. There is also an abandonment of other mythical stories such as the return to Eden or the arrival at the Guaraní "tierra sin mal" (land without evil).

66. "Es preferible acabar de una vez . . . Pero ¡qué difícil es morir!"

67. "Me hallaba sentado a la mesa de un boliche, junto a otros despojos humanos de la guerra, sin ser su semejante. Como en aquel remoto cañadón del Chaco, calcinado por la sed, embrujado por la muerte. Ese cañadón no tenía salida. Y sin embargo estoy aquí. Mis uñas y mis cabellos siguen creciendo, pero un muerto no es capaz de retractarse, de claudicar, de ceder cada vez un poco más . . . Yo sigo, pues, viviendo, a mi modo, más interesado en lo que he visto que en lo que aún me queda por ver."

68. "Alguna salida debe haber en este monstruoso contrasentido del hombre crucificado por el hombre. Porque de lo contrario sería el caso de pensar que la raza humana está maldita para siempre, que esto es el infierno y que no podemos esperar salvación. Debe haber una salida, porque de lo contrario . . ."

69. " . . . Así concluye el manuscrito de Miguel Vera" The ellipsis is in the text and does not indicate an omission.

70. "Era un torturado sin remedio, su espíritu asqueado por la ferocidad del mundo, pero rechazaba la idea del suicidio. 'Un paraguayo no se suicida jamás . . .—me escribía en una de sus últimas cartas—. A lo sumo se dejará morir, que no es lo mismo . . .'"

71. "Y haré que vuelva a encarnarse el habla . . . / Después que se pierda este tiempo y un nuevo tiempo amanezca."

72. Levinas explains further: "I want to stress . . . the consequences of this conception of the *there is*. It consists in promoting a notion of being without nothingness, which leaves no hole and permits no escape. And this impossibility of nothingness deprives suicide, which is the final mastery one can have over being, of its function of mastery" (Levinas, *Time* 50). Nancy reinterprets the Levinasian focus on alterity by generalizing and expanding it: "We might also say that [thinking a secret in which thinking becomes secret onto itself] is a matter of the other   this time, considering a Levinasian source—but of the other insofar as he or she outstrips any assignation *as* or *in* an other of some kind, whether with

a capital or a lowercase *o*. This means not only the *alter*—the other of two—but also the *alienus*, the *allos*, everyone's other, and the senseless" (*Dis-enclosure* 6).

73. Nancy considers this part of the constitutive dis-enclosure of metaphysics: "In truth, metaphysics deconstructs itself constitutively, and, in deconstructing itself, it dis-encloses [*déclôt*] in itself the presence and certainty of the world founded on reason" (*Dis-enclosure* 7).

74. "Nuestras líneas se han estabilizado de una manera muy precaria. Es más bien un equilibrio inestable."

75. "En guaraní, la palabra *arandú* quiere decir *sabiduría*, y significa *sentir-el-tiempo*."

2. THE CHACO WAR AND THE CONSUMPTION OF STATUS

Roa Bastos, *Hijo de hombre* [2012] 262. Translation: "Boquerón is a hard bone to digest. The peristaltic movement of our lines work on swallowing it to no avail. There's something magical about this handful of invisible defenders that resist with a bedeviled, blind obstinacy in the wooded stronghold. It's like fighting against ghosts saturated with an agonizing strength, morbidly sinister, that have surpassed all borders of consumption, of annihilation, of desperation."

1. Standard Oil Company of New Jersey's responses to the Bolivian government's accusations appear in the propaganda pamphlets *Bolivia* and *Confiscation*.

2. In *From Rebellion*, Webber is emphatic in his condemnation of the decree: "Three months into the new MAS [*Movimiento al Socialismo*, "Movement for Socialism"] government Morales announced the nationalization of hydrocarbons through presidential decree 28071. However, it quickly became apparent that 'nationalization' amounted to little more than rhetorical flourish and populist theater" (80). He goes on to say that, after an initial period of legal and practical confusion, the situation became clear: "Under the new contracts and export agreements there has been an undeniable increase in state revenues, which brings to an end the unadulterated giveaways of the Sánchez de Lozada years. It is also clear, however, that the new contracts do not amount to a nationalization of the industry. They reinforce the primary-export model of development and militate against the development of a serious industrialization policy and reconstitution of YPFB [the state-owned oil and gas company]" (82).

3. Incidentally, the skirmish took place during the presidency of Hernando Siles, father of Jorge Siles Salinas. The clash at Vanguardia

is generally considered indicative of early Bolivian aggression, even though his son remembers him as the president who knew how to avoid war.

4. Rodríguez-Alcalá explains further that, in his view, the trauma of war forced Paraguay into the past: "El Paraguay, entonces, en vez de inventarse un plan de vida para el mañana y de ponerse al día en lo atinente a las letras y las artes, regresaba espiritualmente en el tiempo para asistir, imaginativamente, a sus orígenes" (243; Thus Paraguay, instead of inventing a life plan for tomorrow and keeping up to date in matters of arts and letters, went back in time spiritually to attend, imaginatively, to its origins). He goes on to say that the generation around the 1930s "no podía vacar al ocio creador y consagrarse a experimentos literarios" (243; could not take leave to dedicate itself to creative leisure or devote itself to literary experiments).

5. For the former case, see Montaigne's famous essay "Of Cannibals" and other portrayals of "the noble savage." For the latter, see travelogues—the European colonizer, defeated in battle, would be fattened up, then sacrificed in a meal of ritual sacrifice—especially Staden. The frequent mention of cannibalism in colonial mishaps and disappearances, alongside questions of whether the explorers could legitimately (legally and ethically) kill and eat a companion, also enters into the European tradition of just war (Avramescu).

6. I use masculine pronouns because the cases documented in the travelogues involved male cannibals.

7. I use Leslie Bary's translations of the manifesto unless otherwise noted. "Expressão mascarada de todos os individualismos, de todos os coletivismos. De todas as religiões. De todos os tratados de paz" ("Manifesto antropófago" 3).

8. "A luta entre o que se chamaria Incriado e a Criatura—ilustrada pela contradição permanente do homem e o seu Tabu. O amor cotidiano e o modusvivendi capitalista. Antropofagia. Absorção do inimigo sacro. Para transformá-lo em totem" ("Manifesto antropófago" 7). Note that the tree's face in *La laguna H.3*, discussed in chapter 1, also resembles a type of totem.

9. In English in the original. The famous line in which Hamlet contemplates suicide is the same that Levinas discusses when talking about the absurdity of life without exit, briefly addressed at the end of the previous chapter. The connection to the *salida*, "exit," discussed in this chapter, foreshadows "creative tensions" and Bolivia's struggle with the perennial question of the outlet to the sea.

10. Malabou, whose work on futurity informs the last part of this

chapter, writes against Kojève in *Future*. Malabou's work will be used to recover a concept of futurity, drawing on theorizations of that concept from Derrida and Nancy. See also Martinon, *On Futurity*.

11. "una isla de tierra / rodeada de tierra."

12. Note that Urrelo Zárate styles Papá's speech with punctuation but without capitalization. Capital letters have been introduced at the beginning of quotations and paragraphs to improve readability. "Era la guerra. la guerra nunca termina cuando se firma la paz. no termina tampoco con nuestro alimento. continúa aquí. como esas enfermedades que consumen a los viejos. en los corazones de los excombatientes. vuelven a sus casas y la guerra que cargan en sus cuerpos se dispersa. ¡plaf! contagia como una enfermedad a quienes viven ahí. ataca a las esposas. las sacrifica. mata a los hijos. a las hijas. la bala paraguaya ya no es la que mata. ya no es la fiebre. ya no es el paludismo. ya no es el calor del chaco. ya no es el hambre. ya no es la sed. ahora lo que mata es el propio excombatiente y lo hace en su propio hogar. su fuerza es el odio. ahí matan esposas. crimen. era el odio. era el miedo. era la guerra que seguía viva. y aunque se nieguen a creerlo pervive hasta nuestros días. los jóvenes de 1935 ahora ancianos como yo. o casi muertos. o muertos. ahora la guerra mata a los nietos, a los que no saben o no quieren saber del sufrimiento de sus abuelas. esa historia está cerrada. muerta. ahora la guerra es la hipocresía, señorita, y esa mata peor todavía."

13. "¿Por qué a los que fuimos a la guerra nos dicen héroes si sólo matamos gente?"

14. "Grito [que] pareció subir del fondo mismo del cerro."

15. See a more detailed development of aphasia in the section later in this chapter titled "Cannibalism and Metaphysical Synthesis."

16. "Lo que pasa es que en este país todo empeora con el tiempo."

17. Viveiros de Castro argues that the "substance" does not matter, at least in Tupi-group cannibalism. In this case, I would change his choice of the word *substance* to *matter* or *nutritional value* because it is precisely the substance as hypostasis that matters in Christianity, for instance. Viveiros de Castro explains Araweté cannibalism: "What was really eaten in this enemy? The answer could not be his matter or substance, since this was a ritual form of cannibalism where the consumption of (a quantity of) the victim's flesh was effectively insignificant; the extant sources, moreover, only rarely offer testimony that a physical or metaphysical virtue was attributed to the victim's body" (142). While this metaphysical aspect may be lacking in the Araweté or Tupi-group cannibalism more generally, it is definitely present in Urrelo Zárate's novel through the Satanist inversion of Christianity.

18. In interviews and press releases about the novel, Urrelo Zárate refers to vengeance above justice, specifically in the case of eating the wealthy. See M. Paz Soldán; Ossio Lazcano.

19. "Ahí, en ese momento, abriéndose las puertas que siempre estaban cerradas ante nosotros. la paz invadiendo su corazón. tanto amar para qué. tanto sufrir por amar para qué. y de pronto se abre la puerta. y detrás de ella está la felicidad. . . . la nueva vida. 28 de septiembre de 1932, señorita. el nacimiento de todo."

20. "Los que llegaban siempre personas solas. solitarias. arruinadas por la vida. gente con un vacío que no sabían cómo llenar y la carne los ayudaba, los rescataba, los sacaba de ese pozo."

21. "¿Qué cosa da la carne, señorita? ¿qué le da a uno que le abre nuevos caminos? ¿qué cosa contiene que todos renacemos? ¿por qué si antes éramos miedosos y estúpidos después somos la otra cara de eso?

"Después de tragar aparecen las palabras. las mismas que le dije a usted antes que pase lo de su amigo perro loco. iguales. sin modificación. como nunca antes las palabras despertando en mí como después de un sueño. cuál estúpido. cuál ignorante. ahí explotando las palabras sabias. toda mi soledad. todo mi sufrimiento . . . evaporándose. yéndose de mi cuerpo. entonces era eso. entonces pensando todos estos años había estado esperando la carne."

22. Following Derrida's *écriture*, I consider writing and speech to be inextricably linked here and later in this chapter.

23. "Papá abre la boca de nuevo y ahí la calidez, el infinito amor desinteresado, masque, señorita: ahí, el único, y el auténtico amor que valía la pena en este mundo y yo lo estaba sintiendo en vivo, Papá."

24. Translation modified. "Porém, só as puras elites conseguiram realizar a antropofagia carnal, que traz em si o mais alto sentido da vida e evita todos os males identificados por Freud, males catequistas. O que se dá não é uma sublimação do instinto sexual. É a escala termométrica do instinto antropofágico. De carnal, ele se torna eletivo e cria a amizade. Afetivo, o amor. Especulativo, a ciência. Desvia-se e transfere-se. Chegamos ao aviltamento. A baixa antropofagia aglomerada nos pecados de catecismo—a inveja, a usura, a calúnia, o assassinato. Peste dos chamados povos cultos e cristianizados, é contra ela que estamos agindo. Antropófagos" ("Manifesto antropófago" 7).

25. "Después nos sacaron del fortín formados en una fila y cuando creía que nos fusilarían nos perdonaron la vida. . . . Nos dieron de comer, y sacaron fotos a todos los oficiales. Ya cuando estaba prisionero en Asunción un oficial paraguayo me mostró la mía, . . . y yo pensaba ¿cómo no querer [tener la foto]? ¿No era un bonito recuerdo?, ¿no sería

lindo tener algo que me recordara cuando conocí lo que era ser feliz en serio, hijo? . . . A partir de ese momento, todos éramos prisioneros."

26. "Pues no tiene nada, señora Zoila [abuela de Alicia], nada físico, quiero decir . . . para mí que no quiere hablar, ese es el problema."

27. "Pizarnik y Breton, par de cabrones."

28. "No creyendo en la vieja bruja Pizarnik ni en el tarado de Breton."

29. "Por su culpa casi me vuelvo vegetariano."

30. "La carne de los débiles como la de ese muchachito es necesaria para nosotros, señorita."

31. The full description from Marx: "As against this, the commodity-form, and the value-relation of the products of labour within which it appears, have absolutely no connection with the physical nature of the commodity and the material relations arising out of this. It is nothing but the definite social relation between men themselves which assumes here, for them, the fantastic form of a relation between things. In order, therefore, to find an analogy we must take flight into the misty realm of religion. There the products of the human brain appear as autonomous figures endowed with a life of their own, which enter into relations both with each other and with the human race. So it is in the world of commodities with the products of men's hands. I call this the fetishism which attaches itself to the products of labour as soon as they are produced as commodities, and is therefore inseparable from the production of commodities" (*Capital* 165). For more, see *Capital*, ch. 1, sec. 4.

32. Castro-Klarén writes that the seemingly ambiguous question "Tupi or not Tupi?" is not, in fact, ambiguous at all: "Read within its Tupi origins and relocated in the underbelly of Oswald's own claims, the mother lode of the anthropophagic metaphor of the Caraïbe drags in with it powerful forces of alterity and dissemination. The force of the discourse of Tupi anthropophagy, a subalternized knowledge, begins its work by destabilizing the very 'Manifesto antropófago' and its revolutionary claims. It subverts the smooth surface of the prose of the world and pulls it into the trenches, thus creating the uneven furrows of the aphoristic text. Despite the fact that the European root system suffocates the Tupi anthropophagic metaphor in Oswald's deployment, one must ineluctably acknowledge that the answer to the disjunctive 'Tupi or not Tupi?' must indeed be not Tupi on all counts: The nation and the 'sentido ético' as well as the epistemological dimension" (313).

33. In Latin American studies, such a reading falls under the broad label of subaltern studies. The readings presented here and until the end of the chapter should be seen in conversation with this defining moment

in the discipline, with the goal of understanding how to move beyond some of the barriers that the subaltern perspective and methodology encountered.

34. See also the conversation with Derrida in Nancy, "'Eating Well.'"

35. To be sure, Urrelo Zárate's version of capitalism seems to fit better with Levinas's definition of inconvertibility than Malabou's. Malabou pushes beyond the trace toward a "new materialism" (*Plasticity* 61) and nonmessianic conception of time (77), a new conception of hospitality alongside the possibility of deciding the future. This chapter moves to Encina's film in order to move past the impasse of the fetish. Malabou has also been accused, unjustly in my opinion, of the very thing she accuses. According to Galloway, her plastic ontology mimics global transnational capital by being flexible enough to accommodate almost anything, a critique which overly simplifies her use of the term *plasticity*. See Galloway, "Pamphlet 1." If we follow Malabou further, the conception of a plastic future may help advance a materialist deconstruction. The objection that might be raised, as is often done between Marxist and deconstructive traditions, is that such a turn neglects materialism in favor of idealism. As these two chapters on the Chaco War demonstrate, the cultural and political legacies of this war constantly mediate between these two, which is precisely what makes this war such an interesting site of inquiry into the contemporary nature of border conflict.

36. There are many possible connections to the femicides in Ciudad Juárez, infamously fictionalized in Bolaño's *2666*, as unintelligible violence at the border enacted on the female body. Kate Jenckes's analysis of the mouth in *2666* in her book *Witnessing* contributed vital references to this chapter.

37. During the panel "Escrituras de guerra" (War writing) at the 2014 Festival Internacional del Libro de Buenos Aires, Urrelo Zárate told an interesting story. The final days of writing the novel had drained him so much that he started having horrible abdominal pain. A bursting appendix turned out to be the culprit, but he couldn't be treated because the city of La Paz was paralyzed by the gasolinazo protests. The gasolinazo marks a limit in the Chaco War legacy.

38. It is important to note that these social movements gave rise to the radical transformation of Bolivian politics that García Linera celebrates. Increasingly during the historic Morales presidency, however, different blocs of his social movement coalition expressed discontentment, especially visible during the TIPNIS conflict of 2011. The coalition was further strained during the 2019 political crisis, in which

Morales resigned and left the country in what was widely considered a coup, but the election of a MAS candidate after the interim, and dubiously legal, presidency of Jeanine Áñez consolidated the party again. For more see B. Gustafson (247–53).

39. My translation.

40. In her analysis of the film, Tompkins sees this timeline as more dispersed (232–44).

41. "La esperanza te pierde, Ramón." The film is available with Spanish and Guaraní audio tracks, with Spanish subtitles. I use the Spanish subtitles for quotations.

42. "¿Se terminó la guerra, papá?" "¡No, Cándida, mi dolor de pecho!"

43. García Linera's work, mentioned in this chapter, relies on establishing the characteristics of each phase of the revolution and stating that the revolution is currently in its fifth stage. Encina's film undoes all traditional notions of what a phase might be, blending phases into one another with only limited visual cues.

44. I echo Rodríguez-Alcalá's use of the word *future* when describing the reason that Paraguay lacked a significant literary avant-garde, here and at the beginning of the chapter (243). Although the idea of futurity comes into question throughout this chapter (see especially, Martinon), Encina provides aesthetic tools for imagining time as asynchronous with itself and the future as unprogrammatic waiting. Her view aligns with Roa Bastos's use of *arandú*: wisdom and feeling the passage of time (*Hijo de hombre* 258). Together, they suggest an approach to temporality that differs from more traditional views of *past* and *future*.

3. THE SOCCER WAR AND DEMOGRAPHIC STASIS

Dalton, *Taberna y otros lugares* 6. Translation: "The dead become more unmanageable by the day."

1. From Duffield, see in particular *Global Governance* and *Development*.

2. "Es más seguro ya caminar por la luna que por las veredas de Honduras."

3. On vision and perspective, see Virilio.

4. "Por diversos motivos (la masacre de 1932, el desalojo de sus tierras, el desempleo crónico y el hambre), una profunda corriente emigratoria ha salido de El Salvador superpoblado al extranjero. . . . En Honduras, la población salvadoreña ha llegado a más de 350 mil, la mayor parte campesinos pobres, ocupantes en precario de tierras vírgenes de la despoblada Honduras."

5. "Para llevar a cabo la Reforma Agraria que la Alianza para el Progreso demanda, debemos repartir algunas tierras. El problema está en *cuáles* son estas tierras a repartir. Afectar las propiedades de la United Fruit Company norteamericana es tabú. Si tocamos las propiedades de la gran oligarquía terrateniente hondureña, la Reforma Agraria sería comunista. Echar mano a los bosques nacionales, sería muy caro. No quedan, pues, sino las tierras explotadas por los inmigrantes salvadoreños, que son 370 mil hectáreas. Si expropiamos a los guanacos [salvadoreños], mostraremos sentido patriótico, pues recuperaremos para los hondureños tierras en manos extranjeras."

6. For more on the Alliance for Progress as a renewed push for US hegemony in Latin America, especially Central America during the 1960s, see Berger.

7. In another take on the Soccer War from the other side, Honduran Eduardo Bähr writes of a Salvadoran father, drawn to working on United Fruit Company plantations in Honduras. The story "El cuento de la guerra" (The story of the war) explains how the man lost his job after a 1954 strike (14). As he tells the story, he mourns the loss of his two sons, who fought for Honduras against the father's home country of El Salvador during what he repeatedly refers to as "el cuento ese de la guerra" (this here war story). The father's life story links a series of tragedies that uprooted him and led to the loss of his family.

8. "Los salvadoreños ilegales deben salir de Honduras. Que cargue El Salvador con su demografía."

9. "El Presidente de mi país
se llama hoy por hoy Coronel Fidel Sánchez Hernández.
Pero el General Somoza, Presidente de Nicaragua,
también es Presidente de mi país.
Y el General Stroessner, Presidente del Paraguay,
es también un poquito Presidente de mi país, aunque menos
que el Presidente de Honduras o sea
el General López Arellano, y más que el Presidente de Haití,
Monsieur Duvalier.
Y el Presidente de los Estados Unidos es más Presidente de mi país,
que el Presidente de mi país,
ese que, como dije, hoy por hoy,
se llama Coronel Fidel Sánchez Hernández."

10. The leader who lasted longest in the list, Stroessner, began to rise through military ranks in the wake of the Battle of Boquerón, as mentioned in chapter 1, and served as president of Paraguay from 1954 to

1989, thanks in part to his strong alignment with the United States and its repressive anti-communist policies during the Cold War.

11. For an interesting take that reads Adorno's famous remark—"To write poetry after Auschwitz is barbaric"—through the poetry of Paul Celan, see Zilcosky.

12. While anti-aggression pacts dominated postwar policy in Europe and the Americas, philosophy and art were also placed on trial for their part in allowing, even celebrating and encouraging, the violence that shook Europe. The most emblematic case is the rise of Nazism, and famously, Heidegger became a target of criticism because of his inability or unwillingness to recognize the National Socialist project for what it was, typified in the 1933 Rectorate Address "Self-Assertion." Heidegger's exposure, in turn, led to a more extensive critique of Western philosophy, including Levinas's.

13. See, especially, Fried, ch. 1.

14. Lest it seem that the rectorate at the University of Freiburg is the only ethically questionable academic post, Berger's *Under Northern Eyes* shows the university's role in perpetuating US hegemony in the Latin American context.

15. "¿Para quién deberá ser la voz del poeta?"

16. "Cuando sepas que he muerto, no pronuncies mi nombre"; "Flor, abeja, lágrima, pan, tormenta"; "He ganado el silencio." The title of this collection is difficult to translate, as *turno* might indicate a turn or shift, a duty, or someone on call.

17. For more information, see Castellanos Moya, *Roque Dalton*. Castellanos Moya documents Dalton's movements as he returns to armed struggle, filling in details from his research in the Dalton family's private archive.

18. "Todos nacimos medio muertos en 1932 / sobrevivimos pero medio vivos."

19. For more on the 1932 massacre's importance for Dalton, see Pérez, particularly ch. 2, 119–81.

20. My claim that Dalton uses poetry to signal a problem with representation differs from Knight's analysis of *Las historias prohibidas*. Knight argues that Dalton presents a counterhegemonic project with essentially the same model of masculinity as the hegemonic Salvadoran government model. While masculinity is a key part of the "hombre nuevo" paradigm, Dalton's poetry also presents elements that exceed the hegemonic/counterhegemonic dichotomy, even if, as Knight claims, he does not challenge the male/female one.

21. "Los muertos están cada día más indóciles / . . . / Me parece que caen en la cuenta / de ser cada vez más la mayoría."

22. "Tegucigalpa, el 25 de mayo de 1969 (AP). El Ministro de Relaciones Exteriores de Honduras, en un discurso sobre los efectos de la integración económica centroamericana en su país, señaló a la crema dental Colgate salvadoreña como factor de aumento de las caries entre los niños hondureños."

23. "Fuera de los textos y poemas originales, tres textos han sido modificados para lograr los efectos perseguidos por el autor y dos textos aparentemente extraídos de otras publicaciones son apócrifos, escritos también originalmente por el autor. Corresponde a los lectores descubrirlos."

24. This is an argument with but also against Badiou. On the first account, it valorizes Badiou's work on radical acceptance of undocumented migrants. On the latter, it questions the functions of naming and fidelity that extend from Badiou's theory of subjectivity, which one might expect to align clearly with a Marxist poet-militant like Dalton. While there are certain commonalities between Badiou's poetic and political preferences and Dalton's, Dalton's later work has a more nuanced relationship with the militant subject and the field of the political.

25. "XXXVII. Algunos resultados del conflicto (hasta la fecha): Rearme y modernización del ejército salvadoreño bajo la dirección norteamericana"; "Rearme y modernización del ejército hondureño bajo la dirección norteamericana"; "Decenas de miles de salvadoreños vagando con su hambre a cuestas de Honduras a El Salvador y de El Salvador a Honduras. En Honduras ya no tienen tierra. En El Salvador no tienen tierra ni trabajo. No son ni salvadoreños ni hondureños: son pobres."

26. "La falsificación de la historia de esa guerra / es su continuación por otros medios / la continuación de la verdadera guerra que se desarrolló / bajo las apariencias de una guerra entre El Salvador y Honduras: / la guerra imperialista-oligárquico-burguesa-gubernamental / contra los pueblos de Honduras y El Salvador."

27. Beverley also explains, "La idea de 'post-literatura' sugiere no tanto la superación de la literatura como forma cultural sino una actitud más agnóstica ante ella" (398; The idea of 'post-literature' suggests not so much the overcoming of literature as a cultural form but rather an agnostic attitude towards it). The use of the religious term "agnostic" indicates that belief still forms the central concern of the intersection of literature and testimonio.

28. On testimonio and its exhaustion by the mid- to late 1990s, see Gugelberger.

29. For more on the relationship between testimonio and the literary text, see "Aura of Testimonio" in Moreiras, *Exhaustion* 208–38.

30. Mignolo's "Many Faces of Cosmo-polis" explores problems ranging from sixteenth-century Atlantic commerce and the nation state to natural law and human rights discourse and provides a critical genealogy of the European "cosmo-polis." However, it turns into a modified form of the same idea with a slight twist; Mignolo calls for "critical cosmopolitanism," a "globalization from below" ("The Many Faces" 721). He takes up similar themes in "Cosmopolitanism," seeing a critical distance from the cosmopolitan tradition rooted in European thought but concludes by espousing "cosmopolitan localism" ("Cosmopolitanism" 127). While attempting to amplify their distance from Europe, decolonial critics circle back to the same epistemological problems and structures.

31. So-called dirty realism is the most obvious and commercially successful offshoot of this trend, exporting an image of Latin America's violent drug lords and underling *sicarios* to present realism with grit. Books and films with these themes sell well in the Global North and show the shrinking gap between criminals and state actors alongside the rise of paramilitary and extra-legal forces.

32. "[Doña Lena] decía que habíamos hecho bien al expulsar a los salvadoreños de Honduras, aunque después nos atacaran con una guerra alevosa: 'Esa gente es maligna, y como ahora ya no tienen a quien agredir, han decidido matarse entre sí'."

33. "Cerrar puertas y ventanas"; "Arreglar un cerco de piedra que había sido afectado por una correntada."

34. "En algún momento de la noche me pareció oír el ruido del bastón de doña Lena golpeando la loseta del piso, como si ella hubiese andando caminando por la casa, como si yo no hubiese cerrado todas y cada una de las puertas de las habitaciones y del corredor, tal como ella hacía. Los ecos permanecen en las casas aunque ya nadie las habite."

35. "Le dije que alguna vez le escuché a doña Lena comentar que los terrenos de su familia se habían perdido por las interminables disputas entre los herederos y que la reforma agraria les había pegado el tiro de gracia; también le conté que el abogado Mira Brossa [el esposo de doña Lena y abuelo de Eri], cuando fue director del Instituto Nacional Agrario, veinte años atrás, había tenido que repartir las últimas caballerías entre las cooperativas campesinas, algo que doña Lena nunca le perdonó y por lo que lo acusaba de haber sido un 'tonto útil' de los curas comunistas."

36. NAFTA was replaced in 2020 with the United States–Mexico–Canada Agreement (USMCA). In addition to Central American countries, CAFTA includes the Dominican Republic, which joined negotiations later and is now included in a larger agreement, abbreviated CAFTA-DR.

37. "Era extraño escucharla, porque repetía frases que yo me sabía de tanto oírlas a lo largo de los años, pero mezcladas, sin hilación."

38. "Me desperté cuando ella [doña Lena] gritaba, fuera de sí, que esa pareja de traidores [su hija Teti y nieto Eri] la pagaría caro, que su maldición era que errarían sin patria ni posesiones lo que les quedaba de vida. Entonces escuché los golpes enérgicos del bastón en el corredor, como si doña Lena recién se hubiese levantado, enojada porque yo había olvidado trancar las puertas de la casa como era mi deber."

39. "Recordé que aún no había cumplido su voluntad de quemar las carpetas que ella escondía bajo la vieja máquina de escribir y que ahora yo tenía guardadas en el sótano."

40. "Los muertos están cada día más indóciles." See also the reading of Marx's *Eighteenth Brumaire* in Derrida, *Specters of Marx* 118–55.

41. Another of Castellanos Moya's novels, *Insensatez* (Senselessness), directly engages the archive, this time in indigenous accounts of massacres in a human rights report about the Guatemalan civil war. Acosta reads this novel as a conjunction of testimonio and mestizo fiction, confirming these two modes continue to be dominant in Central American fiction, which therefore fails to overcome the testimonio model. My argument here, while only tangentially related to testimonio, is that Dalton's and Castellanos Moya's texts point to a trace that exceeds the fidelity and strong subjectivity inherent in communist-militant and testimonial models.

42. The epigraph is in Spanish prose rather than English verse in *Desmoronamiento*.

43. The next chapter offers a more sustained reflection on temporality through Heidegger's temporal ecstases.

44. For another perspective on the idea of global war, see Williams, "Decontainment," in which the Schmittian *katechon* serves to contain—that is, to border.

45. I examine this idea further in the conclusion of my article "*Polemos*."

46. Marramao explains that the contradictory relationship has destroyed a long-standing political paradigm: "Jurists like Stefano Rodotà have spoken for some time of the 'fragmentation of the sovereign' in an epoch marked by new bioethical and biopolitical problems generated

by the exponential growth of technological innovations that increasingly invest the private and corporeal spheres. More generally, in recent years the conviction has grown that the fall of the Berlin Wall not only marked the end of the Soviet empire and of the bipolar system but has also brought to an end the epoch of the nation state that began with the French Revolution" (97).

4. THE FALKLANDS/MALVINAS WAR AND NEOLIBERAL ECSTASY

Gamerro, *Las Islas* 132. My translation: "The homeland exists on a symbolic level. Basically, it's a metaphor. If you try to make it real all at once, it will evaporate right out of your hands." In this chapter, English translations of Gamerro's *Las Islas* are from Gamerro's *The Islands*, translated by Ian Barnett, unless otherwise noted; all page number references are from the Spanish version of Gamerro's *Las Islas*. All English translations from the novel *Los pichiciegos* are my own and not from the English-translated edition, *Malvinas Requiem*.

1. My translation. "La patria existe a nivel simbólico. Básicamente, es una metáfora. Si uno trata de hacerla real toda de golpe se le evaporará de las manos."

2. "Estado placentero de exaltación emocional y admirativa."

3. "Cristóforo / (el Portador de Cristo)."

4. Note also the parallel with *La laguna H.3* in chapter 1, in which invasion and border fixing recalls Columbus and colonial territorialization.

5. De facto president Leopoldo Galtieri was forced to confront the issue of democracy in his interview with Fallaci. Using the dictatorship's official rhetoric, he defended the impossibility of the vote as preparation for future electoral democracy. Once the pressing issues of the present had been satisfactorily resolved, democratic elections would return to Argentina (Fallaci). Galtieri expected to win the election and legitimize his government on the strength of the recovery of Malvinas.

6. Sarlo's use of the word *colony* also indicates that even an antinationalist group of Argentine settlers invokes a similarly colonial structure.

7. "Y aunque nadie sabía si los Magos eran capaces de matar o no a un pichi o a uno que había sido pichi, por las dudas no lo iban a probar: obedecían."

8. *Death flights* was the name of the state-sanctioned process of dropping bodies of detained citizens into the Río de la Plata from a plane or helicopter so that there would be no forensic evidence of the state's involvement in detainees' deaths. Fogwill's discussion of the disappear-

ances and death flights was a bold step at the time, given the climate of pervasive fear and far-reaching censorship.

9. "'Che Turco . . . ¿te parece . . . ?' '¿Qué?' '¿Que éstos pueden votar?' '¡Éstos no pueden nada!,' dijo el Turco y '¡dormite!'"

10. "Como nadie nombró a los pichis que faltaban, el Turco sacó el tema y les dijo que habían quedado con los ingleses, en garantía, y todos creyeron, o quisieron creer o hacer creer que creían."

11. "Es que el miedo suelta el instinto que cada uno lleva dentro, y así como algunos con el miedo se vuelven más forros que antes, porque les sale el dormido de adentro, a él le despertó el árabe de adentro: ese instinto de amontonar las cosas y de cambiar y de mandar. . . . Y el que lo veía mandando, cambiando y almacenando cosas ni pensaba que atrás de todo eso estaba el miedo. Pero es el miedo el que está atrás mandándote, cambiándote."

12. "Si a él le sobraba querosén, hacía correr la bola de que precisaba querosén, que se acababa el querosén, que todos daban cualquier cosa por el querosén. Después mandaba un pichi desconocido a la Intendencia o al pueblo, o a los ingleses, a ofrecer querosén y volvía lleno de montones de cosas a cambio de un bidón aguado que a él le venía sobrando."

13. In an interview with Kohan, Fogwill accounts for Sarlo's 1994 materialist analysis of *Los pichiciegos* in "No olvidar la guerra de Malvinas" as a response to neoliberal *menemismo*, in which one was free to choose as long as that choice was to stay in the market (Kohan, "Fogwill").

14. "Los dos ingleses, los veintitrés pichis y todo lo que abajo estuvieron guardando van a formar una sola cosa, una nueva piedra metida dentro de la piedra vieja del cerro."

15. Note also that Fogwill was sometimes referred to as Quique, after his middle name Enrique.

16. See Perosino et al. Their book, *La dictadura del capital financiero*, provides evidence of a close relationship between the 1976–1983 dictatorship and corporations that began introducing finance capitalism into Argentina.

17. Caruth's *Unclaimed Experience* is a seminal reference in trauma studies, though much contested since its publication in 1996. Caruth's work serves as a bedrock of literary trauma studies and has been incorporated into studies of Malvinas. However, Malabou serves as the primary theoretical reference here, as we will see later in this chapter. Both theorists draw from Freud.

18. "Dedicándonos por las tardes, si habíamos conseguido algo que valiera la pena, al trueque con los clanes vecinos (comida, pilas, combus-

tible de helicóptero, ropa, latas vacías, turba seca; todo menos el dinero tenía su valor)."

19. The closest anyone comes to escaping is Félix, who, as one of the only English speakers, gets taken to the village to interpret. Because the information that he conveys contradicts what the officers want to hear, Félix is relieved of his duties, allegedly for supporting the enemy's psychological propaganda campaign, and asked to return to his regiment (340). His experience as a wartime translator, cast aside as a traitor, mirrors the Italian phrase "traduttore, traditore," and as a traitor, he returns to the regiments where Gamerro adapts Fogwill's story.

20. "Había aparecido un día pidiendo algo de comer, y no supo decir de qué compañía o regimiento venía. Era un 63, se le notaba en los ojos, y aparentemente se había fugado de su posición por el maltrato o la inquina de algún oficial: era lo más parecido a desertar que podía lograrse en estas Islas de mierda. Al principio debatieron si guardarlo o no, podían castigarlos y la comida ya no alcanzaba, pero con Carlos impulsando el voto lo adoptaron como mascota y como no hablaba ni tenía identificación le pusieron Hijitus."

21. "Para lo cual propone, entre otras cosas, reconquistar Bolivia, Paraguay y Uruguay e invadir Chile y Brasil."

22. Tamerlán and his company reappear in Gamerro's cycle of novels about the legacies of major figures in Argentine history: in order of publication, *Las Islas* (originally published in 1998) about Malvinas; *La aventura* (originally published in 2002) about Eva Perón; and *Un yuppie* (originally published in 2010) about Ernesto "Che" Guevara.

23. "Se vinieron para el Quinto Centenario. Hace unos días empezaron con la maldita carabela, allá afuera, para la Expoamérica 92. . . . ¡Qué bajo hemos caído! Pero tenemos que financiar la tercera fundación, y me parece natural que como en las otras dos anteriores se pongan los españoles."

24. "Mi reino es de este mundo."

25. Freud goes on to complicate this hypothesis, later arriving at the titular idea of something beyond the pleasure principle. More on this later in this chapter, along with more recent interpretations from Malabou and Žižek.

26. "Ahí están todos los datos que necesitás, los hechos, las fechas, los nombres; toda la historia, contada por un afásico con una bala en el cerebro que no tuvo tanta suerte como vos, o más suerte, qué sé yo, andá a preguntarle."

27. My translation; part of this quotation does not appear in the English version. "Una vez me explicaron que sus oídos percibían sus

propias frases sin error, y que eran las nuestras las que se habían vuelto un balbuceo obsceno. ¡No era él quien había perdido el habla, sino todos los demás!"

28. Emilio's aphasia also recalls Alicia's in *Hablar con los perros* in chapter 2.

29. "Me entendía ahora con las máquinas como si fuéramos animales de la misma especie; y la única explicación posible estaba ahí, en ese bulto cruzado por cicatrices que el pelo en el espejo todavía no llegaba a cubrir; el pedazo de la máquina que yo había incorporado para siempre a mi cuerpo."

30. "Eran estas pequeñas cicatrices brillosas lo que mis dedos habían detectado antes, en la oscuridad confundiéndolas con una ilusión táctil fruto de mi embeleso; el mapa que yo había trazado uniendo estos puntos con mis dedos recién ahora empezaba a tomar forma."

31. "Yo, paralizada, no pude ni gritar."

32. "Ese día fue como una revelación para mí, ¿entendés? Como si el hacha me hubiera partido en dos la cabeza a mí. Seguí con la militancia, incluso después del golpe, pero solo por reflejo, en automático."

33. "Sé que en algún momento se me anuló la conciencia, como si hubieran tirado demasiado del cable del enchufe: simplemente se desconectó."

34. According to the *Psychodynamic Diagnostic Manual*'s description of traumatic stress: "Traumatic experience may overwhelm mental capacities, disturb affective experience and expression, and interfere with the capacity for symbolization and fantasy, thus contributing to the breakdown of meaning. It may also interfere with thinking and with the mental processing of trauma-related memories and fantasies. Psychic trauma effects changes in the sense of self . . . and in the quality of interpersonal relationships. Clinical literature has highlighted obligatory repetition and persistent re-experiencing of traumatic events, through recurring nightmares flashbacks/reminiscences, and driven re-enactments of traumatic themes" (PDM Task Force). Gamerro's novel works through this mental processing through symbolization, memory, and fantasy. For a description of the neurological response to traumatic events, see van der Kolk.

35. "Dejamos un espacio preciso cuando nos fuimos, pero allá cambiamos de forma, y al volver ya no encajábamos, por más vueltas que nos dieran, en el rompecabezas; volvimos diez mil iluminados, locos, profetas malditos, y ahí andamos, sueltos por las cuatro puntas del país, hablando un idioma que nadie entiende haciendo como que trabajamos, jugamos al fútbol, cogemos, pero nunca del todo, en algún lugar sabiendo siempre que algo nuestro valioso e indefinible quedó enterrado allá."

36. In her reading of *Las Islas* in her book *Masculinidades en guerra*, Ehrmantraut interprets Félix's condition as hysteria. While this reading aligns with Ehrmantraut's gender focus, PTSD recognizes the similarities between Félix and Gloria's conditions as similar results of internal and external war.

37. "El tiempo para nosotros detenido en un instante como los relojes de Hiroshima."

38. "No te quepa duda. Puedo escribirte un libro."

39. "Empecé con el día en que entré por primera vez a la torre de Tamerlán, o con el día en que los tres canas vinieron para reincorporarme al ejército; no había mucha diferencia: a medida que avanzaba me daba cuenta de que las dos historias habían terminado por fundirse en una como dos ríos se juntan para formar un tercero, o quizás siempre había sido uno solo y era yo el que se había encontrado en dos momentos con dos tramos distintos sin darme cuenta de que el agua era la misma."

40. "Otra torsión a la cinta de Moebius que serpenteando entre dos mundos vueltos uno como dos espejos enfrentados había terminado por encontrarse meramente a sí misma." Barnett adds the serpent eating its tail, echoing "serpenteando" as well as the conspiracy theories of the Asociación Virreinal.

41. MDMA has since been tested as part of a treatment program for PTSD in studies that found it increases tolerance for traumatic memories while encouraging imagination and association (Mithoefer et al.; Oehen et al.).

42. "Che, me parece que vinieron fantásticos estos bichos [las píldoras]"; "¿Dónde los conseguiste?"; "Me llovieron del cielo. Un amigo que vino de España."; "¿Colón?"

43. The reconfiguration of "discovery," especially as "bringing near" things that are already at hand, is a central dynamic in this scene, developed in this chapter through Heidegger's writing on temporality rather than trauma theory.

44. "Una nueva ráfaga de aire tibio soplada desde el nuevo mundo apagó en nuestras bocas las palabras antes de que llegáramos a pronunciarlas, y una lánguida y exquisita dulzura se apoderó de mis extremidades, sujetándolas, entregándome inerme a esas manos irrespetuosas que sin permiso de mi parte empezaron a amasar en una bola la arcilla de mi viejo cuerpo; una nueva identidad nacía temblando a medida que sus dedos hábiles iban desenvainando de ellas las formas del nuevo; las manos de Rodin no habrían dado tanta vida a mis miembros."

45. Translation modified to include some phrases omitted from Barnett's translation. "Las palabras habían caído como los vestidos y en esta

terrible desnudez sin miedo la voz no era más que respiración sonora, el mismo sonido repetido una y otra vez equivalente a toda la literatura, las palabras vertidas en mis oídos no más que prolongaciones de los labios que los besaban. Qué equivocado había estado siempre: no eran las cosas las que se encontraban distanciadas de las palabras; éramos nosotros, y de la misma manera que por primera vez tocaba lo que alcanzaban mis ávidas manos de bebé, por primera vez decía las palabras que hasta ahora apenas había repetido, las decía con todo el cuerpo, no sólo la lengua y la garganta, y la voz . . . la voz era el sentido del tacto yendo por dentro."

46. Translation modified. "Los relojes habían recuperado su autoridad sobre el tiempo, trozándolo minuciosamente con sus precisos cuchillos, los objetos volvían a revestirse de su superficie y los dedos ya no conseguían atravesarla al tocarlos."

47. "Primero caigo en el infierno, después aparezco en el paraíso, y de golpe . . . acá."

48. Žižek's understanding of the post-traumatic subject in "Descartes" differs from Malabou's. His analysis returns to the most basic, "autistic" split subject described by Jacques Lacan. This interpretation allows him to recover the post-traumatic subject in the service of his political project: the return of the commons and a renewed communism. Malabou, on the other hand, favors a sustained inquiry into the nature of the destruction of the subject through a neurological break that has not been accounted for in psychoanalysis, especially in *New Wounded* and *Ontology of the Accident*. She addresses Freud's *Beyond the Pleasure Principle* in the essay "Plasticity."

49. "Estamos ganándole terreno al río. Ganando. ¡Ja! Tanto esfuerzo para comprar espacio cuando lo que necesito es tiempo."

50. My translation. "Hubieran sido amigos, pero se vieron una sola vez cara a cara, en unas islas demasiado famosas, y cada uno de los dos fue Caín, y cada uno, Abel."

51. There are numerous other doubles associated with alternative histories, including the Asociación Virreinal's belief that if the Argentines had invaded the other, less inhabited island, they would have won the war; Félix's video game, seen in this chapter, which shows Argentina always winning at first, then always losing; a veteran's painstakingly detailed model of Stanley/Puerto Argentino, perfected so that his comrades can destroy it and enact their revenge—although the man always claims the model is incomplete because, they suspect, he does not want them to destroy it.

52. "Voy a reventarla [la empresa]. El control pasa a una sociedad anónima, y Canal [el psicoanalista] y yo quedamos apenas como accion-

istas. Ya acordamos la reestructuración. Vamos a rotar todos los espejos, para que nadie sepa muy bien dónde está el jefe. Va a ser una democracia. Una democracia sin pueblo. Esta cosa personalizada y jerárquica es muy vulnerable. El error de la araña."

53. "Una utopía anarquista al revés. Una organización sin jefes donde nadie es libre."

54. For a detailed analysis of the transition between dictatorship and democracy as part of a generalized crisis of sovereignty, see Dove.

55. In Spanish, the islands are called Soledad and Malvina; in English, they are referred to as East and West Falkland.

56. Malabou would not classify Down syndrome as an example of destructive plasticity, since her work focuses on traumatic brain lesions and not genetic anomalies. In particular, she is interested in how brain trauma causes a radical shift in personality, so that the same body might have two radically different personalities—one before and one after the trauma or accident. However, in fiction, the author has more latitude to play with the body, and in Gamerro's fictionalized legacy, Soledad and Malvina appear at the end of the novel to resolve Gloria and Félix's traumatic confrontation with their own death into the everyday.

5. THE FALKLANDS/MALVINAS WAR AND BORDER METASTASIS

Pron, *Nosotros caminamos en sueños* 106. Translation: "'Who are we?' I asked again, and I had the impression that I'd spent the whole war asking myself the same question."

1. "Para competir en suelo inglés, entrenamos en suelo argentino."

2. "Los pibes de Malvinas que jamás olvidaré."

3. I chose *Merriam-Webster* over the *Concise Oxford English Dictionary* for the English definition of *metastasis* because it has a wider range of definitions, more expansive than medical terminology. The *Oxford Dictionary of Literary Terms*, however, has more specific rhetorical definitions and examples.

4. Dialogue sets the date as October 11 without specifying a year. Although I have examined various archival newspapers from the capital on that date, I have not been able to ascribe any particular significance to it beyond its nearness to the October 17 Día de la Lealtad, a Peronist celebration and commemoration.

5. "¡Que se vayan todos! ¡Vamos a la Plaza de Mayo!"

6. The implicit support for Kirchnerism is no accident. Bauer later became director of the Sistema Nacional de Medios Públicos from 2008 to 2013 and director of Radio y Televisión Argentina from 2013 to 2015.

7. "Empezamos a caer y caer y no paramos hasta ahora."

8. "Tuvimos años muy lindos."

9. In the scenes shot on the islands, the film becomes especially heavy-handed with its political views, emphasizing the majority culturally British inhabitants' disdain for Argentines. Esteban confronts his English-speaking guide about uncleared land mines, demanding to know why demining operations were taking so long. Demining was successfully completed in 2020, fifteen years after the film's release ("Falkland Islanders").

10. There are different versions of the film circulating, and not all of them include "Las Malvinas son argentinas" at the end; a full-length copy uploaded to YouTube does not, while the DVD version of the film does. However, all copies have a dedication to the "soldados conscriptos" who fought on the islands, noticeably excluding elective and career military personnel.

11. "Yo me oponía a que los identificaran porque decían que querían traer los cuerpos al continente. Yo me oponía a que los identificaran porque pensé que de mi hijo no quedaba nada. Yo me oponía a que los identificaran porque todos se oponían."

12. The script emerged from Arias's 2014 video installation *Veterans* and later became the 2018 feature-length film *Theatre of War/Teatro de guerra*, analyzed in this chapter.

13. Arias takes the sovereign skewering further in a scene in which the two actors dressed as Galtieri and Thatcher slowly move toward each other to kiss. The scene mocks the closeness of animosity to desire. In another scene, an actor in drag performs a striptease in front of the others, reenacting one of the Royal Marine's stories about the long journey south by sea. Through masks and costumes, Arias uses the surface of the set to explore, exploit, and mock commonly gendered tropes of warfare.

14. For analyses of the play that emphasize empathy and storytelling rather than the interruption of witnessing and identity, see Blejmar and Sosa.

15. The English script reads, "a white backdrop stands in the middle of the stage." I choose the Spanish *sinfín* because it evokes multiple facets of meaning that *backdrop* lacks.

16. Vardoulakis's genealogy of stasis and metastasis through Greek drama are critical here, developed later in this chapter.

17. "Los ingleses no hablan español y los argentinos no hablamos inglés. Pero de alguna forma nos entendimos." All direct quotations from *Minefield/Campo minado* are taken from the published script, which includes two monolingual texts, one in Spanish and one in English. I

reproduce the English in the body of the chapter and the Spanish, if appropriate, in a note. In the performance, all actors spoke their native languages. I saw the play performed on June 9, 2016, at the Royal Court Theatre in London.

18. As Virilio argues in *War and Cinema*, film and war have long benefitted each other. Techniques and optics from film appear in techniques and optics of war. In this way, images of war both reveal and conceal the spectacle of violence. Photos and videos show what is happening but only as supplements since, as Mieszkowski points out, total war cannot be comprehended. Firsthand accounts and images of battlefields may help audiences imagine a war that is otherwise incomprehensible because it exceeds sensory capacity. In Mieszkowski's words: "The authority of total war will truly be threatened only when the scope of the imagination that underwrites its absolutist claims becomes an object of critique" (194). I see Arias's work, especially in *Theatre of War/Teatro de guerra*, as a critique of a tendency to valorize war's totality via an individualized post-traumatic subject instead of decentering war's optics and techniques.

19. "No es contra mí contra quien disparan. Es contra todos."

20. "¡Es tan imbécil que podría pasar por un héroe!"

21. "'¿Quiénes somos nosotros?,' volví a preguntar, y tuve la impresión de que me había pasado toda la guerra haciéndome esa pregunta."

22. "Verás, el problema aquí es que hemos convertido a un amigo en enemigo pero hemos olvidado convertir a nuestro enemigo en amigo. . . . O convertir al amigo de nuestro enemigo en enemigo, o pedirle al amigo de nuestro enemigo que le dijera que fuera nuestro amigo."

23. "'Disculpe, señor, pero ¿quiénes somos nosotros?—preguntó Whitelocke dando un paso al frente—. Quiero decir, ¿usted se refiere a ustedes o a nosotros?,' insistió Whitelocke. '¿Qué ustedes?,' preguntó el Coronel. '¿Qué nosotros?,' respondió Whitelocke. 'Mejor olvídenlo,' suspiró el Coronel Mayor. '¿A quiénes? ¿A ustedes o a nosotros?,' preguntó Sorgenfrei."

24. Curiously, Pron does not use more modern technologies like drones, as US playwright George Brant does in the popular 2012 play *Grounded* about a pilot forced to fly drones instead of jets.

25. "Sorgenfrei, Snowden y los demás estaban reunidos alrededor de un agujero del que no paraban de salir militares argentinos que se rendían tan pronto como alcanzaban la superficie. . . . Se ponían serios y afirmaban que las islas eran argentinas, aunque hasta ese momento no habíamos visto a ningún argentino en ellas y no teníamos idea de si el enemigo era argentino o no: creíamos estar seguros de que nosotros no éramos argentinos y de que teníamos cierto derecho sobre las islas y nos

preguntamos si a partir de ese momento íbamos a tener que pelear contra dos enemigos en vez de contra uno." The omitted part of this quotation discusses how the Argentines enjoyed describing torture but stopped when they realized their audience was not amused.

26. "Éste no es el ejército burocrático del tiempo de sus abuelos. Éste es un ejército moderno que busca la optimización de sus recursos pero elude cualquier clase de traba burocrática: somos una empresa capitalista de exterminio masivo que no escapa a la necesidad de optimizar sus recursos como cualquier otra empresa."

27. "Una bomba había quedado suspendida sobre nuestras cabezas y todos nos habíamos preguntado si eso era algo rutinario en esa guerra o una novedad, inapreciable para quienes—como nosotros—carecían de toda experiencia previa en esa clase de cosas."

28. "Todos mirábamos las oscilaciones de la bomba expectantes y convencidos de que era nuestro fin, que era el momento de decir adiós."

29. "Terrible y magnífica como la Voz de Dios o el Día del Juicio."

30. "El tiempo pareció comenzar a transcurrir de nuevo, como si realmente se hubiese detenido un momento atrás."

31. "¡Deja de robar!"

32. "¡Deja de robar, coño!"

33. "Tampoco hice caso a la voz en la intemperie, que gritaba: '¡Me he cansado así que ya no lo digo más!'"

34. "El soldado se acercó a mí como si quisiera estudiarme más detenidamente y en ese momento noté, y creo que él también lo notó, que existía un cierto parecido entre nosotros: el mismo mechón de cabello que caía sobre la frente, una nariz similar, el mismo color de ojos, cicatrices semejantes provocadas por el frío en las mejillas y en los pómulos, los mismos surcos y las mismas arrugas que nos asemejaban."

35. "Al ver la fotografía que me había extendido, quise mostrarle que yo también tenía una fotografía que había encontrado en un uniforme, mostrarle que él y quienquiera que se hubiera puesto ese uniforme antes que yo habían amado a una y la misma mujer, pero al llevarme la mano al bolsillo interior de la chaqueta sólo palpé la culata de una pistola. Entonces la saqué y disparé dos veces al rostro del soldado, que cayó hacia atrás; al mirar por encima de su cuerpo ese rostro que ya no se parecía al mío noté que en el uniforme llevaba bordado un nombre y que ese nombre todavía se podía leer pese a que la sangre había comenzado a extenderse por todo el pecho. Leí 'Graichen' y pensé en el pedido de O'Brien y tuve la impresión de que todo estaba en orden por fin y encajaba."

36. Note that the woman's photograph recalls earlier representations of how women influence war, such as in the photo in "La paraguaya" in

Augusto Céspedes's *Sangre de mestizos*, discussed in chapter 1. In *Iluminados por el fuego*, discussed in chapter 4, Esteban and Alberto also discuss their partners, and Alberto indicates that just before being transferred to Malvinas he had fought with the woman who would later become his wife.

37. "Entre todas las putas mierdas del mundo esa guerra era sin dudas la peor."

38. "¡Pero si es mi única línea!"

WORKS CITED

Acosta, Abraham. "Of Failed Retreats: Postcolonial Theory and Post-Testimonial Narrative in Central American Writing." *Política común*, vol. 9, 2016, https://doi.org/10.3998/pc.12322227.0009.008.

Adorno, Theodor W. "Cultural Criticism and Society." *Prisms*, translated by Samuel Weber and Shierry Weber, MIT Press, 1983, pp. 17–34.

Agamben, Giorgio. *Stasis: Civil War as a Political Paradigm.* Translated by Nicholas Heron, Stanford UP, 2015.

Anderson, Thomas P. *The War of the Dispossessed: Honduras and El Salvador, 1969.* U of Nebraska P, 1981.

Andrade, Oswald de. "Cannibalist Manifesto." *Latin American Literary Review*, translated by Leslie Bary, vol. 19, no. 38, July–Dec. 1991, pp. 38–47.

Andrade, Oswald de. "Manifesto antropófago." *Revista da Antropofagia*, no. 1, May 1928.

Anzaldúa, Gloria. *Borderlands/La Frontera: The New Mestiza.* 2nd ed., Aunt Lute Books, 1999.

Arendt, Hannah. *On Revolution.* Penguin Books, 1965.

Arendt, Hannah. *The Origins of Totalitarianism.* New ed., Harcourt, 1994.

Arias, Lola. *Minefield/Campo minado.* Translated by Daniel Tunnard, Oberon Books, 2017.

Arias, Lola. *Minefield/Campo minado.* Directed by Lola Arias, 9 June 2016, Royal Court Theatre, London.

Aristotle. *Politics.* Translated by Ernest Barker, Oxford UP, 1998.

Avramescu, Cătălin. *An Intellectual History of Cannibalism*. Translated by Alistair Ian Blyth, Princeton UP, 2009.

Badiou, Alain. *Being and Event*. Translated by Oliver Feltham, Continuum, 2007.

Badiou, Alain. *The Age of the Poets: And Other Writings on Twentieth-Century Poetry and Prose*. Translated by Emily Apter and Bruno Bosteels, Verso Books, 2014.

Bähr, Eduardo. *El cuento de la guerra*. Casasola, 2013.

Barthes, Roland. *Camera Lucida: Reflections on Photography*. Translated by Richard Howard, Hill and Wang, 1982.

Beckett, Samuel. *Waiting for Godot: A Tragicomedy in Two Acts*. Grove Press, 1994.

Benjamin, Walter. "Critique of Violence (*Reflections*)." *On Violence: A Reader*, edited by Bruce B. Lawrence and Aisha Karim, Duke UP, 2007, pp. 268–85.

Benjamin, Walter. "Theses on the Philosophy of History." *Illuminations*, translated by Harry Zohn, edited by Hannah Arendt, Schocken Books, 2007, pp. 253–64.

Berger, Mark T. *Under Northern Eyes: Latin American Studies and U.S. Hegemony in the Americas, 1898–1990*. Indiana UP, 1995.

Berlant, Lauren. *Cruel Optimism*. Duke UP, 2011.

Beverley, John. "Post-literatura." *Nuevo texto crítico*, vol. 7, nos. 14–15, July 1994–June 1995, pp. 385–400.

Beverley, John, and Marc Zimmerman. *Literature and Politics in the Central American Revolutions*. U of Texas P, 1990.

Birnbaum, Daniel, and Anders Olsson. "An Interview with Jacques Derrida on the Limits of Digestion." *e-flux*, vol. 2, no. 1, Jan. 2009, https://www.e-flux.com/journal/02/68495/an-interview-with-jacques-derrida-on-the-limits-of-digestion/.

Blejmar, Jordana. "Autofictions of Postwar: Fostering Empathy in Lola Arias' *Minefield/Campo minado*." *Latin American Theatre Review*, vol. 50, no. 2, spring 2017, pp. 103–23.

Bodin, Jean. *Six Books of the Commonwealth*. Abridged and translated by M. J. Tooley. Blackwell, 1955.

Bolaño, Roberto. *2666*. Anagrama, 2004.

Bolivia (Estado Plurinacional de). "Decreto Supremo 0748." *Gaceta Oficial de Bolivia*, 26 Dec. 2010.

Bolivia (Estado Plurinacional de). "Decreto Supremo 0759." *Gaceta Oficial de Bolivia*, 31 Dec. 2010.

Bolivia (Estado Plurinacional de). "Decreto Supremo 28071: 'Héroes del Chaco.'" *Gaceta Oficial de Bolivia*, 1 May 2006.

Bolivia Takes What It Wants. Standard Oil Company (N.J.), 1941.

Borges, Jorge Luis. "Juan López y John Ward." *Los conjurados*, Emecé, 1985, p. 95.

Borges, Jorge Luis. "Tamerlán (1336–1405)." *El oro de los tigres*, Emecé, 1972, pp. 13–14.

Brant, George. *Grounded.* Samuel French, 2014.

Brown, J. Andrew. *Cyborgs in Latin America.* Palgrave Macmillan, 2010.

Brown, Wendy. *Walled States, Waning Sovereignty.* Zone Books, 2010.

Cable, Vincent. "The 'Football War' and the Central American Common Market." *International Affairs*, vol. 45, no. 4, Oct. 1969, pp. 658–71.

Caruth, Cathy. *Unclaimed Experience: Trauma, Narrative, and History.* Johns Hopkins UP, 1996.

Castellanos Moya, Horacio. *Desmoronamiento.* Tusquets, 2006.

Castellanos Moya, Horacio. *Insensatez.* Tusquets, 2006.

Castellanos Moya, Horacio. *Roque Dalton: Correspondencia clandestina y otros ensayos.* Random House, 2021.

Castro-Klarén, Sara. "A Genealogy for the 'Manifesto Antropófago,' or the Struggle between Socrates and the Caraïbe." *Nepantla*, vol. 1, no. 2, 2000, pp. 295–322.

Cerruto, Óscar. *Aluvión de fuego.* Edited by Carlos D. Mesa G., Plural, 2000.

Cervantes, Miguel de. *El coloquio de los perros.* Nórdica, 2014.

Céspedes, Augusto. *Crónicas heroicas de una guerra estúpida.* Editorial Juventud, 1975.

Céspedes, Augusto. *Sangre de mestizos: Relatos de la Guerra del Chaco.* Nascimento, 1936.

Chesterton, Bridget María. *The Grandchildren of Solano López: Frontier and Nation in Paraguay 1904–1936.* U of New Mexico P, 2013.

Clausewitz, Carl von. *On War.* Edited and translated by Michael Howard and Peter Paret, Princeton UP, 1984.

Confiscation: A History of the Oil Industry in Bolivia. Standard Oil Company of Bolivia, 1939.

Constitución Nacional Argentina. Disposiciones transitorias: Primera. 1994.

Costa du Rels, Adolfo. *La laguna H.3.* Translated by Nicolás Fernández Naranjo, Instituto Normal Superior de La Paz, 1967.

Costa du Rels, Adolfo. *Lagune H.3.* Viau, 1944.

Cote, Stephen C. *Oil and Nation: A History of Bolivia's Petroleum Sector.* West Virginia UP, 2016.

Courthès, Eric. "Hamaca paraguaya. Sinopsis y entrevista a Paz Encina por Eric Courthès." *Carátula* revista electrónica, abril-mayo 2008,

https://www.caratula.net/hamaca-paraguaya-sinopsis-y-entrevista
-a-paz-encina-por-eric-courthes/.

Dalton, Roque. *Las historias prohibidas del pulgarcito*. Siglo XXI, 1988.

Dalton, Roque. *El turno del ofendido*. Casa de las Américas, 1962.

Dalton, Roque. *Taberna y otros lugares*. Casa de las Américas, 1969.

Deleuze, Gilles, and Félix Guattari. *A Thousand Plateaus: Capitalism and Schizophrenia*. Translated by Brian Massumi, U of Minnesota P, 1987.

Derrida, Jacques. *The Politics of Friendship*. Translated by George Collins, Verso Books, 2005.

Derrida, Jacques. *Specters of Marx: The State of the Debt, the Work of Mourning and the New International*. Translated by Peggy Kamuf, Routledge, 2011.

Dove, Patrick. *Literature and "Interregnum": Globalization, War, and the Crisis of Sovereignty in Latin America*. State U of New York P, 2016.

Dowd, Shannon. "*Polemos*: The Struggle between Being and History in Heidegger and Derrida." *Política común*, vol. 13, 2019. https://doi.org/10.3998/pc.12322227.0013.010.

Duffield, Mark. *Development, Security and Unending War: Governing the World of Peoples*. Polity Press, 2007.

Duffield, Mark. "Global Civil War: The Non-Insured, International Containment and Post-Interventionary Society." *Journal of Refugee Studies*, vol. 21, no. 2, June 2008, pp. 145–65.

Duffield, Mark. *Global Governance and the New Wars: The Merging of Development and Security*. Zed Books, 2001.

Durham, William H. *Scarcity and Survival in Central America: Ecological Origins of the Soccer War*. Stanford UP, 1979.

"Ecstasy." *Concise Oxford English Dictionary*, 11th ed., edited by Catherine Soanes et al., Oxford UP, 2008, p. 454.

"Éxtasis." *Diccionario de la lengua española*, Real Academia Española, 2022, https://dle.rae.es/éxtasis.

Ehrmantraut, Paola. *Masculinidades en guerra: Malvinas en la literatura y el cine*. Comunicarte, 2013.

Elden, Stuart. *The Birth of Territory*. U of Chicago P, 2013.

Elden, Stuart. *Terror and Territory: The Spatial Extent of Sovereignty*. U of Minnesota P, 2009.

Esteban, Edgardo. *Iluminados por el fuego: Confesiones de un soldado que combatió en Malvinas*. Sudamericana, 1993.

Esposito, Roberto. *Third Person: Politics of Life and Philosophy of the Impersonal*. Translated by Zakiya Hanafi, Polity Press, 2012.

Evans, Dylan. *An Introductory Dictionary of Lacanian Psychoanalysis*. Routledge, 1996.

"Falkland Islanders Celebrate Being Landmine Free—After Nearly 40 Years." *BBC News*, 14 Nov. 2020, www.bbc.com/news/uk-wales -54894171#.

Fallaci, Oriana. "Galtieri: El general argentino que nunca peleó en una guerra." *El porteño*, vol. 1, no. 8, Aug. 1982, pp. 6–9.

"FIFA multa a Argentina por pancarta sobre las islas Malvinas." *El Comercio–Perú*, 25 July 2014, elcomercio.pe/deporte-total/futbol-mundial/ fifa-multa-argentina-pancarta-islas-malvinas-345520-noticia/.

Finburgh, Clare. "'Violence without Violence': Spectacle, War and Lola Arias's *MINEFIELD/CAMPO MINADO*." *Theatre Research International*, vol. 42, no. 2, July 2017, pp. 163–78.

Fogwill, Rodolfo Enrique. *Los pichiciegos: Visiones de una batalla subterránea*. Interzona, 2006.

Freud, Sigmund. *Beyond the Pleasure Principle*. Translated by James Strachey, W. W. Norton, 1989.

Fried, Gregory. *Heidegger's Polemos: From Being to Politics*. Yale UP, 2000.

Foucault, Michel. *"Society Must Be Defended": Lectures at the Collège de France, 1975–1976*. Translated by David Macey, edited by Mauro Bertani and Alessandro Fontana, Picador, 2003.

Fuentes, Carlos. *La nueva novela hispanoamericana*. Joaquín Mortiz, 1997.

Fukuyama, Francis. *The End of History and the Last Man*. Free Press, 2006.

Galak, Oliver. "No cesan los suicidios de ex combatientes de Malvinas." *La Nación*, 28 Feb. 2006, www.lanacion.com.ar/politica/no-cesan -los-suicidios-de-ex-combatientes-de-malvinas-nid784519/.

Galli, Carlo. *Political Spaces and Global War*. Translated by Elisabeth Fay, edited by Adam Sitze, U of Minnesota P, 2010.

Galloway, Alexander R. "Pamphlet 1: Catherine Malabou, or The Commerce in Being." *French Theory Today: An Introduction to Possible Futures: A pamphlet series by Alexander R. Galloway and the Public School New York*, Public School of New York, 2010, pp. 3–16. http:// cultureandcommunication.org/galloway/FTT/French-Theory-To day.pdf.

Gamerro, Carlos. *La aventura de los bustos de Eva*. Norma, 2009.

Gamerro, Carlos. *Las Islas*. Edhasa, 2012.

Gamerro, Carlos. *The Islands*. Translated by Ian Barnett, And Other Stories, 2012.

Gamerro, Carlos. *Un yuppie en la columna del Che Guevara*. Edhasa, 2011.

García Linera, Álvaro. *Las tensiones creativas de la revolución: La quinta fase del Proceso de Cambio*. Vicepresidencia del Estado Plurinacional, 2011.

Gardner, Lyn. "Minefield: The Falklands Drama Taking Veterans back to the Battle." *The Guardian*, 26 May 2016, www.theguardian.com/stage/2016/may/26/minefield-falklands-theatre-veterans-battle.

Ginés de Sepúlveda, Juan. *Tratado sobre las justas causas de la guerra contra los indios.* Fondo de Cultura Económica, 1986.

Graham-Jones, Jean. "The Translational Politics of Surtitling: Lola Arias's *Campo minado/Minefield.*" *Theatrical Speech Acts: Performing Language: Politics, Translation, Embodiments*, edited by Erika Fischer-Lichte et al., Routledge, 2020, pp. 119–30.

Gramuglio, María Teresa. "Políticas del decir y formas de la ficción: Novelas de la dictadura militar." *Punto de Vista*, no. 74, Dec. 2002, pp. 9–14.

Guerriero, Leila. *La otra guerra: Una historia del cementerio argentino en las islas Malvinas.* Anagrama, 2021.

Gugelberger, Georg M., editor. *The Real Thing: Testimonial Discourse and Latin America.* Duke UP, 1996.

Gustafson, Bret. *Bolivia in the Age of Gas.* Duke UP, 2020.

Gustafson, Lowell S. *The Sovereignty Dispute over the Falkland (Malvinas) Islands.* Oxford UP, 1988.

Hamaca paraguaya. Directed by Paz Encina, Black Forest Films et al., 2006.

Haraway, Donna J. "A Cyborg Manifesto: Science, Technology and Socialist-Feminism in the Late Twentieth Century." *Simians, Cyborgs, and Women: The Reinvention of Nature.* Routledge, 1991, pp. 149–82.

Harvey, David. *The New Imperialism.* Oxford UP, 2005.

Hassner, Ron E. "The Path to Intractability: Time and the Entrenchment of Territorial Disputes." *International Security*, vol. 31, no. 3, winter 2006/07, pp. 107–38.

Havercroft, Jonathan. *Captives of Sovereignty.* Cambridge UP, 2011.

Heidegger, Martin. *Being and Time.* Translated by Joan Stambaugh, revised by Dennis J. Schmidt, State U of New York P, 2010.

Heidegger, Martin. *Introduction to Metaphysics.* Translated by Gregory Fried and Richard Polt, Yale UP, 2000.

Heidegger, Martin. "On the Essence of Ground." *Pathmarks*, edited by William McNeill, Cambridge UP, 1998, pp. 97–135.

Heidegger, Martin. *The Principle of Reason.* Translated by Reginald Lilly, Indiana UP, 1991.

Heidegger, Martin. "The Self-Assertion of the German University: Address, Delivered on the Solemn Assumption of the Rectorate of the University Freiburg; the Rectorate 1933/34: Facts and Thoughts." Translated by Karsten Harries. *The Review of Metaphysics*, vol. 38, no. 3, Mar. 1985, pp. 467–502.

WORKS CITED

Hobbes, Thomas. *Leviathan.* Edited by Edwin Curley, Hackett, 1994.

Iffland, James. "*Las historias prohibidas del pulgarcito* como 'constelación' revolucionaria: Roque Dalton/Walter Benjamin." *Ensayos sobre la poesía revolucionaria de Centroamérica,* Editorial Universitaria Centroamericana, 1994, pp. 131–67.

Iluminados por el fuego. Directed by Tristán Bauer, performances by Gastón Pauls et al., INCAA et al., 2005.

Jameson, Fredric. *The Antinomies of Realism.* Verso Books, 2013.

Jameson, Fredric. *Valences of the Dialectic.* Verso Books, 2009.

Jenckes, Kate. *Witnessing beyond the Human: Addressing the Alterity of the Other in Post-coup Chile and Argentina.* State U of New York P, 2017.

Johnson, Adriana. "Paraguayan Counterlives." *Authoritarianism, Cultural History, and Political Resistance in Latin America: Exposing Paraguay,* edited by Federico Pous et al., Palgrave Macmillan, 2018, pp. 223–46.

Kaldor, Mary. *New and Old Wars: Organised Violence in a Global Era.* Stanford UP, 2012.

Kalimtzis, Kostas. *Aristotle on Political Enmity and Disease: An Inquiry into Stasis.* State U of New York P, 2000.

Kapuściński, Ryszard. *The Soccer War.* Translated by William Brand, Granta Books, 1990.

Klein, Herbert S. *Bolivia: The Evolution of a Multi-Ethnic Society.* 2nd ed., Oxford UP, 1992.

Knight, Jim. "'Más allá de las palabras': Violence, Masculinity and National Identity in Roque Dalton's *Las historias prohibidas del pulgarcito.*" *Bulletin of Hispanic Studies,* vol. 87, no. 6, Jan. 2010, pp. 685–703.

Kohan, Martín. "Fogwill, en pose de combate." *Clarín: Revista Ñ,* 25 Mar. 2006.

Kohan, Martín. "El fin de una épica." *Punto de Vista,* no. 64, Aug. 1999, pp. 6–11.

Kojève, Alexandre. *Introduction to the Reading of Hegel: Lectures on the Phenomenology of Spirit.* Edited by Allan Bloom, translated by James H. Nichols Jr., Cornell UP, 1969.

Lanham, Richard A. *A Handlist of Rhetorical Terms.* U of California P, 1991.

Levinas, Emmanuel. *Time and the Other.* Translated by Richard A. Cohen, Duquesne UP, 1987.

Levinas, Emmanuel. *Totality and Infinity: An Essay on Exteriority.* Translated by Alphonso Lingus, Kluwer Academic Publishers, 1991.

Loraux, Nicole. *The Divided City: On Memory and Forgetting in Ancient Athens.* Translated by Corinne Pache with Jeff Fort, Zone Books, 2002.

Loraux, Nicole. "La guerre dans la famille." *Clio*, no. 5, 1997, https://www.jstor.org/stable/44406238.

Malabou, Catherine. *Changing Difference.* Translated by Carolyn Shread, Polity Press, 2011.

Malabou, Catherine. *The Future of Hegel: Plasticity, Temporality and Dialectic.* Translated by Lisabeth During, Routledge, 2005.

Malabou, Catherine. *The New Wounded: From Neurosis to Brain Damage.* Translated by Steven Miller, Fordham UP, 2012.

Malabou, Catherine. *The Ontology of the Accident: An Essay on Destructive Plasticity.* Translated by Carolyn Shread, Polity Press, 2012.

Malabou, Catherine. "Plasticity and Elasticity in Freud's *Beyond the Pleasure Principle.*" *Diacritics*, vol. 37, no. 4, winter 2007, pp. 78–85.

Malabou, Catherine. *Plasticity at the Dusk of Writing: Dialectic, Destruction, Deconstruction.* Translated by Carolyn Shread, Columbia UP, 2009.

Maldonado-Torres, Nelson. *Against War: Views from the Underside of Modernity.* Duke UP, 2008.

Mares, David R. *Violent Peace: Militarized Interstate Bargaining in Latin America.* Columbia UP, 2001.

Marinetti, Filippo Tommaso. "Manifesto of Futurism." *The Documents of 20th-Century Art: Futurist Manifestos*, edited by Umbro Apollonio, translated by Robert Brain et al., Viking Press, 1973, pp. 19–24.

Marramao, Giacomo. *The Passage West: Philosophy After the Age of the Nation State.* Translated by Matteo Mandarini, Verso Books, 2012.

Martinon, Jean-Paul. *On Futurity: Malabou, Nancy and Derrida.* Palgrave Macmillan, 2007.

Marx, Karl. *Capital: Volume 1.* Translated by David Fernbach, Penguin, 1978.

Marx, Karl. *The Eighteenth Brumaire of Louis Bonaparte.* International Publishers, 2008.

Mattos Vazualdo, Diego. "De aluviones, pozos, mutilaciones y parques: La literatura boliviana de la Guerra del Chaco y la poética de la ausencia." *Revista Iberoamericana*, vol. 82, no. 254, Jan.–March 2016, pp. 157–71.

McGuirk, Bernard. *Falklands-Malvinas: An Unfinished Business.* New Ventures, 2007.

Menchú, Rigoberta, and Elizabeth Burgos-Debray. *Me llamo Rigoberta Menchú y así me nació la conciencia.* Argos Vergara, 1983.

"Metastasis." *Merriam-Webster*, 2021, www.merriam-webster.com/dictionary/metastasis.

"Metastasis." *Oxford Dictionary of Literary Terms*, 2021, https://www.ox fordreference.com/display/10.1093/oi/authority.20110803100 153253.

Mezzadra, Sandro, and Brett Neilson. *Border as Method, or, The Multiplication of Labor*. Duke UP, 2013.

Mi mejor enemigo: Patagonia, 1978. Directed by Alex Bowen, ALCE Producciones et al., 2005.

Mieszkowski, Jan. *Watching War*. Stanford UP, 2012.

Mignolo, Walter. "Cosmopolitanism and the De-colonial Option." *Studies in Philosophy and Education*, vol. 29, no. 2, Mar. 2010, pp. 111–27.

Mignolo, Walter. "The Many Faces of Cosmo-polis: Border Thinking and Critical Cosmopolitanism." *Public Culture*, vol. 12, no. 3, Sept. 2000, pp. 721–48.

Mithoefer, Michael C., et al. "The Safety and Efficacy of ±3,4-Methylenedioxymethamphetamine-Assisted Psychotherapy in Subjects with Chronic, Treatment-Resistant Posttraumatic Stress Disorder: The First Randomized Controlled Pilot Study." *Journal of Psychopharmacology*, vol. 25, no. 4, April 2011, pp. 439–52.

Montaigne, Michel de. "Of Cannibals (1578–80)." *The Complete Essays of Montaigne*, translated by Donald M. Frame, Stanford UP, 1958, pp. 150–58.

Moreiras, Alberto. *The Exhaustion of Difference: The Politics of Latin American Cultural Studies*. Duke UP, 2001.

Moreiras, Alberto. "Infrapolitical Literature: Hispanism and the Border." *CR: The New Centennial Review*, vol. 10, no. 2, fall 2010, pp. 183–203.

Nancy, Jean-Luc. *Dis-enclosure: The Deconstruction of Christianity*. Translated by Bettina Bergo et al., Fordham UP, 2008.

Nancy, Jean-Luc. "'Eating Well,' or the Calculation of the Subject: An Interview with Jacques Derrida." Translated by Peter Connor and Avital Ronell. *Who Comes After the Subject?*, edited by Eduardo Cadava et al., Routledge, 1991, pp. 96–119.

Nancy, Jean-Luc. "Image and Violence." *The Ground of the Image*, translated by Jeff Fort, Fordham UP, 2005, pp. 15–26.

Natero, Vilma. *Héroes de Malvinas*. 2001, Plaza Islas Malvinas, Ushuaia, Argentina. Bronze sculpture wall.

Oehen, Peter, et al. "A Randomized, Controlled Pilot Study of MDMA (± 3,4-Methylenedioxymethamphetamine)-Assisted Psychotherapy for Treatment of Resistant, Chronic Post-Traumatic Stress Disorder (PTSD)." *Journal of Psychopharmacology*, vol. 27, no. 1, Jan. 2013, pp. 40–52.

Ossio Lazcano, Marcela. "Hablar con los perros, de Urrelo." *La Prensa*, 27 July 2011.

Palermo, Vicente. *Sal en las heridas: Las Malvinas en la cultura argentina contemporánea*. Sudamericana, 2007.

Lambert, Peter, and Andrew Nickson, editors. *The Paraguay Reader: History, Culture, Politics*. Duke UP, 2013.

Paz Soldán, Edmundo. "La imagen fotográfica, entre el aura y el cuestionamiento de la identidad: Una lectura de 'La paraguaya' de Augusto Céspedes y *La invención de Morel* de Adolfo Bioy Casares." *Revista Iberoamericana*, vol. 73, no. 221, 2007, pp. 759–70.

Paz Soldán, Marcelo. "Entrevista a Wilmer Urrelo." *Ecdótica*, 20 Aug. 2007, https://ecdotica.com/entrevista-a-wilmer-urrelo/.

PDM Task Force. *Psychodynamic Diagnostic Manual*. Alliance of Psychoanalytic Organizations, 2006.

Pérez, Yansi Y. *The Poetics of History in the Work of Roque Dalton*. 2007. Princeton U, PhD dissertation.

Perosino, Celeste, et al. *La dictadura del capital financiero: El golpe militar corporativo y la trama bursátil*. Continente, 2014.

Philips, Stephen John. *Elastic Architecture: Frederick Kiesler and Design Research in the First Age of Robotic Culture*. MIT Press, 2017.

Plato. *The Republic: The Dialogues of Plato*. Translated by B. Jowett, vol. 2, 4th ed., Oxford UP, 2010.

Pous, Federico. *Eventos carcelarios: Subjetivación política e imaginario revolucionario en América Latina*. A Contracorriente, 2022.

Presidencia de la Nación Argentina [Cristina Fernández de Kirchner]. "Homenaje a los caídos y ex combatientes de Malvinas." *YouTube*, uploaded by Casa Rosada – República Argentina, 2 May 2012, https://www.youtube.com/watch?v=lSlyQp9NAoM.

Pron, Patricio. *Nosotros caminamos en sueños*. Penguin Random House, 2014.

Pron, Patricio. *Una puta mierda*. El Cuenco de Plata, 2007.

Querejazu Calvo, Roberto. *Masamaclay: Historia política, diplomática y militar de la Guerra del Chaco*. Empresa Industrial Gráfica E. Burillo, 1965.

Rama, Ángel. *La ciudad letrada*. Ediciones del Norte, 1984.

Relaciones chileno-argentinas: La controversia del Canal Beagle: Una selección cartográfica. Impr. Atar, 1979.

Rivera, José Eustasio. *La vorágine*. Edited by Juan Loveluck, Biblioteca Ayacucho, 1993.

Roa Bastos, Augusto. *Hijo de hombre*. El perro y la rana, 2008.

Roa Bastos, Augusto. *Hijo de hombre*. Rev. ed., Debolsillo, 2012.

Roa Bastos, Augusto. *El naranjal ardiente (Nocturno paraguayo), 1947-1949.* Alcándara, 1983.

Rodríguez-Alcalá, Hugo. "El vanguardismo en el Paraguay." *Revista Iberoamericana*, vol. 48, nos. 118–119, June 1982, pp. 241–55.

Rodríguez Matos, Jaime. *Writing of the Formless: José Lezama Lima and the End of Time*. Fordham UP, 2017.

Rosenberg, Fernando. *After Human Rights: Literature, Visual Arts, and Film in Latin America, 1990–2010*. U of Pittsburgh P, 2016.

Rozitchner, León. *Malvinas: De la guerra sucia a la guerra limpia: El punto ciego de la crítica política*. Losada, 2005.

Sakai, Naoki. *Translation and Subjectivity: On "Japan" and Cultural Nationalism*. U of Minnesota P, 1997.

Sapienza, Antonio Luis. *The Chaco Air War 1932–35: The First Modern Air War in Latin America*. Helion, 2018.

Sarlo, Beatriz. "No olvidar la guerra de Malvinas. Sobre cine, literatura e historia." *Punto de Vista*, vol. 17, no. 49, 1994, pp. 11–15.

Schmitt, Carl. *The Concept of the Political*. Translated by George Schwab, expanded ed., U of Chicago P, 2007.

Schmitt, Carl. *The Nomos of the Earth in the International Law of the Jus Publicum Europaeum*. Translated by G. L. Ulman, Telos Press, 2003.

Schmitt, Carl. *Political Theology II: The Myth of the Closure of Any Political Theology*. Translated by Michael Hoelzl and Graham Ward, Polity Press, 2015.

Schmitt, Carl. *Theory of the Partisan: Intermediate Commentary on the Concept of the Political*. Translated by G. L. Ulman, Telos Press, 2007.

Shakespeare, William. *Pericles*. Edited by Suzanne Gossett, Arden Shakespeare, 2004.

Shakespeare, William. *The Tragedy of Hamlet Prince of Denmark*. Edited by Sylvan Barnet, Signet Classics, 1998.

Siles Salinas, Jorge. *La literatura boliviana de la Guerra del Chaco*. U Católica Boliviana, 1969.

Siles Salinas, Jorge. *Sí, el mar: La negociación boliviano-chilena de 1986–1987*. Plural, 2012.

Solé Zapatero, Francisco Xavier. "'. . . ¡Y se los tragó el Chaco!' El pozo, de Augusto Céspedes (metáfora de una 'guerra estúpida' entre Bolivia y Paraguay)." *Revista de pensamiento crítico latinoamericano*, vol. 3, no. 12, July–Sept. 2012, http://ri.uaemex.mx/bitstream/han dle/20.500.11799/100140/28.%20%2522%27%c2%a1...Y%20se%20

los%20trago%cc%81%20el%20Chaco%21%27-%20El%20pozo...
ra%20estu%cc%81pida%e2%80%9d%20entre%20Bolivia%20y%20
Paraguay%29.pdf.

Sontag, Susan. *On Photography*. Picador, 1977.

Sosa, Cecilia. "*CAMPO MINADO/MINEFIELD*: War, Affect and Vulnerability—a Spectacle of Intimate Power." *Theatre Research International*, vol. 42, no. 2, July 2017, pp. 179–89.

Staden, Hans. *Hans Staden's True History: An Account of Cannibal Captivity in Brazil*. Edited and translated by Neil L. Whitehead and Michael Harbsmeier, Duke UP, 2008.

Strachan, Hew. "The Changing Character of War." Europaeum Lectures. 9 Nov. 2006, Graduate Institute of International Relations, Geneva, Switzerland.

Strachan, Hew, and Sibylle Scheipers, editors. *The Changing Character of War*. Oxford UP, 2011.

Theatre of War/Teatro de guerra. Directed by Lola Arias, performances by Lou Armour et al., Gema Films, 2018.

Thénon, Susana. "Poema con traducción simultánea español-español." *La morada imposible*, edited by Ana M. Barrenechea and María Negroni, vol. 1, Corregidor, 2001, pp. 152–53.

Thomas, Robert N., and Don R. Hoy. "A Demographic Perspective to El Salvador's Internal Struggle." *Yearbook (Conference of Latin Americanist Geographers)*, vol. 14, 1988, pp. 38–42.

Thucydides. *The Peloponnesian War*. Translated by Martin Hammond, Oxford UP, 2009.

Tompkins, Cynthia. "Life Is and Is Not: Paz Encina's *Hamaca paraguaya*." *Experimental Latin American Cinema: History and Aesthetics*, U of Texas P, 2013, pp. 232–44.

"*Top Gear* Crew 'Chased by Thousands and Ordered out of Country.'" *BBC News*, 4 Oct. 2014, www.bbc.com/news/entertainment-arts -29488770#.

Urrelo Zárate, Wilmer. "Escrituras de guerra." Festival Internacional del Libro de Buenos Aires, 25 Sept. 2014, Museo de Arte Latinoamericano de Buenos Aires, Buenos Aires, Argentina. Panel.

Urrelo Zárate, Wilmer. *Hablar con los perros*. Alfaguara, 2011.

Van der Kolk, Bessel. *The Body Keeps the Score: Brain, Mind, and Body in the Healing of Trauma*. Penguin Books, 2014.

Vardoulakis, Dimitris. "The Ends of Stasis: Spinoza as a Reader of Agamben." *Culture, Theory and Critique*, vol. 51, no. 2, July 2010, pp. 145–56.

Vardoulakis, Dimitris. *Sovereignty and Its Other: Toward the Dejustification of Violence.* Fordham UP, 2013.

Vardoulakis, Dimitris. *Stasis before the State: Nine Theses on Agonistic Democracy.* Fordham UP, 2017.

Vardoulakis, Dimitris. "Stasis: Beyond Political Theology?" *Cultural Critique,* vol. 73, no. 1, fall 2009, pp. 125–47.

Villalobos-Ruminott, Sergio. "Literatura y destrucción: Aproximación a la narrativa centroamericana actual." *Revista Iberoamericana,* vol. 79, no. 242, Sept. 2013, pp. 131–48.

Virilio, Paul. *War and Cinema: The Logistics of Perception.* Translated by Patrick Camiller, Verso Books, 1989.

Vitullo, Julieta. *Islas imaginadas: La guerra de Malvinas en la literatura y el cine argentinos.* Corregidor, 2012.

Viveiros de Castro, Eduardo. *Cannibal Metaphysics: For a Post-Structural Anthropology.* Edited and translated by Peter Skafish, Univocal, 2014.

Webber, Jeffery R. *From Rebellion to Reform in Bolivia: Class Struggle, Indigenous Liberation, and the Politics of Evo Morales.* Haymarket Books, 2011.

Weber, Max. "Politics as Vocation." *Weber's Rationalism and Modern Society: New Translations on Politics, Bureaucracy, and Social Stratification,* edited and translated by Tony Waters and Dagmar Waters, Palgrave Macmillan, 2015, pp. 129–98.

Williams, Gareth. "Decontainment: The Collapse of the Katechon and the End of Hegemony." *The Anomie of the Earth: Philosophy, Politics, and Autonomy in Europe and the Americas,* edited by Federico Luisetti et al., Duke UP, 2015, pp. 159–73.

Williams, Gareth. *The Other Side of the Popular: Neoliberalism and Subalternity in Latin America.* Duke UP, 2002.

Withnall, Adam. "1936 Nobel Peace Prize Medal to Sell at Auction after Appearing in South American Pawn Shop." *The Independent,* 13 Mar. 2014, www.independent.co.uk/news/world/americas/1936 -nobel-peace-prize-medal-to-sell-at-auction-after-appearing-in -south-american-pawn-shop-9189969.html.

Zilcosky, John. "Poetry after Auschwitz? Celan and Adorno Revisited." *Deutsche Vierteljahrsschrift für Literaturwissenschaft und Geistesgeschichte,* vol. 79, 2005, pp. 670–91. https://doi.org/10.1007/BF03374610.

Zimmer, Zac. "The Passage of Savage Capitalism: Time, Non-Place and Subjectivity in Fogwill's Narration." *Journal of Latin American Cultural Studies,* vol. 15, no. 2, Aug. 2006, pp. 143–58.

Žižek, Slavoj. "Descartes and the Post-Traumatic Subject." *Filozofski Vestnik*, vol. 29, no. 2, 2008, pp. 9–29.

INDEX

Guaraní, 20, 42-43, 47, 67, 184n58, 185n65, 192n41
Guattari, Félix, 163
Guerriero, Leila, 141-43
Gurkha, 151-54, 156

Hablar con los perros (Urrelo Zárate), 14, 63, 66; antithesis, cannibalism and, 50-55; about Battle of Boquerón, 46, 47; fetishism, cannibalism and, 59-63; metaphysical synthesis, cannibalism and, 55-59
Hamaca paraguaya (film), 14, 47; Chaco War narratives in, 67-72
Hamlet (Shakespeare), 49
Haraway, Donna J., 119
Harvey, David, 64, 178n15
Hassner, Ron, 7
Hegel, Georg Wilhelm Friedrich, 50, 58
Heidegger, Martin, 9, 26-27, 42, 180n25, 180n27, 184n59, 194n12; Carl Schmitt and, 81-82; Levinas's criticism of, 90; Nazism and, 9, 82, 194n12; about role of polemos, 81-82
Heraclitus, 9, 81-82, 100, 176n11
"Héroes del Chaco," 45
Heroic tales of a stupid war. *See Crónicas heroicas de una guerra estúpida* (Céspedes)
heterolingual address, Sakai's definition of, 152-53
heterolingual community, 153
Hijo de hombre (Roa Bastos), 13, 17, 184n58, 184n64; El Zurdo's theory of Chaco War, 17-18; fragmentary portrayal of Paraguayan history, 40-43; narration of Chaco War, 13, 21-23; Noguera's theory of Chaco War, 18-19
Hitler, Adolf, 9
Hobbes, Thomas, 21, 142, 145
"hombre nuevo" paradigm, 194-95n20
Hoy, Don, 74
human rights, 140, 143; abuses

under dictatorship, 139-40; in Falklands/Malvinas, 136-37, 138; international law, 135; military-industrial complex and, 155
Hundred Hours War. *See* Soccer War
hypostasis, 13, 39; Céspedes's "El pozo" from *Sangre de mestizos*, 25-30, 37; in Christianity, 13, 20-21; Costa du Rels's *La laguna H.3*, 30-35, 38; Levinas's use of, 180n27; in philosophy, 20; problem of assumption of, 36; Roa Bastos's *Hijo de hombre*, 21-23, 40-43

Iffland, James, 86
Iluminados por el fuego (film), 137, 139-40, 143, 147, 150
"Image and Violence" essay (Nancy), 148-49
imperialism, 153, 155; British, 14-15, 136; dismantling in Malvinas, 132; European, 107; Spanish, 14-15, 109, 115
inconvertibility, 62-63, 191n35
Inferno (Alighieri), 33
Insensatez (Castellanos Moya), 197n41
Inter-American Treaty of Reciprocal Assistance (1947), 80
Introduction to Metaphysics (Heidegger), 82

Jameson, Fredric, 8, 39
Jenckes, Kate, 191n36
John Paul II (Pope), 6
Johnson, Lyndon, 80

Kaldor, Mary, 100
Kalimtzis, Kostas, 53
Kant, Immanuel, 26, 91
Kapuściński, Ryszard, 76, 77, 83, 84
katechon, 197n44
Kirchner, Cristina Fernández de, 133
Kirchner, Néstor, 133-34
Knight, Jim, 194-95n20
Kohan, Martín, 110, 120, 199n13
Kojève, Alexandre, 50, 188n10

Palermo, Vicente, 103, 122, 134
"paradigm of war," 9–10
Paradise in the new world. *See El paraíso en el nuevo mundo* (Pinelo)
Paraguayan hammock. *See Hamaca paraguaya* (film)
The Paraguayan woman. *See* "La paraguaya" (Céspedes)
pata pila, 29
Pérez, Yansi, 86
Pericles (Shakespeare), 99
personhood, 137, 154, 159; primacy of, 154; spiritual, legal, and biological, 143
petroleum. *See* oil
pilas. See pata pila
Pinelo, Antonio de León, 21
Pinochet, Augusto, 6
Pizarnik, Alejandra, 59
Plá, Josefina, 46
plasticity, 63, 191n35
Plasticity at the Dusk of Writing (Malabou), 62
Plato, 9, 28–29, 99, 176n10, 178n9, 180n28
"Poema con traducción simultánea español-español" (poem by Thénon), 105, 107; mistranslated metaphors of conquest about Falklands/Malvinas War, 107–9
points de capiton, 179n24
polemos, 6, 8–9, 11–12, 16, 76, 81–82, 100, 132, 159, 170, 173
political/politics: Athenian, 9, 38; Clausewitz's proposition of, 8, 77–78; myths about Chaco War, 21–22; culture and, 12, 154, 172–74; family as threshold, 38–39; identity, 100; picture of, 35, 36, 38; realism and, 22; representation and, 21, 79, 82–83, 90–93, 136; theory of Chaco War, 35–36
political theology, 6, 9, 13, 25, 39, 168, 172
Political Theology II (Schmitt), 176n10
Politics (Aristotle), 9
Politics of Friendship (Derrida), 176n10

post-literature, 90, 195n27
post-traumatic stress disorder (PTSD), 107, 202n36
post-traumatic subjectivity, 150
primitive accumulation, 22. *See also* Marx *and* Harvey
Principle of Reason (Heidegger), 180n25. *See also nihil est sine ratione*
Proceso de Reorganización Nacional, 104
Pron, Patricio, 15, 137, 161, 164, 206n24. *See also Nosotros caminamos en sueños* (Pron)
Prudencio, Roberto, 26
psychic trauma, 201n34. *See also* trauma
Psychodynamic Diagnostic Manual, 201n34
PTSD. *See* post-traumatic stress disorder

Querejazu Calvo, Roberto, 19
Quijano, Aníbal, 152

Rama, Ángel, 179n19
realism and literature, 91–92
Relaciones chileno-argentinas, 176n6
remalvinización, 134
Republic (Plato), 9
revolution: Bolivia (1952), 23, 52; Bolivia (MAS) and revolutionary phase, 64; in Central America 84, 91; and civil war, 145; in France 143, 198n46
Rey Rosa, Rodrigo, 91
Rio Treaty. *See* Inter-American Treaty of Reciprocal Assistance (1947)
ritual cannibalism, 46, 50, 55, 62, 63
Rivera, José Eustasio, 35
Roa Bastos, Augusto, 13, 17, 33, 44, 67, 179n24, 184n58; about Chaco's oil deposits issue, 19; about Chaco War, 20, 21–23, 50; explanations for war in novels, 18; magical realism in writings, 178n14; use of *arandú*, 43, 192n44. *See also Hijo de hombre* (Roa Bastos)

Rodríguez-Alcalá, Hugo, 46, 187n4, 192n44
Rodríguez Matos, Jaime, 177n15
Rosenberg, Fernando, 139–40
Royal Dutch Shell, 19
Rozitchner, León, 109, 111
Rulfo, Juan, 67

Saavedra Lamas, Carlos, 182n40
Sakai, Naoki, 151–53
Sangre de mestizos (Céspedes), 13, 208n36
Sarlo, Beatriz, 110–11
Satanism in Hablar con los perros, 51–53, 188–89n17
savage hybridity, 177n13
Schlossmann, Siegmund, 147
Schmitt, Carl, 7, 9, 160, 175n4, 176n10, 178n13; claims for international law, 19; Concept of the Political, 54, 81; criticism of sovereignty after Second World War, 11–12; about fiction of political origin, 21–22; about role of polemos, 81–82
Second World War, 9, 76, 79–81
self-determination, 11, 19
Senselessness. See Insensatez (Castellanos Moya)
Sepúlveda, Juan Ginés de, 48
Shakespeare, William, 49
Sí, el mar (Siles Salinas), 179n20
Siles Salinas, Jorge, 23–25, 179n20, 182n47
sinfín, 148–50, 205n15
Smith, Adam, 22
Snowden, Edward, 163
Soccer War, 13, 14, 73, 135, 171; CACM impact, 74; Dalton's writing of demos about, 89–93; about demography and history, 79; Desmoronamiento about, 93–98; domestic and international pressures, 75–76; history of, 73–74; labor, migration, and documentation in, 16; "La guerra es la continuación" about, 78,

87, 89; Las historias prohibidas del pulgarcito about, 77–79, 83–89; map of guerrilla training areas, 74–75, 75, 171; naming of, 77; rise of nationalist modes of belonging, 76; and sovereignty in literature, 79–83; sovereignty without demos, 98–102
"Socialist Discussion Group". See Grupo de Discusión Socialista
Soldado argentino sólo conocido por Dios (Argentine soldier known only to God), 142
Soledad Island, 204n55, 204n56
Solé Zapatero, Francisco Xavier, 35
Son of man. See Hijo de hombre (Roa Bastos)
sovereignty, 6–7, 11–12, 35–39, 110–13, 160, 168, 170–74, 176n12, 183n49; as basis of claims, 13, 25–26, 123, 134–37, 140–43, 148–49, 172; in Beagle Conflict, 4–6; without demos in Soccer War, 98–102; European political theological models, 171; Falklands/Malvinas Islands and, 103–7, 129, 132, 134–55; Hobbesian mask of, 145; limits of, 102, 136, 164; Chaco and 18–19, 21; national and international legal systems, 7, 204n54; Soccer War and, 79–83
Staden, Hans, 187n5
Standard Oil Company of New Jersey, 19, 45
stasis, 6, 39, 43, 52, 86; in ancient Athens, 25; Aristotle's views of, 176n10; border war as, 171; Central American, 14; as stagnation, 7–8; Kalimtzis's views of, 53; Latin American border conflicts, 169; Loraux's views of 9, 24, 38, 52, 179n18; medical definition of, 96; of photographic image, 29; Agamben's approach to, 38–39; question of conflict and democracy, 173; rhetorical stasis, 11, 12; as internal conflict, 8–10; in Soccer War, 102; as displacement, 10–12;